Wales and World War One

Wales

and

World War One

Robin Barlow

Gomer

Published in 2014 by
Gomer Press, Llandysul, Ceredigion, SA44 4JL

ISBN 978 1 84851 885 8

This book is published with the financial support of the
Welsh Books Council.

Printed and bound in Wales at
Gomer Press, Llandysul, Ceredigion

To

Monica, Mari, Tom and Alun

Contents

A note on Proper Names

The spelling of all place names is taken from *Rhestr o Enwau Lleoedd: A Gazetteer of Welsh Place Names*, E. Davies (ed.), Cardiff, 1975.

The contemporary spelling of the Welsh Regiment (not Welch Regiment) and Royal Welsh Fusiliers (not Royal Welch Fusiliers) is used throughout.

Abbreviations

CAS	Carmarthenshire Archives Service
CO	Commanding Officer
GOC	General Officer Commanding
ILP	Independent Labour Party
IWM	Imperial War Museum
MP	Member of Parliament
MFGB	Miners' Federation of Great Britain
NLW	National Library of Wales
PRC	Parliamentary Recruiting Committee
PRO	Pembrokeshire Record Office
SWMF	South Wales Miners' Federation
TNA	The National Archives
WAC	Welsh Army Corps
WNEC	Welsh National Executive Committee
WO	War Office

Acknowledgements

—⁓—

Thanks to the following institutions and individuals for their kind permission to reproduce photographs:

Adrian James
Anglesey County Record Office
Bangor University Archives
Caernarfon Record Office
Ceredigion Archives
Flintshire Record Office
Gwent Record Office
Imperial War Museum
National Library of Wales
Powys County Archives
Roger J. C. Thomas

Introduction

—·⁓w⁓·—

THE FIRST WORLD WAR is still highly controversial. During the commemoration of its outbreak, arguments flared up once again as to how the war should be interpreted. For some it will always be a futile and wasteful war, a view shaped and reinforced by the poetry of writers such as Wilfred Owen and Siegfried Sassoon. Horrified by the casualties, the conflict is seen in terms of what Owen described as the 'pity of war'. For others, Britain necessarily went to war to prevent a militarist, expansionist enemy achieving hegemony in Europe and thus endangering British security. The war was certainly not seen as being futile at the time, despite the loss of life which was a necessary but unfortunate corollary.

During the First World War 272,000 Welshmen enlisted in the army and some 31,000 of these men sacrificed their lives. They joined not only the well known Welsh regiments (Royal Welsh Fusiliers, South Wales Borderers, Welsh Regiment and Welsh Guards) but also virtually every other regiment of the British Army. Others served in the Royal Navy, the Mercantile Marine and the Royal Flying Corps. They fought in every theatre of the war including Belgium and northern France, the Dardanelles, the Middle East, Africa and China. Men died heroically in battle, or more prosaically from disease and accidents, both at home and abroad.

This book aims to describe and explain what happened on the home front in Wales during the war and what happened to Welshmen (and women) abroad. What was the contribution of Wales to the war and was this a distinct contribution? Thousands of books have been published on the First World War with 'Britain' in the title, yet one will search in vain through the index of nearly all of them for references to 'Wales', or indeed 'Scotland' and 'Ireland'. Unfortunately, the old cliché still applies, 'For Wales, see England'.

In Wales on the outbreak of war, there were many different responses and reactions to the conflict, which is the main theme examined in Chapter 1. There is plenty of evidence to show that many Welsh people, especially those in the more rural areas, did not fully grasp the reasons for the declaration of war, nor understand what was at stake. They saw it very much as England's war, being fought between the major powers, of which Wales just happened to be a part. However, this group remained the silent minority. In Wales, as in all combatant nations, the voices of dissent were drowned by a chorus supportive of the decision to resort to arms. As this group contained leading local and national politicians, newspaper editors, clergymen and businessmen, it is not difficult to see why this view prevailed. It was widely believed that the war would be over quickly and that victory would not require any fundamental change to the established way of life. The one factor which did resonate in Wales was the defence of the neutrality of Belgium, where it was possible to identify with the plight of a similarly small nation being bullied by a more powerful neighbour.

In the nineteenth and early twentieth century, the Nonconformist tradition had ensured that militarism and war were denounced from the pulpit at every opportunity. Joining the army was not a path followed by many in Wales, apart from the landed aristocracy at one end of the socio-economic scale and the destitute and poor at the other. The growing influence of the socialist movement, especially in south Wales, saw war as a capitalist construct to allow the rich to get richer and thus to be avoided at all costs. Although recruitment from Wales was proportionately less than from England, Scotland and Ireland, it is still surprising that as many Welshmen volunteered as actually did so. How this was achieved is considered in Chapter 2. The establishment of the Welsh Army Corps and its relative success in attracting Welshmen to a distinctly Welsh formation is examined in Chapter 3. Although this book is not intended to be a military history, how the Welsh regiments fared in battle, seen through the eyes of individual combatants, is important. Chapters 4 and 5 look at the Battle of Mametz and the Gallipoli campaign. Although all of the Welsh regiments relied on others from outside the Principality to bolster their ranks, the extent to which particular national features and characteristics were retained, is the theme of Chapter 6. This might, at times, have only been the Welshmen's willingness to sing; partaking in the familiar ritual of hymn-singing would have immediately transported them from the front line to the familiarity of home, family and chapel. The fact that the War Office accommodated the use of the Welsh language within the armed forces and that Nonconformist ministers were attached to the Welsh regiments, were victories both for Lloyd George and the Welsh nation.

It is easy to overstate the extent and depth of opposition to the war in Wales. The result of the by-election in Merthyr Boroughs in 1915, when the jingoistic Charles Stanton heavily defeated James Winstone, paints a clear picture of where most people's loyalties lay. Chapter 7 charts the opposition to the war, such as it was. It is often forgotten that roughly half of those who served in the army in the war only did so because they were called up; they did not volunteer, they were compelled. Given the effects that the introduction of conscription was to have on the Liberal Party, it is surprising that compulsion was passed through Parliament with little opposition. Military tribunals were introduced for those seeking exemption from military service; dealing with the appeals was a gargantuan task and frequently unappreciated. Chapter 8 examines the decisions of the tribunals, showing that in rural Wales exemptions were the rule rather than the exception.

The First World War has often been called the most literary of wars, which is certainly true quantitatively if not qualitatively and with no other war has the writing of combatants so influenced popular perceptions and understanding of the conflict. The Welsh contributions to this body of work are examined in Chapter 9. Total war, a concept unimagined in August 1914, meant that what happened on the home front was fundamental to the successful prosecution of the war. Various social, religious, economic and political aspects of the home front are examined in Chapters 10, 11 and 12. Those who had a good war were the agricultural labourers, the coal miners, working women and the Labour Party; for the Liberal Party and the coal mining industry, their decline dates from the war years.

In 1914, Wales was a self-confident, culturally aware nation, which successfully embraced social, class and religious differences. This confidence was manifested in the recent successful establishment of institutional symbols such as the National Library, the National Museum and the University of Wales. When war broke out, Wales felt bound to play her part, not only as part of the Empire, but in her own right. Wales's participation must be seen from the perspective of the nation's quest to establish its national identity with increased international engagement. In 1914, the cost of doing so could not have been imagined.

Chapter 1

'Have you been asleep or something? War has been declared'

The response in Wales to the outbreak of war

—⚬—

ON BANK HOLIDAY MONDAY, 3 August 1914, 50,000 day-trippers descended on Barry Island. Many went to watch and listen to a grand band competition on Nell's Point, others to picnic on the grass or to stroll on the beach. Similar scenes would have been witnessed throughout Wales as the crowds sought to take advantage of the benign summer weather at coastal resorts like Mumbles, Aberystwyth, Llandudno and Tenby. To the vast majority of the population, lulled by years of peace, the prospect of a European war seemed distant and unlikely. The political skies seemed as cloudless as those of the coastal resorts. There were hopes that the Anglo-German naval rivalry would soon diminish and that the beneficial effects of trade and commerce would encourage peace among nations once again. For Lloyd George, as for the great mass of his countrymen in July 1914, 'blue skies and serene horizons alone seemed to lie ahead'.[1] The Labour politician Norman Angell had written the best-selling book (in both Britain and Germany), *The Great Illusion,* in which he argued that the 'Great War' would never come because countries were too economically interlinked. Two recent studies have similarly emphasized the relative calmness in Europe: Florian Illies, maintains that far from teetering on the edge of the abyss, the generation of 1913 was surprisingly carefree; the title of Christopher Clark's study of how Europe went to war in 1914, *The Sleepwalkers* (2012) is self-explanatory.[2]

Morgan Watcyn-Williams was a student in Swansea in June 1914 and discussed the situation with friends:

> We read of the murder of the Archduke, and the tension in Europe
> … one of [my friends] … insisted that it meant war and that before
> a month was out we would be in it. I was vehement in my protests.
> 'The thing's impossible, man. Neither the Churches nor the Trades
> Unions will stand for it. Keir Hardie is certain the workers will strike
> against war'.[3]

When war was declared on 4 August 1914, the vast majority of the population of Wales was unable to comprehend the reasons for it, knew little of the web of treaties and alliances binding European countries and certainly had no perception of the nature of the war that was to come. Emlyn Davies thought that the Welsh people were 'rudely shocked and much confused when the declaration of war was announced'.[4] Lilly Powell, aged twelve on the outbreak of war, remembered, 'I'd gone down to Morriston to get the evening paper and there were crowds everywhere and all sorts of hullabaloo and I asked my friend what all the fuss was about and she said, "Have you been asleep or something? WAR has been declared!"'[5]

Dai Dan Evans, like all miners, had been looking forward only to a three-day bank holiday break from the pit:

> Nobody expected the war to come, I mean from little villages.
> Obviously the people that were in Parliament and people that
> were studying politics knew the trends and knew that there was
> something in the offing. But to the ordinary man in the street and
> to the children and teenagers, particularly, it would never dawn on
> them. So when the First World War was declared it was a shattering
> blow, see. It came like a bolt from the blue as far as the mass of the
> people were concerned.[6]

In north Wales, whilst leading public figures aligned themselves squarely behind the government's policies, the response of the general public was much more muted. Kate Roberts, writing about the slate-quarrying area of Caernarfonshire commented, 'when war broke out no one knew what to make of it.' Cyril Parry, in his study of Gwynedd in the Great War, thought the ordinary people of Gwynedd 'were unaware of the reasons for the declaration of war, they knew nothing about the government's diplomatic policies and, conditioned by years of peace, they experienced the greatest difficulty in perceiving the reality of war and assessing its implications for them.' War was 'an interesting game that was fascinating to watch.' Parry also argues that the Welsh-speaking communities in the north responded to the outbreak of war in a different way to the English-speaking regions because of their religious and cultural traditions. Many within the Welsh-speaking communities were unable to identify with the war, or contribute to the pro-war consensus, because of a newly kindled awareness of different values, norms and perceptions.[7]

On the first day of the war, the *Western Mail* printed a cartoon, 'The Call of Patriotism', depicting Dame Wales blowing her patriotic horn. The text read:

> Welshmen! 'In the hours of danger our Navy asks for coal. It shall not ask in vain. We will show the world that the blast of my horn, resounding in the hills of Wales, can be responded to by men as patriotic as any the world can boast!'[8]

The south Wales miners made a clear statement of their confrontational attitude by refusing the entreaties of the newspaper, and the Admiralty's request for them to forego their bank holiday to work on 3, 4 and 5 August. They were adamant that coal stocks were not dangerously low as had been claimed and that they were therefore entitled to take their annual break.[9] Few of the south Wales pits produced coal over the holiday, with the unlikely exception of those at Llwynypia, an area not renowned for moderation in its industrial relations. However, within a week, the South Wales Miners' Federation (SWMF) agreed that its members should work for an extra hour per day to help the national cause. Virtually every colliery complied with the request, the one understandable exception being Senghenydd, which had recently experienced its own Armageddon when 439 men had died in a horrific explosion. The colliery manager had just received a paltry fine for the disaster, which hardened the resolve of the men not to comply with the request to work extra hours.

On 8 August 1914, the Chancellor of the Exchequer, David Lloyd George, published a bilingual 'Appeal to Wales', listing the 'three plain duties which should be felt in all reverence and solemnity in our

David Lloyd George.

innermost hearts this day.' Firstly, no one was to 'foolishly obstruct the efforts of the government to keep stable the finances of the country', with fears of a run on the banks uppermost in Lloyd George's mind. Secondly, no one should buy more food than they needed, in response to reports of hoarding and panic buying of staple foodstuffs. It had been reported that in Cardiff the price of bread, meat and sugar had all risen in the first few days of the war, following a sharp rise in demand. Finally, employers were urged to keep up levels of employment during the period of economic uncertainty, immediately following the outbreak of war.[10]

Suspicion, fear and panic were the result of a failure to understand what the declaration of war actually meant to the residents of Wales. In Neath, shops owned by Germans who had lived in the town for many years were attacked and looted.[11] Spy stories spread like wildfire. On 7 August, Edward Davies from Hengoed was caught sketching the sentries patrolling around Barry Fort. He was seized and held on suspicion of being a spy. It turned out that he was sketching for art classes at the Barry summer school; nonetheless, his drawings were destroyed and he was given a 'severe reprimand.'[12] In Cardiff and Barry, German sailors were immediately rounded up and kept under guard. On 5 August the German steamer *Ulla Borg* had entered the Bristol Channel heading for Barry Docks, unaware that war had been declared. Her crew was interned and the ship held as a war prize, later to be auctioned off and renamed *Mary Baird*.[13] In Abercynon, a German hairdresser named Otto Kruger, who had been living and working in the town for eighteen months, was arrested and charged under the Official Secrets Act. Porthcawl golf club expelled all 'alien enemy members'; in the case of one of them, his clubs were commandeered, auctioned off and the profit given to the Prince of Wales Fund.[14] On 14 August the *Cambrian News* reported that 'two weather-stained and bronzed men arrived on foot at Aberayron on

Royal Welsh Fusilier with the regimental mascot in Llandeilo prior to the outbreak of war.

(NLW, D. C. Harries Collection)

Tuesday evening and as one of them was wearing spectacles they were taken to be German spies. When they retired to rest under the stars at night they were awakened by a police officer and arrested.' It transpired that the two men were on a walking holiday; one was a doctor from Bristol and the other a clergyman from Southwark Cathedral.[15]

The Welsh provincial press was generally in full support of the government's declaration of war, which was perhaps more a reflection of the controlling interests of the newspaper industry, than of the views of the readers. On 7 August, the *Carmarthen Journal* reported that 'no sooner had the rumour of war become current than this old barrack town was afire with enthusiasm. Wherever one went it was nothing but war.' The paper reported that Llandovery was in 'a state of seething excitement', whilst in Ferryside only 'great excitement prevailed'. The *Amman Valley Chronicle* reported 'patriotic fervour', also confidently predicting that, 'modern warfare tends to make the clash of nations a brief affair'. A year would be 'an outside estimate' for the duration of the war. The *Herald* group of newspapers in north Wales did not initially follow the establishment line and on 4 August advocated the well-rehearsed liberal anti-war stance. An editorial argued that 'the Tory Party is the party of the arms manufacturers, and they are the only ones who will make their fortunes through blood-letting'.[16]

The *Welsh Outlook* was much more circumspect:

> At the bottom of our hearts, probably most of us believed that a European war could only become real to us in the pages of Mr. H.G. Wells ... Even now [September 1914] we cannot realize it, we find ourselves reading the headlines of newspapers, and we have to force our imaginations to realise that it is not a novel we are reading ... With the German people as with the Russian people, we are sympathetic, gradually, even the least cultured amongst us are learning to know and admire their literature and music; it is only their ruling classes who have caused this war ... we wish to protest against all manifestations of that ignorant and malicious spirit that can despise a whole nation. Let us remember that the Germans believe as strongly as we do that they are defending their country, and the whole world, against wilful aggression ... In both countries [i.e. Wales and Germany] heroic sacrifices are being made, in both countries the appalling tragedy of war is equally felt.[17]

In the same edition of the *Welsh Outlook*, portraits of Bach, Beethoven, Kant and Goethe were published, under the strangely prescient heading 'Lest we Forget'. The editorial concluded, 'the Junker class is not all Germany nor "blood and iron" their universal motto.' One month later, the tenor of the writing had hardened when it was claimed that the 'genius of all four [i.e. Bach, Beethoven, Kant and Goethe] is pre-eminently human – human before it is German'. It was the Germany of the past to which Welshmen owed their respect and gratitude; the Germany of 1914 was 'its exact antithesis'.[18]

For a week before the outbreak of war, a peace meeting had been planned for 6 August, to be held in the Market Hall, Aberdare. The chief speaker was to be Keir Hardie, MP for the constituency, and the chair was to be taken by Charles Butt Stanton, the rabid syndicalist and headstrong miners' agent for the Aberdare district of the SWMF. With the declaration of war two days prior to the meeting, the predominant mood of the locality changed to one which seemed to be broadly in support of the government's actions. Hardie and his supporters felt uneasy, but decided nevertheless to fulfil their commitment to the meeting and indeed to their conscience. Stanton, with remarkable alacrity, switched horses and was to become the apogee of jingoism as the war progressed. He refused to attend the meeting, which was subsequently chaired by Edmund Stonelake. Stanton was reported as saying:

> In times of distress and trouble I stand in with my country. We are in the throes of a gigantic war, and therefore our solemn duty is to be patriotic and strain every nerve to emerge out of it with credit to the history of our past as Britishers.[19]

At the ill-tempered meeting, Hardie managed to speak for about twenty minutes but found it hard to make himself heard above the patriotic songs and hostile interruptions. He was physically jostled by the crowd, many of whom were miners, but he was not actually assaulted. It has been asserted, somewhat erroneously, that the traumatic scenes at Aberdare so upset Hardie that they hastened his death the following year, whereas he was clearly used to such a brouhaha, describing those who had disrupted the meeting as having attended 'to have some fun'. [20] Hardie had, however, totally misjudged the prevailing mood of his constituents; when Edmund

Stonelake told him that local feeling was intensely in favour of the war, 'a look of surprise and astonishment came into his face'. When Hardie left the meeting, he was accompanied to Aberdare railway station by a police inspector, where access to the platform was via a door from the waiting room. The police inspector unwisely stepped through the door first in front of Hardie, thereby receiving the salvo of eggs and vegetables hurled by a group which had walked along the track into the station and was waiting in readiness for the MP to open the door.[21] The Merthyr Boroughs constituency, which for thirty-two years (1868–1900) was represented in Parliament by Henry Richard the renowned 'apostle of peace', had shown itself to be firmly in favour of the conflict with Germany. Stanton's new-found patriotism and moderation led him to sever all connections with the Independent Labour Party and to appear at numerous recruiting meetings and rallies throughout south Wales. In July 1915 he attempted to prevent the miners from taking strike action in their dispute with the coal owners.

Charles Stanton was not alone in ditching pre-war views and becoming an advocate of the conflict with Germany. Ted Gill, a left-wing miners' leader was to speak at numerous recruiting meetings, as did another former miners' leader and current MP, William Abraham (Mabon). At a recruiting meeting in Pentre in February 1915 he stated:

> The cruelty and butchery of the Germans' mode of warfare is appalling, and the waste and suffering in their wake is heartrending. All this must be stopped, and for that purpose we want all the eligible young men to join the ranks of the British Army … I trust that the appeal that is now being made will meet with an enthusiastic immediate response.[22]

David ('Dai') Watts Morgan, the moderate Rhondda miners' leader was another whose patriotic zeal came as a surprise. On 4 August 1914 he enlisted as a private in the 10th Battalion (1st Rhondda) Welsh Regiment, later to be commissioned and eventually to reach the rank of lieutenant-colonel. He excelled as a 'recruiting sergeant' both in the Rhondda and north Wales, where his proficiency in the Welsh language was invaluable. He had sworn in 4,510 men (mostly miners) to the armed forces by March 1915 and a further 10,000 by the end of the war. In 1917 Watts Morgan was posted to northern France where he was three times mentioned in dispatches and appointed DSO in 1918. After the armistice, for his contribution to recruiting, he was presented with a cheque for 100 guineas and a service revolver. The *Western Mail* dubbed him 'The Organiser of Victory', but Lieutenant-Colonel David Watts Morgan CBE, DSO, MP, JP was also fondly known by his mining constituents as 'Dai Alphabet'.

The response of the academic community to the outbreak of war was largely one of support, with varying intellectual justifications. Sir Henry ('Harry') Reichel, Principal of University College of North Wales, Bangor and of German extraction, thought the German attack was an unparalleled example by a civilized nation of 'cold-blooded wickedness', based on intellectual training and scientific efficiency.[23] For Professor Henry Jones, it was the 'moral splendour' of the sacrifice which appealed: 'never had the history of the world shown so much spirit of Christianity'.[24] T.F. Roberts, Principal at Aberystwyth, though supporting the war, had no wish to disparage 'what Germany has achieved, and yet under happier auspices will achieve'.[25] Lord Lloyd Tyrell Kenyon, Senior Deputy Chancellor of the University of Wales, praised students who had enlisted: 'all honour to them. Their studies may be delayed, but their minds will be enlarged'.[26] T.A. Levi, a lecturer in law in Aberystwyth, went as far as to tell law students that if they enlisted, 'he would guarantee that their examination would be passed for them.'[27]

One of the most unsavoury incidents of the war was to centre on the University College of Wales, Aberystwyth, and its treatment of Professor Hermann Ethé. He had joined the College staff in 1875 and was one of the few scholars with an indisputably international reputation. He customarily taught six languages (Hebrew, Sanskrit, Arabic, Italian, French and German) also offering to read with students in other oriental languages. However, Ethé made little effort to blend into the restricted society in which he found himself, nor to

Cartoon of Prof Hermann Ethé by the cartoonist 'ap Rhobert'.

(Howard Lloyd Roberts)

9

become a British citizen; after forty years in Aberystwyth he still had a thick German accent and despite his linguistic skills he never learnt Welsh. In a largely teetotal town, he drank openly and with relish, claiming the only word of Welsh that he needed was 'cwrw' (beer). Whilst these characteristics may partly explain later events, they do not excuse or exonerate his persecutors.

On the outbreak of war, Ethé and his English-born wife were making their annual visit to Germany. After initially being refused permission to travel back to Wales, the College authorities intervened on Ethé's behalf and he returned to Aberystwyth on 14 October 1914. He was met at the railway station by the principal, the registrar and three students in order to demonstrate that the University and student body were willing to welcome him back. These intentions were laudable, but served merely to stoke the fires of spy-mania and Germanophobia that were blazing through towns the length and breadth of Wales. Rumours – both true and false – of German atrocities during the advance through Belgium were thought to have further hardened local public opinion. The following day a mob of 2,000 assembled in the square in front of Siloh chapel to be addressed by Dr T.D. Harries, a magistrate and former mayor, and T.J. Samuel, a solicitor and town councillor. Dr Harries demanded that all enemy aliens should be driven out of the town, but he warned 'do not touch them for they stink of German sausage. Put them in the sea to clean them, and then send them off by train'.[28] The mob processed up Caradoc Road to Ethé's house, headed by a union jack mounted on a long pole, where angry scenes followed. Ethé was fortunately not at home, having fled to his wife's family in Reading. Professors Marshall and O.T. Jones tried to remonstrate with the mob, but they were howled down. Attention

IN MEMORY OF HERMANN ETHÉ
PROFESSOR OF GERMAN. DISTINGUISHED ORIENTALIST
& LOYAL SERVANT OF THE COLLEGE
FROM 1875 TO 1914

Dedicated 1974

Memorial plaque to Prof Hermann Ethé, in Aberystwyth University.

then turned to Professor Schott who, it was claimed, played the German national anthem every night on his piano. He was in fact from Bradford and had lived all his life in Britain, although his wife was German. When a union jack was found flying outside his house the fickle mood of the townsmen changed and he was given 'three cheers'.

At a public meeting soon afterwards, the College authorities were denounced for according Ethé 'a welcome' and his dismissal from the staff was demanded. However, the College came out of the whole sorry affair with slightly more credit than the town when three of Ethé's colleagues paid him over £200 from their own pockets, as all his savings were tied up abroad and he was not receiving his university salary. A member of the College Council, F. Llewelyn Jones, then made moves to deprive Ethé of his professorial chair. This was only avoided when he agreed to resign and accept a small pension. Ethé lived in Reading and ironically carried out important work for both the India Office and British Museum during the war. He died in 1917, never having returned to Aberystwyth or to the College which he had served with such distinction for almost fifty years. The official historian of the College concluded: 'With all due allowance for the disturbed temper of the times, the picture of a brute mass of townspeople, spurred on by public men, hounding out a harmless old scholar in his seventies is utterly shameful'.[29]

There were contrasting reactions to the outbreak of war from Wales's two foremost sporting organisations: the Welsh Rugby Union (WRU) and the Football Association of Wales (FAW), perhaps reflecting the socio-economic make-up of their governing bodies. On 27 August 1914, the general committee of the WRU passed a resolution that 'it is the duty of all [rugby] football players, where practicable, immediately to join one of his Majesty's forces' and all international fixtures for the foreseeable future were cancelled. The WRU felt that rugby players would make good soldiers:

> Considering that our players comprise … the very pick of men eligible for service in the Army, and considering that Welshmen have the reputation for not being wanting in either patriotism or pluck, we feel we shall not appeal in vain … If only every man in every First XV in Wales were to enlist, what a magnificent body there would be at the service of our country.[30]

On 1 September, both Cardiff and Swansea rugby clubs abandoned all fixtures for the season, followed by Llanelli RFC the following day. The New Dock Stars RFC enlisted en bloc, plus the whole of their committee.

The FAW, in contrast, decided to play on, as did the Football Association in England. This decision attracted a great deal of criticism in the press and a letter to the *South Wales Daily News* was typical:

> It is unimaginable that people could look on at a game of football and forget themselves in the ecstasy of a winning goal at the moment when their comrades, maybe brothers, are making gallant and stupendous efforts at the front, even sacrificing their lives for the life of a nation.[31]

The president of the FAW justified the continuation of fixtures by arguing that soccer occupied an important place in the life of the nation and that its discontinuation would only produce undesirable results. In the early months of the war most of the regional papers in south Wales, such as the *South Wales Argus*, refused to cover matches, although reports began to creep back in during 1915. It may have been that the military authorities gave tacit approval to the continuation of soccer matches, because this gave easy access to large numbers of potential recruits from working class communities. A Welsh League match between Swansea Town and Llanelli in September 1914 attracted a crowd of 7,000, almost all of whom would have been eligible for enlistment. The crowd was subjected to six speakers – including the mayor, the club chairman and the local recruiting officer – extolling the virtues of joining up. During the season 1914-15, attendances

Recruiting poster.

at matches fell by an average of 50 per cent, which had severe financial repercussions for many of the smaller clubs. Mardy AFC, for example, who played in the Southern League, was forced to close before the end of 1914. Cardiff City, Merthyr Town and Swansea Town survived the war, but other clubs were less fortunate.[32]

The press in Wales was broadly supportive of the war, becoming increasingly so as 1914 wore on. Aled Gruffydd Jones, in his detailed study of the press in Wales, maintains that the pressure to conform to the pro-war mood in 1914 was as overwhelming in Wales as it was elsewhere in Britain, as even 'the most progressive of the liberal and nationalist journalists and publishers turned their talents to support the war effort'.[33] Jones identified three responses to the outbreak of war: uncritical support, principled opposition and initial reluctance that later transformed into patriotic enthusiasm. The *Western Mail* clearly fell into the first category along with *Welsh Outlook*, O.M. Edwards's *Cymru*, and the denominational weeklies *Y Tyst*, *Y Goleuad*, *Herald Cymraeg* and *Genedl*. *Y Beirniad* gave its support to the war throughout its duration. It had begun publication in 1911 and was influential amongst academic and university circles despite its circulation of only around 1,000. Sir John Morris-Jones, a highly respected and leading Welsh scholar writing in *Y Beirniad*, believed that Germany had sold its soul to the devil. In an appeal to the people of Wales, in both English and Welsh, he declared that the war was not only being fought against German military aggression but also against the most extreme form of ungodliness ever to possess a nation. *Y Goleuad*, a title purchased by the governing body of the Calvinistic Methodists in July 1914, under the editorship of E. Morgan Humphreys, offered a critical voice whilst remaining broadly behind government policy. Later in the war, Humphreys published articles critical of Lloyd George and his support for conscription which eventually led to his dismissal from the editorship. The chairman of the editorial committee, Revd John Williams Brynsiencyn and Lloyd George's staunchest Welsh supporter, was the one who pulled the trigger. In north Wales, Frederick Copplestone's *Herald* group of newspapers responded to the outbreak of war with traditional liberal, anti-war arguments. However, by 11 August the papers printed Lloyd George's 'Appeal to Wales' and by 18 August a special telegraph service had been

Recruiting poster.

installed to improve the papers' war coverage. By 13 October the papers had begun to openly support the war, quoting Lloyd George's justification of it being a war to defend the small nations of the world. Before the year was out, leader columns were beating the patriotic drum as loudly as any other.[34] Those publications opposed to the war included *Seren Gomer, Y Gwleidydd Newydd* and most notably, later in the war, *Y Deyrnas*.

In Wales, as in the rest of Britain, war led to pressure being exerted on editors and publishers to conform to the pro-war consensus through the control of content. A Press Bureau was established early in the war to provide the government with a means of channelling and co-ordinating the news. Surprisingly, Lord Riddell of the *Western Mail* protested vigorously about such state interference and control, whilst the editor of the *Merthyr Express* thought that 'the control and censorship of war news by the government is a great boon for the public … It will prevent the publication of flesh-creeping, jumpy despatches.'[35]

Reactions to the outbreak of war in Wales were not uniform, nor were they necessarily accurately represented by the press. Adrian Gregory has recently challenged the largely unexamined assumption that British popular attitudes to the onset of hostilities were jingoistic and enthusiastically pro-war. [36] He correctly argues that discussion of responses to the war in Britain have been blind to major divisions in Edwardian society, particularly region, nation, class and gender. Such generalisations about 'the Welsh' similarly must be broken down where differences of language, employment, religion and location are equally relevant. Gregory argues that the evidence for mass enthusiasm *at the time* is surprisingly weak, probably owing more to contemporary beliefs of the excitability of mass society than to any empirical evidence. The image of 'war fever' has received significant support from the memoirs of politicians such as Lloyd George, who wrote of the 'warlike crowds that thronged Whitehall and poured into Downing Street, whilst the Cabinet was deliberating on the alternatives of peace or war'. The decision to go to war was taken by a small number of men, Gregory argues, but the idea that it was in response to, and in tune with, the prevailing national sentiment, became a useful way of spreading the blame and avoiding questions of personal culpability.

NOTES

[1] Kenneth O. Morgan, *Rebirth of a Nation: Wales 1880–1980* (Oxford: Oxford University Press, 1982), p. 155.
[2] Florian Illies, *1913: The Year Before the Storm* (London: Clerkenwell, 2013); Christopher Clark, *The Sleepwalkers: How Europe Went to War in 1914* (London: Allen Lane, 2012).
[3] Morgan Watcyn-Williams, *From Khaki to Cloth* (Caernarfon: Calvinistic Methodist Book Agency, 1949), p. 43.
[4] Emlyn Davies, *Taffy Went to War* (Knutsford: Knutsford Secretarial Bureau, 1975), p. 1.
[5] Keith Strange, *Wales and the First World War* (Cardiff: Mid-Glamorgan County Council, no date), p. 1.
[6] Ibid.
[7] Cyril Parry, 'Gwynedd and the Great War, 1914–1918', *The Welsh History Review*, 14/1 (1988), 78–117.
[8] *Western Mail*, 5 August 1914.
[9] *Western Mail*, 6 August 1914.
[10] *Western Mail*, 8 August 1914.
[11] Strange, *Wales*, p. 1.
[12] Alun Robertson, 'A Welsh Seaside Town at War', in J. Dixon (ed), *Front Line Articles on the Great War by Members of the South Wales Branch, Western Front Association* (Caerphilly: Cwm Press, 1996), pp. 2-4.
[13] Ibid.
[14] *Western Mail*, 19 July 1916.
[15] *Cambrian News*, 14 August 1914.
[16] Quoted in Aled Gruffydd Jones, *Press, Politics and Society: A History of Journalism in Wales* (Cardiff: UWP, 1993), p. 205.
[17] *Welsh Outlook*, September 1914.
[18] Ibid.
[19] *Merthyr Express*, 8 August 1914.
[20] *The Pioneer*, 31 October 1914.
[21] Anthony Mòr O-Brien, 'Keir Hardie, C.B. Stanton, and the First World War', *Llafur*, 4/3 (1986), 31-42.
[22] *Western Mail*, 6 February 1915.
[23] J. Gwynn Williams, *The University of Wales, 1839–1939* (Cardiff: University of Wales Press, 1997), p. 167.
[24] Ibid.
[25] Ibid.
[26] Ibid.
[27] Ibid.
[28] *Western Mail*, 16 October, 1914.

[29] E.L. Ellis, *The University College of Wales, Aberystwyth, 1872-1972* (Cardiff: University of Wales Press, 1972), p. 172.

[30] David Smith and Gareth Williams, *Fields of Praise: The Official History of the Welsh Rugby Union, 1881–1981* (Cardiff: University of Wales Press, 1980), p. 201.

[31] *South Wales Daily News*, 3 September 1914.

[32] Martin Johnes, *Soccer and Society, South Wales 1900-1939* (Cardiff: University of Wales Press, 2002), p. 53.

[33] Aled Gruffydd Jones, *Press, Politics and Society*, p. 204.

[34] Ibid., p.205.

[35] Ibid., pp. 206-7.

[36] Adrian Gregory, 'British "War Enthusiasm" in 1914', in Gail Braybon (ed.), *Evidence, History and the Great War: Historians and the Impact of 1914-18* (Oxford: Oxford University Press, 2003), 67-85.

Chapter 2

'Honour, Glory, Adventure ...'

Voluntary recruitment in Wales

—◊◊◊—

ONCE WAR WAS DECLARED on 4 August, the process of mobilising all available men from the Reserves, Special Reserves and Territorial Force began as quickly as possible. Railway stations throughout Wales became the focal point of every town and village as soldiers hastily rejoined their units. Frank Richards, ex-regular soldier and Royal Welsh Fusiliers reservist, was working as a timberman's assistant in a coal mine. On the evening of 4 August he was drinking in a pub when he heard that war had broken out and that the 'Sergeant of Police was hanging up a notice by the post office, calling all reservists to the colours ... This caused a bit of excitement and language, but it was too late in the evening for any of us to proceed to our depots so we kept on drinking and yarning until stop-tap.'[1]

In August 1914, Harlech was full of summer visitors including a young regular army officer, Major Reid, who was on holiday with his wife, three children and a nanny. O. Wynne Hughes remembers:

> On the Bank Holiday Sunday a telegram for Major Reid arrived at the Post Office. News of this soon travelled around Harlech and the telegraph boy was followed, as always, by a crowd of children, keenly inquisitive about news so exciting that it couldn't wait for the normal post ... By the afternoon the news had swept around the town that Major Reid had been recalled to his regiment and would

be leaving shortly. Spectators gathered and waited. Soon a pony and trap arrived. Major Reid came out, now transformed in khaki, got into the trap and, waving goodbye to a tearful wife and children, was driven away to catch the five o'clock train. It was a short burst of excitement for the children of Harlech, made a little sad with the departure of his family a few days later, and saddened still further some weeks afterwards when news came through that he had been killed in France.[2]

Harold Owen, an Anglo-Welshman who was educated in London but spent his holidays in Penmaenmawr, was a member of the territorial unit, 6th Battalion Royal Welsh Fusiliers. The unit was on annual camp in Aberystwyth prior to the outbreak of war, but on 3 August had been ordered to strike camp and return to north Wales. Ominously, all bayonets were taken down for sharpening. Men from all over north Wales assembled at Conway Morfa camp before Owen's battalion was sent to Northampton for further training:

> Never in the history of Llandudno Junction has there been such excitement amongst the inhabitants as when the 5,000 territorials were entrained at the railway station. Large crowds of inhabitants witnessed the departure and they showered gifts upon the men, some of them forsaking their own Sunday dinners and bringing it on plates to the soldiers.[3]

On 5 August Lord Kitchener was appointed as Secretary of State for War; he immediately began to dominate the proceedings in the Cabinet, with a clear vision of how long he expected the war to last and the size of army needed to achieve victory. The following day, Parliament gave approval to increase the size of the army to 500,000 men, with an immediate appeal for 100,000 volunteers. This was the first of Kitchener's 'New Armies'; he was aiming for four such armies, giving him twenty-four divisions in addition to the six formed by the existing regular army.

At the outbreak of the First World War, Britain had a relatively small, highly trained, professional army, numbering only 247,432 officers and men. Approximately one third of this number was in India in August 1914. This army was in marked contrast to those of the other belligerents:

Austro-Hungary could call on more than 3,000,000 men, France 4,000,000, Germany 4,500,000, and Russia nearly 6,000,000. Britain saw its navy as its prime defence and unlike many European nations, had no tradition of conscription. The army needed 35,000 recruits each year and yet only once between 1908 and 1913 did it exceed 30,000. The Territorial Army, portrayed by its founder Lord Haldane as the 'nation in arms', recruited equally badly: in 1913 it was almost 67,000 men below its establishment of 312,000 with a 12.5 per cent annual wastage rate.[4]

On 1 November 1918, British troops in France (not including colonial troops), amounted to 1,497,198 officers and men, while the British army everywhere at the same date totalled 2,075,275 (again not including colonial troops). To this should be added another 1,383,311 British officers and men stationed at home in November 1918, giving a grand total of 3,458,586. The British army had increased fourteen times in size during the period of the war. By the time of the armistice in 1918, nearly 5,000,000 men had enlisted in the British Army during the war, and when this is added to the pre-war force, and the various reserve formations, it gives a total of 5.7 million soldiers, or 22.1 per cent of the male population of the United Kingdom.[5] This expansion of the British army is seen to be, and quite rightly so, one of the most significant phenomena of the war. The willingness of men to enlist in the army altered the pattern of the previous one hundred years.

The statistical question of just how many men from Wales served in the armed forces, especially in comparison to England, Scotland and Ireland, has proved to be a thorny issue for historians. The evidence for the army, however, is unequivocal, although it is frequently misquoted and misrepresented. Between the outbreak of war and 11 November 1918, 272,924 men from Wales (including Monmouthshire) enlisted in the British army. In the same period, England contributed 4,006,158 men, and Scotland 557,618. Using estimates of the total population in July 1914, official statistics calculated that 11.57 per cent of England's total population enlisted, compared to 11.50 per cent of Scotland's total population, and 10.96 per cent of Wales's population.[6] Taking enlistment as a percentage of estimated male population in July 1914, England contributed 24.02 per cent, Scotland 23.71 per cent, and Wales 21.52 per cent. When the figures for voluntary enlistment are examined, a similar picture emerges: 6.61 per cent of Scotland's estimated population in July 1914 voluntarily enlisted, compared to 6.04 per cent for England, and 5.83 per cent for Wales.[7]

The crucial factor about all these statistics is that Wales consistently lags behind both England and Scotland in all aspects of enlistment. However, countless Welsh historians (and historians of Wales), notably led by Kenneth O. Morgan, have reversed this league table and consequently concluded, on the basis of an erroneous interpretation of the statistics, that the vast majority of people in Wales gave their full and whole-hearted support to the First World War. It is also frequently claimed, again erroneously, that the Welsh supported the war to a greater degree than the men of England and Scotland. Morgan maintained that 'the overwhelming mass of the Welsh people cast aside their political and industrial divisions, and threw themselves into the war with a gusto'.[8] Furthermore, patriotic fervour 'reached heights of hysteria in Wales rarely matched in other parts of the United Kingdom'.[9] In an earlier work he argued that 'the whole-hearted support that Welshmen of all parties and creeds gave to the war itself' was in 'striking contrast to the divisions of the recent past'.[10] Morgan concluded that 'Welshmen, indeed, enlisted in such vast numbers that the proportion of the male population engaged in the armed forces (13.82 per cent) eventually outstripped that for either England or Scotland'.[11] In fact, Morgan was doubly wrong, in that his inaccurate percentage figure refers to the total population of Wales, not the male population.

The myth of the superiority of the Welsh effort has been perpetrated by other historians following Morgan's lead (and often his vocabulary). For example, Gareth Elwyn Jones has written, 'when war broke out in 1914 it was generally popular. Recruitment was proportionately higher in Wales than in England or Scotland'.[12] J. Graham Jones wrote that, 'the majority of Welshmen, sympathising deeply with the plight of the small, defenceless nations on the Continent, responded to the call to arms with a vigour and enthusiasm which were little short of miraculous. The readiness of Welshmen to join the armed services at least equalled that of the Scots and the English.' He referred also to the 'patriotic frenzy of 1914'.[13] Philip Jenkins stated that Wales 'responded to the outbreak of war with considerable enthusiasm, and some 280,000 men would serve, a proportionately higher number than either England or Scotland'.[14]

Gwynfor Evans made the distinction that the 'British Welsh' warmly welcomed the war, but still calculated that, 'it was Wales that sent the highest proportion of men into the armed forces'.[15] More recently, it has been stated that, 'proportionately, more Welsh men and boys were to serve in the armed forces between 1914 and 1918 than either English or Scots'.[16]

Kenneth Morgan's assertion that the Welsh recruiting effort outstripped that of England and Scotland has therefore had a marked effect on later historical writing, interpretation and analysis. However, Morgan's figures were based on statistically flawed evidence, taken from a work published in 1919, edited by two ex-Ministry of Information propagandists, Ivor Nicholson and Trevor Lloyd-Williams, entitled *Wales: Its Part in the War*.[17] In turn, their recruitment figures were based on the speech by Sir Auckland Geddes to the House of Commons on 14 January 1918, in his capacity as Director of Recruiting.

When trying to assess whether the willingness of men to volunteer is evidence of broad Welsh support for the war, it is important to try and ascertain exactly who was volunteering. According to the census of 1911, there were significant numbers of migrants to the very Welsh counties which were at the forefront of voluntaryism. In Glamorgan, 17.30 per cent of the county's population had been born in England, whilst in Monmouthshire the figure was 22.40 per cent. Between 1891-1901, there were 37,861 migrants from England to Glamorgan, and between 1901-11 there were 75,719.[18] The vast majority were employed in the coal industry, which consistently showed high levels of enlistment. Furthermore, the migrants were predominantly male, single and under thirty-five years of age – the most likely profile of a volunteer. It can also be argued that the English migrants would have had fewer familial and societal ties to their new locality, thus predisposing them to be more likely to volunteer. This is not to say that some Welshmen had migrated to England and would join up there, but in nothing like the numbers which would have been travelling in the other direction. For example, of those from the 10th (1st Rhondda) Battalion Welsh Regiment, who had died between August 1914 and December 1916 (and would therefore almost certainly been volunteers), 18.4 per cent had been born in England. The figure for the 13th (2nd Rhondda) Battalion Welsh Regiment was 21.1 per cent. On the basis of these statistics it is possible to argue that around 20 per cent of the Welsh volunteers were actually English, furthering the argument that Welsh support for the war was not quite so full of 'gusto' as has been claimed.

While Wales did provide proportionately fewer men for the army than England or Scotland, this still begs the question as to why just over 145,000 Welshmen volunteered for the armed forces when the liberal, Nonconformist tradition of Wales was strongly anti-militarist. In the nineteenth century, the regular army was seen as a refuge for the destitute and desperate, and for those who were unemployable in any other occupation. The ranks were overwhelmingly English, working-class and at least nominally Anglican. Low pay, poor food and accommodation and harsh discipline (flogging was only abolished in 1881) ensured that recruiting rarely met its annual targets. In 1913, Welshmen made up only 1.8 per cent of the regular army, compared to 78.6 per cent from England, 7.6 per cent from Scotland and 9.1 per cent from Ireland.

D. Parry-Jones, writing of Carmarthenshire just before the First World War, commented that 'the soldier was a rare and somewhat suspect bird in my boyhood days. It was not considered respectable to join the army or the navy or to go down the mines … My mother would have died of a broken heart had any of us joined the army.' Parry-Jones's uncle Jim shocked and disgraced his family when he joined the army, dashing his family's hope that he would go on to a career in the ministry. Direct communication was severed, he was regarded as the prodigal son and his existence was hardly ever referred to.[19] When Emlyn Davies joined the 17th Battalion Royal Welsh Fusiliers in 1915 he couldn't break the news to his mother for two days: 'she suspected there was something out of the ordinary. She thought I had been sacked. It was a terrible shock to her when I did eventually pluck up the courage to enlighten her. Until my departure, and probably long afterwards, she was in a state of near collapse'.[20] Trevor Royle commented that 'traditionally Welsh people looked askance at the armed forces as a means of making a living … nineteenth century Nonconformist preachers had taught their congregations to condemn militarism'.[21] The Welsh Regiment, the South Wales Borderers and the Royal Welsh Fusiliers, whilst nominally representing the Principality, had little direct link with Wales in the nineteenth and early twentieth centuries; all three regiments relied on English recruits to remain up to strength. By contrast, there were fifteen Scottish regiments and seven Irish regiments in the same period. In 1896 a recruiting march undertaken by the Royal Welsh Fusiliers proceeded from Anglesey to Wrexham via Dolgellau and Llangollen. It produced just one recruit who almost immediately was to buy his discharge through a collection taken in his chapel.[22]

The *Welsh Outlook* commented that 'our fathers believed that war under any circumstance was unjustifiable' and any young man who enlisted was 'regarded as a slacker or worse'.[23] Kate Roberts, in her novel *Traed Mewn Cyffion* (*Feet in Chains*), set in the slate-quarrying area of north Wales, wrote dismissively that 'one here and there belonged to the militia, but they were not ones to be proud of'. Ifan Gruffydd, writing of Anglesey, thought that the few who joined the army were regarded as social outcasts 'having chosen the life to escape from the responsibility of living respectably'. Furthermore, 'soldiers and armies and all things military were distant and alien to us at the time, they belonged to the English and the making of war was England's work with us hearing of her achievements'.[24] Robert Graves observed that 'the chapels held soldiering to be sinful and in Merioneth the chapels had the last word'.[25] Whilst Wales provided proportionately less men for the armed forces than either England or Scotland, given the radical, anti-militarist ethos which was embedded in the nation's character, it is perhaps surprising that the recruiting sergeants had any success at all.

Nonconformist intellectuals and early twentieth-century nationalists regarded the Welsh as a naturally peaceful and pacific people, innately anti-militarist. John Ellis has argued persuasively that Wales and its people were not predisposed to pacifism, nor was there a deeply held historical opposition to war and anything which hinted of militarism. He maintains that Wales had a far more complicated relationship with war than this image allows and that 'the Welsh have at times been enthusiastic supporters and participants in war and the British imperial enterprise'[26] Ellis dismisses the argument that the level of support for war in any period corresponds to the degree of decline of Welshness and the increase of Anglicization. He argues that Welsh national identity is 'Janus-faced', contested by two competing images alternately defining the Welsh as a pacific people and as a martial race. There is ample historical evidence of the latter in the characters of Llewelyn Olaf and Owain Glyndŵr and the skills on the battlefield of Welsh soldiers fighting at Crécy and Agincourt. During the nineteenth century, however, a major change took place in the Welsh national character forcefully led by the Nonconformist clergy, which rejected military traditions in favour of a new identity which embraced Christianity and peace. Henry Richard, the first Welsh Nonconformist MP, known as the 'Apostle of Peace' came to represent this new character. Welsh national identity and the cause of peace were to become inextricably linked in this period. Ellis argues that there were the beginnings of an invigoration of the Welsh martial tradition in the early twentieth century, which was to be fully used by the propagandists of the Great War. Lloyd George was to declare that the Welsh martial spirit had been merely 'slumbering' and 'the great warlike spirit that maintained the independence of these mountains for centuries woke up once more.'[27] Thus the war was being fought to defend religion and the rights of small nations, causes which were still consistent with the principles of Welsh patriotism.

Recruitment for the army in Wales was based on three pre-war recruiting areas which broadly conformed to county boundaries. The 23rd (Wrexham) area covered the six north Wales counties, namely Anglesey, Caernarfon, Denbigh, Merioneth, Flintshire and Montgomeryshire, while the 24th (Brecon) area covered mid-Wales, and the 41st (Carmarthen) area covered south and west Wales including Carmarthenshire, Glamorgan and Monmouthshire. Recruiting returns for the three areas are contained in the Ministry of National Service papers showing that a total of 122,995 men volunteered for the regular army and territorial force in Wales, between 4 August 1914 and the end of December 1915. In the Welsh Army Corps papers there are daily recruiting returns for Wales for the first three months of the war. These figures are not always consistent with those of the recruiting areas, but they do reflect the trends of recruitment. In total, 272,924 men from Wales served in the army during the war, in addition to the many thousands who joined the Royal Navy and Naval Reserve, for which accurate figures are not available.

The statistics of voluntary recruitment clearly show that in Wales, as in Scotland and England, there was not the 'rush to the colours' that has often been portrayed. There are very few illustrated books on the First

World War that do not have a picture of a long snake of cap-wearing men, waiting patiently outside a recruiting office. However, it was only in the final week of August 1914 that the number of recruits reached over 500 per day in Wales, with the main peak occurring in the first ten days of September. Peter Simkins, in his detailed study of the raising of 'Kitchener's Army', noted that 'the provinces were slower to respond to the call to arms', and indeed one third of all those who enlisted in Britain on 8 August did so at Great Scotland Yard. On 9 August, London produced 1,100 recruits which was almost half the national total for the day.[28] In Wales on this day only fifty-eight men enlisted.

The outbreak of war caused uncertainty, both in the workplace and in the home. While some men felt able to join up immediately, most needed time to settle their affairs, perhaps ensuring that their jobs would be held open for them at the end of the war – whenever that might be. Furthermore, married men were initially concerned about separation allowances, which had previously been paid monthly in arrears. At the end of August it was announced that all new recruits would be entitled to such allowances and from September 1914 they would be paid weekly. A married man was entitled to 12s. 6d per week, plus 2s. 6d per child for the first three children and 2s. per child thereafter. A further factor which slowed enlistments early in the war was that the creaking administrative machinery of a pre-war army could not cope with the number of recruits coming forward. Throughout August new recruiting offices were being hastily opened in towns such as Llanelli, Tumble and Ammanford, with nineteen in Glamorgan, to deal with the influx of volunteers.

Early in the war there was still a fairly rigid adherence to the physical requirements: men had to be between eighteen and thirty, a minimum height of 5 ft 3 ins, a chest of 32 ins with a range of 2 ins on deflation, a minimum weight of 110 lbs, good eyesight and teeth that would not cause malnutrition. A Parliamentary Report on recruitment published after the war admitted that recruiting had become so brisk in early September that the difficulties of housing, feeding and clothing the men became unmanageable, and it was deemed advisable that a 'brake should be put on'. While the height regulation was raised and lowered, other physical requirements were conveniently ignored as the war progressed. William David Roberts, a fifteen-year-old steel worker from Swansea, enlisted into the 6th Battalion Welsh Guards, claiming to be nineteen years and three months. He was wounded on the Somme in July 1916, his post-war discharge papers proving he was born in 1899. One of the youngest to lose his life was Private Richard Flynn from Milford Haven, 9th Battalion Welsh Regiment, who was killed at the Battle of Loos on 25 September 1915, aged fifteen. His name appears on the Loos Memorial, which forms part of the wall surrounding Dud Corner Cemetery. The town of Carmarthen claimed to have supplied the youngest recruit for the British army, who joined the Welsh Regiment at thirteen years and nine months.

Robert Graves recalled that when he was attached to the 2nd Battalion Welsh Regiment 'the recruits were mostly men either over-age or under-age ... or with some slight physical disability'.[29] In his first platoon of forty men no less than fourteen in the roll gave their age as forty or over; Fred Prosser, a painter in civilian life was actually fifty-six. The oldest of all, James Burford, a collier and fitter, was sixty-three. Prior to the war he had last fired a rifle in anger in Egypt in 1882 and when he had tried to re-enlist in the South African war he had been told he was too old.[30] On the wall of the church of St John the Baptist in Cardiff there is a memorial plaque to Sergeant Charles O. Winn who died on active service on 22 May 1918, aged fifty-eight. He served with the Army Service Corps and was buried at Mikra British cemetery at Kalamaria. Under the banner of 'King and Country', those in recruiting offices were happy to accept the answers of volunteers at face value, even when the physical evidence in front of their eyes proved otherwise.

In Wales, as in England and Scotland, the peak of voluntary recruitment took place in the period 25 August–10 September 1914. On Wednesday 3 September, 33,204 men enlisted throughout Britain, with 2,180 in Wales. On the following day 1,941 recruits enlisted in Wales, but then the number fell for two days to under 1,000 before rising again to over 1,100 per day on 8, 9, 10 September. On 3 September, the *Western Mail* commented:

> It is evident that the people have awakened at last to the unprecedented dangers to which the country is exposed, and that there is now a keener desire to assume a personal share of the burden of national defence ... the people of this country are patriotic enough at bottom, but they do not live in an atmosphere of patriotic fervour. While in

Glamorgan and Monmouthshire the authorities have been active enough ... there is a lamentable want of organised effort in other parts of Wales.

Many recruiting stations were unable to cope with the sudden influx of volunteers. A.E. Perriman presented himself for enlistment in Newport at the end of August; he passed his medical, was given 1s. 'tip' and then sent home to await notice to report. This did not come for a fortnight, when he was told to rendezvous at the central cattle market, 'a right place believe me'. Around one hundred men found themselves being 'pushed around like cattle by drovers masquerading as sergeants'. Headed by a local band they marched through the town to the cheers of the crowd lining the streets en route to the railway station. They were treated as 'national heroes'. When they reached the headquarters of the South Wales Borderers in Brecon, conditions soon brought them down to earth:

> The washing facilities and toiletry were disgusting. There was no hot water available. On each floor was a two-handled tank of considerable proportions which was filled, or thereabouts during the night by barrack room occupants. In the morning it had to be carried away and emptied by [a] room orderly with [the] help of a volunteer. Reveille at 6 a.m. followed with beating of drum and blaring bugle in the barrack rooms made further sleep impossible ... to the Mess for breakfast. This consisted of a pint size basin of tea, undrinkable because of grease from previous meals, floating on top, which almost turned one's stomach, chunks of bread, pieces of margarine and fat bacon.[31]

When someone complained about the tea, the sergeant replied, 'There's nothing wrong with that', as he proceeded to 'stir the offending beverage with two somewhat grubby fingers'.

In north Wales, recruitment in the Welsh-speaking areas was consistently lower than in the English-speaking areas. In August 1914, one recruiter complained that 'ten days yielded but the paltry total of sixty men for Kitchener's Army in Caernarfonshire', while another complained that 'no one registered in the regular Army in Anglesey during the last week of September'.[32] In October 1914, when Sir Henry Lewis visited markets in Menai Bridge and Caernarfon, he noted that there were 'hundreds of young men at both places who ought to be drilling and serving their country in a crisis'.[33] The slate-quarrying areas were criticised by the Caernarfonshire Recruiting Committee for poor enlistment rates, especially as many quarrymen were on short time, and thus had a clear economic incentive to enlist. One contributor to the *Manchester Guardian* argued that the enlistment rates were low in these areas because the quarryman's 'education is almost entirely Welsh and religious'.[34]

Across Wales, a sharp decline in volunteers had followed in the second half of September, after the early rush, with daily totals dwindling to an average of 200. The same pattern of recruitment occurred in England and Scotland. In September 1914, 462,901 men volunteered for the regular army and territorial force, with 23,449 coming from Wales. It is, of course, difficult to draw too many conclusions from these figures because the conditions under which men were enlisting constantly changed. Separation allowances, the stringency of medicals, and even the bounty paid to recruiters (originally 2s. 6d, but reduced to 1s.) altered during the early months of the war and subsequently had an effect on the flow of volunteers. It can be argued, therefore, that it was not solely the enthusiasm or commitment of the volunteers for the war which altered, but the conditions under which they were enlisting. The various authorities were struggling to find the right balance between military requirements, civilian enthusiasm and political expediency.

The boom of voluntary recruitment was an extraordinary phenomenon but short-lived. The Welsh Army Corps figures in their 'Statement of Recruiting in Wales' show only 4,891 enlistments in Wales between 1 October and 26 October 1914, which is when the figures end. In the last week of the recorded figures, enlistments had fallen to only 170 per day, with the nadir being reached on 26 October with eighty-two enlistments. There was disquiet both locally and nationally at these declining figures, and although the army stood at over one million men at

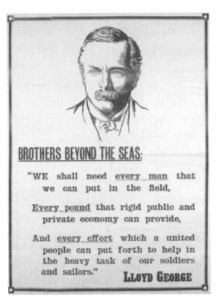

A David Lloyd George recruiting poster, used in both England and Wales.

the end of November 1914, Parliament had sanctioned a growth to two million men. In Wales, prior to conscription, a monthly total of 8,000 or more volunteers was only reached in October 1914, November 1914 and January 1915. In September and December 1915 the monthly total fell below 3,000.

What had caused this slow down in volunteers? Firstly, there is clear evidence that recruitment was affected by the economic situation. When war was declared, orders in both home and foreign trade were withheld or cancelled, large numbers of factories went on short-time, and there was an abrupt and considerable curtailment of production. However, by the end of September 1914, prospects of employment showed a considerable up-turn compared to August. While it is impossible to be certain of a causal relationship between the strength of the economy, employment, and enlistment rates, there is no doubt that as employment opportunities in Wales fell in August and early September 1914, enlistment increased, and this pattern reversed itself from October 1914 onwards, with employment opportunities increasing and enlistments falling.

The second reason for declining enlistments in Wales in the autumn of 1914 can be explained by a growing realisation that the war would not be 'all over by Christmas' and that the conditions under which recruits were trained were far from ideal. A good example of this was provided by a recruit from Llanelli, who had enlisted in the town with the Royal Field Artillery, and was immediately sent to Woolwich. Clearly this army did not march on its stomach, as food was reported to be a major source of complaint. Breakfast was one-sixth of a loaf of bread, lunch was potatoes and stewed meat, and tea was a repeat of breakfast. Knives and forks were scarce, and their meals were eaten using only fingers; this was matched by those who served up the meals, as the orderly who served the potatoes used, 'his hands only in the process'. After some days at Woolwich, the recruits were ordered to Shorncliffe where training began. Reveille was at 5.30 a.m. with parade at 6.00 a.m., followed by a swim in the sea and a four or five mile march, all before breakfast. No uniforms or kit were issued and the men had only the clothes they stood up in, consequently lice and vermin were rampant in the tents in which the recruits were living. Such reports were hardly likely to encourage men to rush to the recruiting offices, even if this particular new recruit typically concluded his letter by

Gwnaeth ef ei ddyledswydd
A wnewch CHWI?

Parliamentary Recruiting Committee
poster No 20, showing Lord Frederick
Roberts VC, hero of military campaigns
in India, Afghanistan and South Africa.
(He did his duty. Will you?)

Parliamentary Recruiting Committee
poster No 31. (To the Army, boys of
Wales! Hated is the man who does not
hate the enemy of his country. Wales
for ever!)

saying, 'in spite of all these defects, the men are in splendid spirits'.[35]

Throughout the period of voluntary enlistment, the Parliamentary Recruiting Committee (PRC), which met first at the end of August 1914, was broadly responsible for trying to maintain a satisfactory flow of recruits. In Wales, responsibility was delegated to a Welsh National Executive Committee based in Cardiff, with a system of county recruiting committees and sub-committees to organize activities at a local level. The county committees relied on the voluntary support and co-operation of local community leaders such as JPs, ministers of religion, aldermen and other local politicians, under the chairmanship of the lord lieutenant of the county. The programme lacked strategic direction, consequently counties responded with varying degrees of enthusiasm, often relying heavily on the efforts of committed individuals.

The PRC quickly set up a publications sub-department, which was to produce twenty million leaflets and two million posters by the end of March 1915. After some pressure by the Executive Committee of the Welsh Army Corps, and the support of the clerk to the PRC, R.H. Davies, a series of Welsh posters became available in November 1914. The first (PRC No 15), produced against a green background with white type and a yellow and black border, was headed 'Y DARN PAPUR' (The Scrap of Paper). It showed a reproduction of the seals and signatures of the representatives of Britain, Belgium, Austria, France, Russia and Germany from the Treaty of London of 1839, which guaranteed Belgian independence and neutrality. It stated, 'Mae'r Ellmyn wedi tori eu llw, gan anrheithio Belgium' (The Germans have broken their pledge and are ravaging Belgium) and concluded, 'Ymrestrwch heddyw' (Enlist today). The second poster (PRC No 20) depicted a large framed portrait of the recently-deceased Lord Frederick Roberts, winner of the Victoria Cross and hero of military campaigns in India, Afghanistan and South Africa. The next Welsh poster (PRC No 22) showed little understanding of what was needed locally with the entreaty 'Dewch gyda mi, fechgyn!' (Come along, boys!), supported by a quotation by General Sir Horace Smith-Dorrien. It was not until December 1914 that the PRC produced two posters which were more specifically aimed at Welsh recruits. PRC No 30 was printed against a yellow background, within a green border of daffodil stems and PRC No 31 had red text overlaid across an outline map of Wales.

The other area in which the PRC was actively engaged was the organization of meetings, initially to promote British involvement in the war, but also to try and persuade members of the audience to enlist. Public meetings, at the beginning of the twentieth century, were an established method of launching various projects from the parochial to the national; they would generally have been well attended, seen almost as a form of public entertainment. A meeting, typical of those early in the war, took place at Maesteg rugby ground on 5 September, 1914. Prior to the gathering, the Hibernian Band, the Caerau Silver Band, the Salvation Army and the Boy Scouts paraded through the main streets of the town. Speeches were given by local dignitaries including Revd M.H. Jones and Vernon Hartshorn. The latter

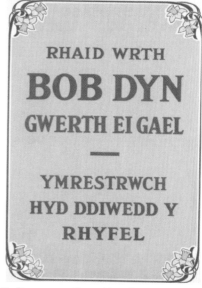

RHAID WRTH

BOB DYN

GWERTH EI GAEL

—

YMRESTRWCH HYD DDIWEDD Y RHYFEL

Parliamentary Recruiting Committee poster No 30. (We must have every worthwhile man – register until the end of the war.)

declared that the war was one of democracy against autocracy and he supported the government in their declaration of war, if only to support the smaller nations in their fight for liberty. A resolution was passed urging all able-bodied men young men to join the armed forces and 'cheers were raised' for the British army and navy. The meeting concluded with the singing of the hymn 'Bydd myrdd o ryfeddodau' (There will be a myriad of wonders), whereupon 'hundreds of young men announced their intention of joining Kitchener's Army'.[36] On the following day, it was reported that nearly 3,000 young men attended a meeting at the Tredegar Olympia and 'many young men gave in their names as recruits'.[37]

In north Wales one of the most significant features of the recruiting meetings was the coalition of two elites drawn from their respective English-speaking and Welsh-speaking communities. Predictably, the most loyal and fervent support for the government's policies came from the leading members of the English-speaking community, who occupied strategic roles in local society not only as holders of high civic offices, but also as owners and managers of land and large commercial enterprises such as the slate quarries. However, the contribution of this group was necessarily limited because of their inability to speak Welsh and the fact that they were perceived by most local inhabitants as a class apart. Thus the support and involvement of the Welsh-speaking members of the pro-war coalition proved to be vital.[38] Recruiting meetings attracted large audiences, as in south Wales, though similarly it is hard to know just how many recruits were actually secured. Cultural leaders such as Sir O.M. Edwards, Professors J. Morris Jones, E.V. Arnold and H. Milner-Barry of the University College of North Wales, and Profesor R. Morris of Bala Theological College all spoke frequently at meetings, as did leading ministers of religion such as Revds John Williams, Brynsiencyn, R. Silyn Roberts (also the editor of the *Welsh Outlook*), T.C. Williams, Gwynoro Davies, H. Berriw Williams and O. Selwyn Jones. Political leaders such as Sir Henry Lewis of Bangor, Ellis Jones Griffith MP and Ellis W. Davies MP, also appeared at many meetings, which were generally conducted in Welsh.

In 1915 as recruiting levels continued to fall, more innovative approaches were tried. On 5 April 1915 a parade was organized through the streets of Cardiff, involving 5,000 schoolchildren who had fathers or brothers fighting in the armed forces. A banner held by one child read, 'My Daddy is at the front, what is yours doing?'[39] On April 17, an international rugby union match was organized by the military authorities at Cardiff Arms Park, between a Welsh XV and an International XV, drawn mainly from England and Scotland. Nearly all those who played had previously been capped by their respective countries; nine of the Welsh team and all those in the combined team were members of the armed forces. Successfully combining the two religions of Wales was the pack leader Revd Lieutenant Alban Davies, chaplain to the 6th Battalion Welsh regiment. All servicemen in uniform were admitted free, while others paid 6d to stand or 1s. 6d to sit. Recruiting sergeants were on duty throughout the game and anyone who enlisted on the day was given free admission. Prior to the match, the crowd was entertained by the bands of the 3rd Battalion Welsh Regiment and the 3rd Cameron Highlanders, while at half-time 'stirring appeals were made to the spectators to join the forces'. Despite all these efforts only sixty volunteers came forward on the day, but it was estimated that over 1,000 did so in Cardiff during the following week.[40] In early May, the 3rd Battalion Welsh Regiment sent a recruiting party to Manchester. Over 500 recruits were obtained in one week, necessitating a special train being commissioned to bring the men to Wales. This was followed by a procession through the streets of Cardiff, headed by a banner proclaiming 'See what Manchester did in one week for the Welsh Regiment. Now, Cardiff, what will you do?'[41]

On 22 May 1915 a boxing carnival was held at Cardiff Arms Park, attracting a crowd of 8,000, which included both military bouts and professional exhibition contests. The top billing was a twenty round bout between Driver Joe Johns from Merthyr Tydfil and Arthur Evans from Tirphil in the Rhymney Valley, fighting for the Welsh lightweight championship. It was fittingly won by the military man. Only thirty-eight volunteers came forward during the day, with a further fifty-three on Monday 24 May. This poor response provided further evidence for those who saw the only answer to the manpower shortages of the armed forces to be compulsory military service. At a recruiting conference called by the Mayor of Swansea in mid-May 1915, speaker after speaker advocated compulsion as the only solution.[42]

By mid-1915, public attitudes towards the war were changing both in Britain generally and in Wales. Growing casualty lists, disillusionment with the reasons for fighting and a more realistic appreciation of the realities of twentieth century warfare all played their part. It was therefore hardly surprising that voluntary enlistment was falling to a point where there was not going to be enough men coming forward to fight the war to a successful conclusion. Evidence of official concerns about the level of volunteers was again shown by the raising of the maximum age of enlistment from thirty-eight to forty, and the lowering of the minimum height to 5 ft 2 ins, both in June 1915.

By the end of December 1915, 122,995 men from Wales had volunteered for the army, out of a total of some 2.5 million throughout Britain. Historians continue to debate why so many men, more or less enthusiastically, volunteered to fight, especially as at most times those from Wales certainly did not willingly become soldiers. Most explanations for this phenomenon centre on the degree of militarism which existed in Edwardian society, pre-conditioning and pre-disposing men to enlist when war was declared. Ian Beckett has written that 'the British public had been conditioned in advance to meet the challenge of war through the militarization of the British public schools and youth organisations, through the influence of the press and popular literature, even through the industrial militancy of the Edwardian age.' Commonly held ideas of war, of patriotism, and of duty therefore created a collective frame of mind which was receptive to calls for enlistment when war broke out.[43]

It can be argued that the situation in pre-war Wales would not have been greatly dissimilar to that in other parts of Britain. The publishing revolution of the 1880s ensured that newspapers and periodicals were more widely available and more widely read than ever before. Undoubtedly authors such as G.A. Henty, R. Haggard, W.H.G. Kingston, R.M. Ballantyne and P.F. Westerman would have been read, all of whom alluded to the glory of the empire, patriotism, and the manly and healthy-minded pursuit of fighting wars. The popular press, popular entertainment such as the music hall and even the infant cinema did similar service in transmitting nationalistic themes. *The Boys' Own Paper*, *Chums* and *The Captain* would have peddled similar ideas, and would have been read

Troops of the 2nd Battalion South Wales Borderers, on the road to the trenches in the rain at Montauban, October 1916.
(Imperial War Museum)

by the youngsters of certainly the urban areas of south Wales. Queen Victoria's Diamond Jubilee, the outbreak of the South African War, the relief of Mafeking and the Coronations of King Edward VII and George V were as enthusiastically celebrated in Newport, Merthyr Tydfil or Milford Haven, as they were in the towns of England. It can be argued that the concept of fighting wars in distant lands, if not the actuality, would have found some favour in industrialised Wales.

The growth of youth organizations in the late nineteenth century, and early twentieth century, it is claimed, provided a fertile breeding ground for the future volunteers for the First World War. Such movements were often based on a loose military structure, were uniformed, and were frequently founded and led by ex-military men. Most importantly, they

A toby jug depiction of David Lloyd George, Minister of Munitions from May 1915.

emphasised and reinforced the attributes of duty, honour and patriotism which were so important to the voluntary recruiting movement.[44] The Boys' Brigade, founded in 1883, had branches in south Wales and whilst claiming religious rather than militarist aims, still continued to drill with dummy rifles until 1924. The Church Lads' Brigade, founded in 1891, was openly militaristic. Tudor Lewis from Carmarthen remembers joining the Brigade when he was eleven years old, meeting twice a week in the town barracks. They wore khaki uniforms, were issued with rifles and often marched through the town led by a bugle band.[45] In August 1914, at least two battalions of the Brigade from all over Wales, went on a camp to Dawlish in Devon, where they were involved in drill parades, military-style manoeuvres and mock battles. One of the battalions was made up of five hundred boys, most of whom apparently were Welsh-speaking.[46]

Another explanation often cited for encouraging Welsh volunteers was their sympathy with Belgium as a similarly small nation, being pushed around by its larger and more powerful neighbour. In Lloyd George's oft-quoted speech at the Queen's Hall on 19 September, 1914 he referred to the war as a noble fight by all the 'five-foot-five nations' such as Wales, Belgium and Serbia, to defeat the German military caste. Robert Graves recalled being outraged by the 'Germans' cynical violation of Belgian neutrality', although he can hardly be held up as typifying the mood in Wales. The average Welsh volunteer was probably more likely to have agreed with 'Bill', the author of Herbert Read's model letter home: 'Well, they say it's all for little Belgium, so cheer up, says I: but wait till I gets hold of little Belgium'.

There were those who saw war as an intrinsically valuable human endeavour, beneficial for both society and the individual. Saunders Lewis, writing to Margaret Gilcriest, told of how glad he was to leave for the war, dreaming in an 'absurd young way of winning strength, character, power, conviction, – and especially depth'.[47] A.E. Perriman, a supervising surveyor with a firm of architects in Newport, was swayed to enlist by the general mood of the time: 'Soon there appeared on hoardings all over the country, posters portraying Kitchener, with pointed finger ... Stirred by the call, with a colleague ... [we] decided to offer our services, and went along to the recruiting office'.[48] Others, who worked long hours in appalling conditions for low wages, and who rarely left their own neighbourhood except for an occasional day out at the seaside, saw the war as a unique opportunity for travel and excitement. Oliver Powell from Tredegar commented, 'Oh yes, a great patriot I was, bloody glad to get out of the pit. I thought we would have a good time, have a good adventure, it was supposed to be over by Christmas'.[49] Another miner, B.L. Coombes, was keen to volunteer to escape the 'machine roars and long hours' of the pit.[50] Irving Jones of the 10th Battalion Welsh Regiment was also working in a colliery:

> There were people joining up, you know, and I thought, oh well – my brother-in-law, we discussed it and we decided to join up. We thought, well, a holiday maybe, you know, that's what we thought. We'd beat the Germans in about six months. That's what we thought.[51]

Volunteers on Llandrindod Wells station, c1914.

(Courtesy of Powys County Archives)

It was not only manual workers who sought to escape from their workplace. Ll. Wyn Griffith, aged twenty-four when war broke out, was employed as a civil servant in the inland revenue:

> I was a Welshman, and my contemporaries were enlisting in the Royal Welch Fusiliers. They were escaping from offices, shops, farms and factories, from the humdrum duties of civilian life to which I was condemned. I cannot remember that I ever thought of soldiering as anything but a better way of life than sitting at a desk: Killing or being killed was something that might happen to someone else. None of my contemporaries thought that there was anything 'noble' about joining the armed forces. It was what your friends were doing, and it was only natural that you should do the same, if you could.[52]

Captain Macdonald and RSM Jones of the 15th Battalion (London Welsh) Royal Welsh Fusiliers with a pet dog in the trenches at Fleurbaix, 28 December 1917. *(Imperial War Museum)*

Men in Wales volunteered for all manner of reasons: some were undoubtedly stirred by the patriotic call to arms and the concept of national duty had real meaning for them; some saw the war as an escape from hard physical employment, a chance for adventure and excitement; and others enlisted for economic reasons. As Peter Simkins wrote 'Probably only a small number had a single overriding motive for enlistment, most recruits being driven to join by a combination of external pressures and personal desires and loyalties'.[53] Furthermore, different factors will have had a greater relative importance at different times during the period of voluntary enlistment.

The naivety of many volunteers is typified by the letters home of Private A.J. Turner, who enlisted with the South Wales Borderers: 'now at last the day had come. Honour, glory, adventure, probably a decoration or two, family adulation – it all lay ahead'. The reality of 'prison haircuts, scrubbing floors and tables, "spud bashing", cleaning cook-house utensils, cleaning latrines, and when these tasks were completed, other utterly useless duties were invented' soon hit home.[54] However, the miseries of training at Kinmel Park were nothing compared to the unknown horrors that lay ahead.

NOTES

[1] Frank Richards, *Old Soldiers Never Die* (London: Faber and Faber, 1930), pp. 9-10.

[2] O. Wynne Hughes, *Every Day was Summer: Childhood Memories of Edwardian Days in a Small Welsh Town* (Llandysul: Gomer Press, 1989), p. 117.

[3] *The North Wales Weekly News*, 3 September 1914.

[4] Peter Simkins, *Kitchener's Army: The Raising of the New Armies, 1914-16* (Manchester: Manchester University Press, 1988), pp. 17-20.

[5] *Statistics of the Military Effort of the British Empire during the Great War* (London: HMSO, 1922), p. 364.

[6] Ibid., p. 363.

[7] *General Annual Report on the British Army (Recruiting) for the period from 1st October 1913 to 30th September 1919*, PP 1921, XX, Cmd 1193.

[8] Kenneth O. Morgan, *Rebirth of a Nation: Wales, 1880–1980* (London: Oxford University Press, 1982), p. 159.

[9] Morgan, *Rebirth of a Nation*, p. 161.

[10] Kenneth O. Morgan, *Wales in British Politics, 1868–1922* (Cardiff: University of Wales Press, 1980), p. 275.

[11] Morgan, *Rebirth of a Nation*, p. 160.

[12] Gareth Elwyn Jones, *Modern Wales, A Concise History, 1485–1979* (Cambridge: Cambridge University Press, 1984), p. 256.

[13] J. Graham Jones, *The History of Wales* (Cardiff: University of Wales Press, 1990), pp. 135-7.

[14] Philip Jenkins, *The History of Modern Wales, 1536-1990* (London: Longman, 1992), p. 343.

[15] Gwynfor Evans, *Land of My Fathers* (Talybont: Y Lolfa, 1992), p. 429.

[16] David Ross, *Wales, History of a Nation* (New Lanark: Geddes & Grosset, 2005), p. 222.

[17] I. Nicholson and T. Lloyd-Williams (eds), *Wales: Its Part in the War* (London: Hodder and Stoughton, 1919).

[18] Philip N. Jones, 'Population Migration into Glamorgan, 1861–1911: a Re-assessment', Prys Morgan (ed.) *Glamorgan County History, VI* (Cardiff: Glamorgan History Trust Ltd, 1988), pp. 173–202.

[19] David Parry-Jones, *Welsh Country Upbringing* (London: Batsford, 1948), p. 94.

[20] Emlyn Davies, *Taffy Went to War*, (Knursford: Knutsford Secretarial Bureau, 1975), p. 2.

[21] Trevor Royle, *Anatomy of a Regiment: Ceremony and Soldiering in the Welsh Guards* (London: Michael Joseph, 1990), p. 26.

[22] Michael Glover, *That Astonishing Infantry: Three Hundred Years of the History of the Royal Welch Fusiliers (23rd Regiment of Foot) 1689–1989* (London: Leo Cooper, 1989), p. 57.

[23] *Welsh Outlook*, October 1914.

[24] Ifan Gruffydd, *Gŵr o Baradwys* (Dinbych: Gwasg Gee, 1963), p. 115.

[25] Robert Graves, *Goodbye to All That* (London: Cassell, 1957), p. 82.

[26] John Ellis, 'A pacific people – a martial race: pacifism, militarism and Welsh national identity', in Matthew Cragoe and Chris Williams (eds), *Wales and War: Society, Politics and Religion in the Nineteenth and Twentieth Centuries* (Cardiff: University of Wales Press, 2007), 15-37.

[27] Ibid., p. 28.

[28] Simkins, *Kitchener's Army*, p. 49.

[29] Graves, *Goodbye to All That*, p. 94.

[30] Ibid., p. 95.

[31] IWM, letters of A.E. Perriman, 80/43/1.

[32] Cyril Parry, 'Gwynedd and the Great War, 1914–18', *The Welsh History Review*, 14/1 (1988), 78–117.

[33] Ibid.

[34] Ibid.

[35] *Llanelly Mercury*, 17 September, 1914.

[36] *Western Mail*, 7 September 1914.

[37] Parry, 'Gwynedd'.

[38] Ibid.

[39] *Western Mail*, 5 April, 1915.

[40] *Western Mail*, 24 April, 1915.

[41] *Western Mail*, 12 May, 1915.

[42] *Western Mail*, 17 May, 1915.

[43] Ian Beckett, 'The British Army 1914-18: the Illusion of Change', in John Turner (ed.), *Britain and the First World War* (London: Unwin Hyman, 1988), 99-116.

[44] See J.O. Springhall, *Youth, Empire and Society* (London: Croom Helm, 1977); P. Wilkinson, 'English Youth Movements 1908–1930', *Journal of Contemporary History*, 4/2 (1969), 3-24.

[45] Personal testimony to the author.

[46] *Carmarthen Journal*, 7 August 1914.

[47] Mair Saunders Jones (ed.), *Letters to Margaret Gilcriest* (Cardiff: University of Wales Press, 1993), p. 241

[48] IWM, letters of A.E. Perriman, 80/43/1.

[49] Keith Strange, *Wales and the First World War* (Cardiff: Mid-Glamorgan County Council, n.d.) p.5.

[50] B.L. Coombes, *These Poor Hands* (Cardiff: University of Wales Press, 2002), p. 88.

[51] Strange, *Wales and the First World War*, p. 5.

[52] Ll. Wyn Griffith, 'The Pattern of One Man's Remembering', in George A. Panichas (ed.), *Promise of Greatness* (London: Cassell, 1968), 286–294.

[53] Simkins, *Kitchener's Army*, p. 185.

[54] IWM, Papers of A. J. Turner, 81/21/1.

Chapter 3

Lloyd George's Welsh Army Corps

The foundation and recruitment
of the 38th (Welsh) Division

—◆—

O N SATURDAY 19 SEPTEMBER at the Queen's Hall, London, the Chancellor of the Exchequer, David Lloyd George, addressed the leaders of all Welsh organisations and denominations in the capital. It was one of the seminal speeches of the war, being a familiar mixture of bombast, hyperbole, questionable historical allusions and emotional appeals to patriotic instincts, but delivered with customary conviction and eloquence. Its greatest significance, however, lay in the fact that it was the first occasion at which Lloyd George had publicly spoken in support of the war and was thus widely reported in both the Welsh and English press. Privately, he was scathing of his audience at the Queen's Hall saying 'they made him sick.' Apparently, 'they were far too stodgy and "comfortable" – "you had to talk your way through layers of fat".'[1]

Although Lloyd George was initially depressed with his speech and thought it was a failure, he was soon buoyed by the press reaction on the following Sunday and Monday. In his speech he had referred to 'the great peaks of Honour, Duty, Patriotism, and, clad in glittering white, the great pinnacle of Sacrifice pointing like a rugged finger to Heaven'.[2] Such sentiments appealed to the Conservative Party even more than to his own Liberal Party and showed a marked change from his position five weeks previously when he had urged his wife not to let their eldest son volunteer too hastily for the war.

Lloyd George declared his commitment to all-out war, characterising the enemy in the shape of the Prussian *Junkers* as the 'road-hog of Europe', and predicting the allies would advance from 'terror to triumph'. With an eye on the wider Welsh audience, he declared that the war was a noble fight by all the 'five-foot-five nations' such as Wales, Belgium and Serbia, to defeat the German military caste. He appealed to the 'race that faced the Norman for hundreds of years in their struggle for freedom, the race that helped to win the battle of Crécy, the race that fought for a generation under Glyndwr', to form a Welsh Army in the Field. [3]

The Welsh Army Corps (WAC) had its genesis in these 'inspiring words', which awakened the 'old marshal ardour and patriotism of the Cymry which for centuries had been slumbering'.[4] Lloyd George was 'overwhelmed with letters of congratulation' for his speech. Prime Minister Asquith, apparently with tears in his eyes, said it was a 'wonderful speech'; Sir Edward Grey apparently wept when he read the peroration; the Chancellor of the Duchy of Lancaster, Charles Masterman, said it was, 'the finest speech in the history of England'.[5]

Two days after the Queen's Hall speech, on 21 September 1914, Lloyd George called a conference of prominent Welshmen at 11 Downing Street to explore further the possibilities of forming a Welsh Army Corps. The Chancellor's idea was 'quickly translated into a living reality' with the formulation of a Provisional Committee of nine members, with the Earl of Plymouth as Chairman, and career civil servant Owen W. Owen as Secretary. The other members of the Committee were Lord Mostyn, Lord Kenyon, Major-General Sir Ivor Herbert, Sir David B. Jones, Reginald McKenna, William Brace, R.T. Jones and Lloyd George himself.[6] After this initial meeting, and organising the Conference in Cardiff on 29 September 1914, the Provisional Committee never met again.

Fears were soon expressed about the idea of a separate Welsh formation, despite the fact that Lord Kitchener, the Secretary of State for War, had recently sanctioned the creation of an Ulster Division. Kitchener invariably viewed proposals for national and semi-national formations with a great deal of caution, until he was sure that they would fit into the established framework of the army and would not remain as separate entities of their own. In his memoirs Lloyd George originally claimed that Kitchener had vetoed the idea of a Welsh Army Corps, although there is no supporting evidence for this.[7] It would not have been a surprise if Kitchener had done so given his view expressed to Asquith: 'no purely Welsh regiment is to be trusted; they are ... always wild & insubordinate & ought to be stiffened by a strong infusion of English or Scotch'.[8] However, on 23 September 1914, it was formally announced that the Secretary of State for War had sanctioned the formation of a Welsh Army Corps.

Lloyd George and Kitchener clashed again in the Cabinet, on 28 September 1914, over the question of sending Nonconformist chaplains to the front. Kitchener did not want to face the difficulty of accommodating all shades of religious belief in the Army, but Lloyd George realised the importance to recruitment for the future WAC of gaining Nonconformist support. Lloyd George compared the situation to native Indian troops, Sikhs and Gurkhas, who were allowed to have priests of their own faith in their regiments. He also accused Kitchener of wanting to send a 'Church of England Army to the front', which would effectively bar half the Welsh nation. Kitchener eventually backed down and asked Lloyd George to supply a list of the Nonconformist denominations.[9]

On 29 September 1914, over 2,000 politicians, religious leaders, trades unionists and industrialists were invited to a conference in Cardiff to consider further the formation of a Welsh Army Corps. After numerous speeches a resolution was unanimously passed 'that Wales, including Monmouthshire, be constituted a military administrative area for the purpose of recruiting and raising the necessary men to form a Welsh Army Corps'.[10] The scale of the proposed force was therefore set at two divisions, the normal size at the time for a formation designated as an army corps. Lloyd George's role as a catalyst for the WAC was crucial. He firmly subscribed to the view that a small nation had an inalienable right to recognition as a separate entity and that Wales ought to be recognised as 'one of the sister nations that entered the lists in defence of the liberties and freedom of other small nations'.[11] Following the meeting in Cardiff on 29 September 1914, Lloyd George played little further part in the affairs of the WAC, but without his Queen's Hall speech and original involvement the WAC would never have been formed.

The new WAC National Executive Committee (WNEC) met for the first time on 2 October 1914 at the Law Courts in Cardiff, acutely aware of the difficulties which would arise in its relationship with the Territorial

Force Associations and the Regular Army, both of whom were competing for the same potential body of recruits. By 30 September 1914 it had been estimated that between 40,000-50,000 men had already volunteered from Wales for the Regular Army, Territorial Force and the Navy. To raise an essentially 'Welsh' army corps was therefore going to be a formidable undertaking, given that the peak of voluntary enlistments had already been reached earlier in the month. Furthermore, there was an added misunderstanding about the extent to which the WAC would embrace units already recruited in Wales, which was never satisfactorily resolved.[12]

At the next meeting on 5 October 1914, the WNEC presented to a representative of the War Office, Major-General P. Jeffreys, a list of recommendations which they hoped would allow recruitment to get off to a positive start. The WNEC requested that the three Welsh battalions, about to become Kitchener's 4th New Army, should become part of the WAC, as should the partly-formed pals battalions from the Rhondda, Swansea and north Wales. In addition, the battalions of Welshmen it was hoped to raise in London, Liverpool and Manchester should also join the WAC. The WNEC undertook to clothe, house and feed the recruits until

Soldiers in a training camp in Pembrokeshire.   *(Courtesy of the Roger J. C. Thomas Collection).*

they were taken over by the War Office while the latter would provide the necessary arms and equipment. As a further boost to recruitment, the WNEC recommended that the height limit be reduced to 5ft 3 ins for the WAC.[13] The initial response from the War Office to these requests was not encouraging causing the Chairman of the WNEC, Lord Plymouth, to consider seriously abandoning the whole idea of a Welsh Corps. It was not until 10 October, that the War Office finally sanctioned the raising of, 'the necessary troops in Wales and Monmouthshire and from Welshmen resident in London, Liverpool and Manchester to form a Welsh Army Corps, consisting of two Divisions'.[14]

However, the key request made to Major-General Jeffreys at the meeting on 5 October, to allow the partially complete Welsh battalions to become part of the WAC was dismissed. The War Office decided every effort had to be made to complete recruitment of existing Welsh units before volunteers were encouraged to enlist in the new entity of the Welsh Army Corps. The municipal and pals battalions from Swansea, north Wales and the Rhondda were allowed to be included in the WAC, and the new units raised for the WAC would become part of the Welsh Regiment, South Wales Borderers, and Royal Welsh Fusiliers. As a final concession, it was agreed that the height standard for the vertically challenged Welsh would be reduced to 5 ft3 ins (not the usual 5 ft 5 ins), although the minimum chest measurement of 34½ ins remained the same.

Against this uncertain background, the WNEC had to begin to plan its campaign of recruitment and at least there were some optimistic signs when the Swansea, Rhondda and north Wales battalions began to reach their full complement. The units based in England were not so fortunate: the Liverpool Battalion faced great opposition from the Liverpool Pals and was disbanded in early December; the Manchester Battalion made little headway and the London Welsh Battalion did not gain official authorisation until the end of October 1914.[15] By the end of October, it was therefore hardly surprising that the WAC had only secured 3,000 recruits.[16]

At the meeting of 2 October, a key decision was taken which was to shape the structure and effectiveness of WAC recruiting. It was resolved that recruiting should be carried out on a county basis, with the intention of raising 40,000 men to form an army corps, tapping into 'county patriotism'.[17] Sir Ivor Herbert issued two memoranda to the lords lieutenant explaining how the 'County Committee Scheme' would work. The lord lieutenant of the county was to be at the head of each county committee, which would also include representatives of employers and employees, ministers of religion and leading public men and operate through the machinery of the county councils. Service units would be created for each county on the plan of the territorial force and these units would be clothed, billeted and trained by the county committee, whose expenses would be met by the WNEC. The county committees were to ensure that all recruits were supplied with boots, a greatcoat, two flannel shirts, two pairs of socks, one towel, one piece of soap, a knife, a fork and a spoon, because it had been found that, 'the want of these necessary articles had been the cause of great discomfort, and even serious insanitary conditions.'[18]

The WAC produced a memorandum entitled 'What County Committees ought to Know', stating that recruits should be 'free from organic disease', have 'free use of their limbs', and have no deformities. Furthermore, recruits should 'not be deficient in intelligence', have no speech impediments, and from their general appearance be likely to 'stand the fatigue and exposure of active service without breaking down'. Mindful of the problems that had been caused by the non-payment of allowances, the WAC instructed that providing men produced marriage certificates and children's birth certificates, separation allowances were to be paid weekly at a local Post Office, 'without any delay'. A wife was entitled to 12s. 6d per week, and wife and children 15s. rising to 22s. for a wife and four children.[19] Each county was to be given a quota of recruits to raise, based on the figures in the 1911 Census.

A second memorandum from the WAC, dated 15 October 1914, urged that county committees should be formed in Breconshire, Denbighshire, Glamorgan, Pembrokeshire, Radnorshire, Merionethshire and Carmarthenshire, all of whom had so far failed to respond.[20] Recruiting meetings were seen to be vital, especially in the open air in market places, where recruiting officers were to be available to immediately enlist men. Route marches were also to be encouraged to show off the Army, and bilingual posters and leaflets were to be distributed.[21] Sir Ivor Herbert, when writing the second memorandum, was clearly aware how

The 38th (Welsh) Division being inspected on the seafront at Llandudno, 2 May 1915.

vital it was to emphasise the particularly Welsh nature of the new Corps. He hoped that there would be much greater control over the selection of officers in Welsh-speaking districts, to ensure that the men would not be officered by monoglot English-speakers, reducing the willingness of men to enlist. Herbert had also proposed that there should be Welsh-speaking recruiting officers.[22]

It must be remembered that the WAC was beginning its recruiting campaign at the very time that the number of volunteers was beginning to show a marked decline. The 3,000 men in the WAC at the end of October 1914 had largely come via the pals battalions which had become incorporated into the WAC. The North Wales Battalion became the 13th (Service) Battalion, Royal Welsh Fusiliers; the Rhondda Battalions became the 10th (Service) Battalion Welsh Regiment and the 13th (Service) Battalion Welsh Regiment; the Swansea Battalion became the 14th (Service) Battalion Welsh Regiment. The various battalions were formed into three infantry brigades which then made up the major part of the 43rd Division (later renumbered as the 38th Division). The commanding officers of the three brigades were Brigadiers-General

Owen Thomas (113th Brigade), R.H.W. Dunn (114th Brigade) and Ivor Philipps (115th Brigade). Thomas and Philipps were both founder members of the WAC Executive and both owed their appointment to Lloyd George's influence and involvement. In her diary, Frances Stevenson records a meeting between Lloyd George and Kitchener on 30 October 1914 at which both men expressed concern about the possible new commanding officer of the 113th Brigade. Kitchener asked Lloyd George if he had anyone in mind, and when he suggested Owen Thomas, Kitchener 'rather fell in with the idea.' The appointment process was, to say the least, lackadaisical:

> He [Kitchener] asked where the Colonel [Owen Thomas] was, & when he heard he was in the building, sent for him & appointed him Brigadier-General on the spot. C. [Lloyd George] said it was a most dramatic touch, & very magnanimous on K.'s [Kitchener's] part as he must have known that it was the Colonel who had been supplying C. with complaints about the W.O. [War Office] & Welsh Army corps. C. was very pleased with the appointment. The new Brigadier seemed rather dazed at his sudden elevation.[23]

Owen Thomas, a Welsh speaker and reserve officer at the time of his appointment, was a colourful character. He had been a captain in the local militia and volunteered to fight in the South African war in 1899. He was employed to survey the agricultural prospects of southern Africa and later became managing director of a land development company in Kenya. During the recruitment campaign, it was estimated that he addressed over 150 recruiting meetings and was personally responsible for raising many thousands of men. Being too old for active service, he lost his training command in 1916. Thomas was to suffer immense personal tragedy in the war, losing three sons: Lieutenant

Brigadier-General Owen Thomas with his three sons, Trevor, Robert and Vincent; all three were to lose their lives in the war.

Trevor Thomas, Royal Welsh Fusiliers, killed in France, 10 January 1916; Flight Commander Robert Newton Thomas, Royal Welsh Fusiliers and Royal Flying Corps, died in Gaza, 23 July 1917; and, Flight Commander Owen Vincent Thomas, Royal Welsh Fusiliers and Royal Flying Corps, killed in a night flying accident in England, 29 July 1918. All three are commemorated on a memorial plaque at Llanfechell, Anglesey.[24]

Ivor Philipps had ended his professional military career in the Indian Army as a relatively junior officer more than ten years before the outbreak of war. More recently he had been MP for Southampton, although he was of Pembrokeshire stock. His appointment to command the 115th Brigade in November 1914, followed by rapid promotion to Major-General and command of the Welsh Division within two months, owed much to Lloyd George repaying a favour. Before the war, Lord St Davids, Ivor Philipps's older brother, had offered to lend Lloyd George a considerable sum of money at a time when his financial position was precarious. Lloyd George had apparently never forgotten St Davids' generosity.[25] The nepotism continued when Lloyd George's son Gwilym was appointed as Philipps's *aide-de-camp* – a posting well away from the dangers of the front line. Philipps was to lose his command of the 38th Division in an ignominious manner after the first two days' fighting at the battle of Mametz in 1916.

The County Committee scheme was a bold move by the WNEC but it failed to stimulate recruitment, largely because local organizations failed to take up the baton. Why was this? Firstly, and most obviously, the concept of 'county patriotism' did not appeal either to those who were charged with setting up the County Committees (i.e. the lords lieutenant) or to those who were resident in the individual counties. There is little evidence that many men joined the WAC because it was specifically a Welsh Corps, although the prospect of joining any pals battalion officered by Welshmen, was an attraction to some. However, for others it was the desire to escape from a socially restrictive and parochial environment which led them to enlist and thus it was a primary objective to join a regiment or corps which had as few connections with Wales as possible. Consequently, men from Wales joined units as diverse as the Gordon Highlanders, Royal Munster Fusiliers, Queen's Own (Royal West Kent) Regiment, Duke of Edinburgh's Wiltshire Regiment, Royal Scots' Fusiliers, Lancashire Fusiliers, and the Devonshire Regiment.

Secondly, the intention that County Committees were to train, clothe and billet units would have caused alarm amongst many at a local level. By early October 1914, there was a significant amount of work already taking place through such organisations as the Red Cross and the Prince of Wales Relief Fund, as well as aid for Belgian refugees and the running of recruiting meetings. It is hardly surprising that the lord lieutenant of a county would shy away from the enormous administrative and logistical problems of dealing with the clothing, billeting and training of up to 1,500 men. The scale of such an operation can be judged from the clothing issue of the 15th Battalion Welsh Regiment, between its inauguration as a unit, and 15 May 1915. In this period it issued 3,339 pairs of boots, 1,334 greatcoats, 1,411 caps, 2,981 pairs of woollen drawers, 1,301 khaki jackets, 1,415 grey (brethyn llwyd) jackets, 1,342 hairbrushes, 782 pairs of braces, 1,255 shaving brushes, 1,370 combs, 4,485 pairs of socks, 4,204 shirts and 1,376 razors. The WAC papers contain literally thousands of files concerned with the basic details of clothing and housing the recruits. The administrative burden shouldered by the secretariat under Owen Owen was staggering and £1.75 million of public money was authorised and spent by the WAC.

The severe difficulties encountered in clothing and equipping the men who joined the WAC were magnified by the decision to issue uniforms of brethyn llwyd or Welsh homespun.[26] This decision had been made for eminently sound reasons: necessity forced a solution to the shortage of uniforms, and brethyn llwyd was thought to be readily available; to have a distinct, locally-made uniform clearly helped the WAC to promote itself as distinctly Welsh, and different from other units in the army; and finally, the manufacture of cloth provided a much welcomed boost to the local economies of south, west and north Wales. However, the decision to utilise brethyn llwyd was not met with universal approval, especially by senior, regular officers. Lieutenant-Colonel Ivor Bowen, who had been instrumental in raising the 15th Battalion Royal Welsh Fusiliers (1st London Welsh) refused to allow his unit to wear brethyn llwyd, and Brigadier-General Owen Thomas, commanding the 1st Brigade, was initially antagonistic to the cloth, but eventually withdrew his opposition.[27]. The actual colour of brethyn llwyd is uncertain. Various samples survive in the WAC archive, attached to correspondence, and range from blue grey, to grey, to khaki, to brown. The final choice of colour is uncertain, and it may well be that there were variations of colour in the actual uniforms, with supplies coming from so many different mills.

In practice, the issue of uniforms – whether of brethyn llwyd or not – in the autumn of 1914, when the recruiting authorities were inundated with volunteers, was a constant headache. It proved virtually impossible to find sufficient uniforms from existing stores, or to manufacture new ones quickly enough. After joining the 11th Battalion South Wales Borderers A.E. Perriman's experience was fairly typical:

> Each in turn was issued with such kit as was available … The turn-out was one of the funniest sights I have ever seen. I almost collapsed with laughing, even at myself. The uniform was that for fatigue duties. It consisted of a blue loose-fitting tunic and trousers to match, a blue Glengarry with two small brass buttons, service boots, etc. My tunic would have fitted a bloke with a 50" chest; and my 36" left plenty of room for expansion. The trousers however, with a 25" inside leg for my 29" left much to be desired. In addition I was issued with size 9 boots instead of size 6 for which I had asked. The Glengarry was loose-fitting with my nice crop of hair, but after the military short back and sides, the damn thing wouldn't stay on.[28]

Many recruits continued to wear their civilian clothes (with the War Office paying an allowance of 10s. per man), and others were even issued with postman's dark blue uniforms as a temporary measure. This was known as 'Kitchener blue' and further stocks of such cloth were produced and issued to recruits after restyling the uniforms in a more military manner. Old and obsolete clothing was also often issued to recruits. This included scarlet jackets of Boer War vintage, canvas fatigue overalls and full-dress tunics, normally only worn on ceremonial parades. Even in early 1915, the 11th Battalion Welsh Regiment had some men parading in civilian suits, cloth caps, trilby hats and bow ties.

The administration of all matters concerning clothing and equipment was handled by the WAC Secretariat, and overseen by the Clothing and Equipment Committee, under the chairmanship of D.A. Thomas (later 1st Viscount Rhondda). The Committee met fifteen times between 23 October 1914 and 7 May 1915, and issued 1,837,411 articles at a total cost of £372,708 6s 7d.[29] Despite the interest (and controversy) created by the issue of brethyn llwyd, examination of the issue of 'clothing and necessaries' produced by the WNEC, shows that traditional khaki was still the standard issue. In total, the WAC issued 74,768 jackets, yet only 8,440 were of brethyn llwyd, whilst 60,578 were khaki and 5,750 were Kitchener blue; 68,276 pairs of trousers were issued, with 8,440 of brethyn llwyd, 54,086 of khaki and 5,750 of Kitchener blue. Of the

Shoulder badge of the 38th (Welsh) Division.

39,283 greatcoats issued, the vast majority (37,587) were khaki, and the remainder were Kitchener blue; none was of brethyn llwyd.[30] Economic considerations may have ruled the day, because brethyn llwyd worked out to be more expensive than traditional khaki. A brethyn llwyd jacket cost almost £1, and trousers 9s 10d. The equivalent khaki jacket cost 14s. 6d, with trousers at roughly the same price as brethyn llwyd. As the War Office maximum grant for clothing and equipping one dismounted soldier was £8 15s. 3d in November 1914, costs would clearly have been important, despite the desire to have a distinctive Welsh uniform.

Brethyn llwyd uniforms were gradually replaced by khaki, as alternative supplies became available, although some soldiers were still wearing brethyn llwyd as late as December 1915, immediately prior to their departure overseas. As testimony to the durability of the cloth, when the WAC discarded the brethyn llwyd uniforms, the authorities utilised the uniforms again for new recruits to use during their training period. Although the WNEC never achieved its aim of clothing as many of the troops as possible in uniforms of native homespun, the decision to use brethyn llwyd did allow the WAC to claim the distinctiveness of a special uniform, produced in Wales, for Welsh soldiers. As a recruiting tool, this was useful, but as an administrative exercise it had proved a nightmare.

Shortages of uniforms were not the only problem faced by the WAC. Equipment of all types was also scarce, but the WAC had less room for manoeuvre when issuing guns and accoutrements. Clive Hughes cites the example of the 16th Battalion Welsh Regiment, which received sixty drill rifles in January 1915, followed by 500 more in April 1915. None of these was capable of being fired, and it was only in August that eight weapons, capable of firing a round, were issued.[31] The Commanding Officer of the WAC's 2nd Brigade, Brigadier-General R. Dunn, was clearly frustrated by the failure of the War Office to provide even unserviceable rifles to the battalions of his brigade. He wrote to Western Command:

> Some Battalions have been formed for over 2½ months, and have had no instruction in handling arms. I therefore request I may be permitted to purchase 1,600 ash poles, 5ft 6ins long, and 1 5/8 in thickness at a cost of £30 … for preliminary instruction in the above subject and in bayonet fighting.[32]

For a man from Wales who had enlisted in the WAC in October or November 1914, perhaps responding to a recruiting poster in Welsh invoking the words of Dafydd ap Gryffudd, or to the patriotic pleas of a recruiting meeting, which warned of the dangers of imminent German invasion, life in the armed forces would probably have been very different to what he expected. He would have signed up, and then have been sent home awaiting instructions to proceed to north Wales. He would have remained in his civilian clothes, though probably issued with a Welsh badge of the WAC to identify him as a soldier. On reaching north Wales, his training would have consisted almost entirely of route marches and drill, as the area was totally unsuitable for military training. His rifle training would have been carried out with what resembled a broomstick, a walking stick, or if he was very lucky a dummy rifle. If he was in the artillery, no horses were available for training until April 1915, and he would have practised limbering and unlimbering with pairs of bus wheels on which were mounted telegraph poles. Boredom and drunkenness were rife. Eventually, he would have proceeded to Winchester, after six or seven months, and then begun more relevant military training, eventually being sent overseas in December 1915 (although the last members of the 38th Division did not embark until March 1916), some thirteen months after joining up, with the words perhaps still ringing in his ears, that 'it will all be over by Christmas [1914]'.

By the end of February 1915, the strength of the WAC was 20,000 men, and consequently the aim of raising two divisions had been half accomplished. The 1st Division of the WAC, under the command of Major-General Sir Ivor Philipps became the 43rd (Welsh) Division on 10 December 1914, and was then renumbered as the 38th (Welsh) Division on 29 April 1915. The new 38th Division was entitled to use the additional title 'Welsh', the Division being the only complete Welsh formation in the New Army, and with the 36th (Ulster) Division, was one of the few to be officially permitted a sub-title. The Division was in training in Winchester from August to November 1915, and then left for overseas service in December 1915. Most men would therefore have had a minimum of nine months training in north Wales and Hampshire before seeing active service.

The meetings of the WNEC in March and April 1915 were totally dominated by the perceived need to reorganise the structure of recruiting

Lloyd George, the British Minister of Munitions, acknowledging the cheers from British troops on emerging from a captured German dug-out at Fricourt, 12 September 1916.   *(Imperial War Museum)*

in Wales if the aim of forming a 2nd Division was to be achieved. The WNEC felt that the competition between the old regular army battalions, the new Kitchener battalions, the territorial force and the WAC was counter-productive. In March 1915 only 2,600 men had signed up for the WAC, which was the lowest monthly total since its inception. In April 1915, 3,700 men signed up, in May 3,300 and in June 5,400. By the end of June 1915, the strength of the WAC stood at 35,000 men. The London correspondent of the *Western Mail* thought that the growth of the WAC was 'a miracle of organization and a wonderful demonstration of the glowing patriotism of the youth of Wales'.[33] On 14 July 1915, the WNEC again discussed whether a 2nd Division of the WAC should be formed. Members of the Committee were split. One group felt that it was only by keeping the unity of the WAC and forming a 2nd Division that recruiting could be successfully continued. Another group within the Committee agreed with the Army Council, that providing reserves for existing units was more important than forming new battalions. The civilian members of the WNEC were in the former camp, and the military members largely in the latter.[34] The WNEC did not meet again, despite a pressing need for a decision for the future of the 2nd Division, until 27 October 1915, over three months since the previous meeting. Lord Derby, the Director-General of Recruiting, was in attendance; he stated that the War Office view was that new units were not desirable and that every effort was necessary for the recruitment of reserves. Consequently, the WNEC decided that recruiting for the WAC should be formally brought to a close. No 2nd Division would be formed, whilst the reserve infantry units such as the 18th, 20th, 21st and 22nd Battalions, Royal Welsh Fusiliers passed out of the WAC's control.[35] By the end of October 1915, the WAC had raised approximately 50,000 men, and the WNEC had achieved the objective it originally set itself in October 1914.

In September 1914, the WNEC had calculated that there were 404,726 men aged between twenty and forty in Wales. In persuading approximately 50,000 of them to join the WAC, in competition with other branches of the armed forces, success as an effective recruiting channel was achieved. If the War Office had allowed the WAC to begin recruiting immediately in October 1914, without first having to fill up existing units beyond its control, there is little doubt that its impact and efficacy as a

Men of the 15th Battalion Royal Welsh Fusiliers (London Welsh) outside their dug outs in the trenches at Fleurbaix, 28 December 1917, with snow on the ground. *(Imperial War Museum)*

channel of recruitment would have been far greater. The stuttering and uncertain start of the WAC led to suspicion and wariness both locally and nationally. The question – which remains impossible to answer – is whether the 50,000 men who joined the WAC would have joined the armed forces in any case? A cautious conclusion is that the specific nature of the WAC with its national character, distinctive uniform and Welsh officers, probably served as an attraction to some men who otherwise would not have contemplated joining the 'English Army'.

NOTES

[1] A.J. P. Taylor (ed.), *Lloyd George, a Diary by Frances Stevenson* (London: Hutchinson, 1971), p. 2.

[2] *The Times*, 20 September 1914.

[3] Ibid.

[4] Welsh Army Corps, *Report of the Executive Committee* [hereafter WAC/REC] (Cardiff: Western Mail, 1921), p. 3.

[5] Taylor, *Lloyd George Diary*, pp. 2-3.

[6] WAC/REC, p. 4.

[7] David Lloyd George, *War Memoirs of David Lloyd George* (London: Odhams Press, 1938), p. 452.

[8] Michael and Eleanor Brock (eds), *Asquith: Letters to Venetia Stanley* (Oxford: Oxford University Press, 1982), p. 298.

[9] Taylor, *Lloyd George Diary*, pp. 3-4.

[10] WAC/REC, p. 12.

[11] WAC/REC, p. 5.

[12] NLW, WAC, C11/22, Minute Book of the Welsh Army Corps National Executive Committee [hereafter NEC Minute Book], 2 October 1914.

[13] NLW, WAC, C11/22, NEC Minute Book, 5 October 1914.

[14] NLW, WAC, AW/98, Letter from GOC, Western Command, 10 October 1914.

[15] NLW, WAC, C12/16, file 'Sir Ivor Herbert', Lord Derby to Sir Ivor Herbert, 21 December 1914.

[16] WAC/REC, p. 40.

[17] NLW, WAC, C11/22, NEC Minute Book, 2 October 1914, 5 October 1914.

[18] NLW, WAC, C12/35, Memorandum to Lords Lieutenant, 3 October 1914.

[19] NLW, WAC, C12/10, undated.

[20] NLW, WAC, C12/11, Memorandum Outlining the Steps to be Taken Preliminary to Active Recruiting for the Welsh Army Corps, 15 October 1914.

[21] NLW, WAC, C12/30, Welsh Army Corps Recruiting Campaign, undated [contents indicate early October 1914].

[22] NLW, WAC, C12/11, Memorandum Outlining the Steps to be Taken Preliminary to Active Recruiting for the Welsh Army Corps, 15 October 1914.

[23] Taylor, *Lloyd George Diary*, pp. 8-9.

[24] See David A. Pretty, *Farmer, Soldier & Politician: the Life of Brigadier-General Sir Owen Thomas, MP, Father of the Welsh Army Corps* (Wrexham: Bridge Books, 2011).

[25] Taylor, *Lloyd George Diary*, p. 24.

[26] For a full account of this topic, see C. Hughes, 'The Welsh Army Corps 1914-1915: Shortages of Khaki and Basic Equipment Promote a National Uniform', *Imperial War Museum Review*, 1 (1986), 91-99.

[27] NLW, WAC, Box 16, Owen Owen to Miss F. Stevenson, 7 January 1915.

[28] IWM, letters of A.E. Perriman, 80/43/1.

[29] WAC/REC, p. 40.

[30] The WAC also issued 42,457 cardigans, 78,236 pairs of drawers, 83,501 pairs of boots, 174,799 badges, 111,212 shirts, 114,860 pairs of socks, 70,675 towels and 40,594 toothbrushes.

[31] Hughes, 'The Welsh Army Corps'.

[32] NLW, WAC, AW/98, Brigadier-General R. Dunn to HQ Western Command Chester, 13 January 1915.

[33] *Western Mail*, 30 April 1915.

[34] NLW, WAC, C11/22, NEC Minute Book, 14 July 1915.

[35] NLW, WAC, C11/22, NEC Minute Book, 27 October 1915; WAC/REC, pp. 28-29.

Chapter 4

'A Menacing Wall of Gloom'

The 38th (Welsh) Division
and the Battle of Mametz Wood

—⁓⁓—

T HE NAME OF MAMETZ WOOD, perhaps like those of Aberfan or
Senghenydd, is embedded deep in the Welsh psyche, immediately
conjuring up images of needless loss of life, bravery, chaos and self-
sacrifice. It was here that the 38th (Welsh) Division was first tested in
battle; here that the volunteer army experienced the reality of war for the
first time. If one visits Mametz Wood today, the landscape has hardly
changed from one hundred years ago, with the thick undergrowth and
heavy tree canopy still evident. There are clear reminders of what has gone
before: shell craters, shallow trenches and other earthworks are clearly
visible, with remnants of rusting barbed wire in amongst the bracken.
One of the most striking sights is the Welsh Division memorial – a vivid
red dragon, tearing at barbed wire, atop a three metre granite plinth –
which faces across the open fields to Mametz Wood, passively guarding
the memory of the Welshmen who died here. The memorial was made by
Welsh sculptor and blacksmith, David Petersen and was unveiled on 11
July 1987. The regimental badges of the South Wales Borderers, the Royal
Welsh Fusiliers and the Welsh Regiment are sculpted into the plinth.

The 38th Divisional headquarters officially opened in Colwyn Bay on
19 January 1915, while the various battalions had gradually been moving
to north Wales since early December 1914. A programme of military
and physical training began, which was severely hampered by a lack of

A Brigadier-General and Staff officers studying a map in Mametz Wood, July 1916. Note the thickness of the undergrowth and the difficulties presented to any advancing troops.

(Imperial War Museum)

equipment, especially rifles. It was decided to give little training in trench warfare as it was thought that there would be no difficulty in learning that in France. Sergeant A.E. Perriman remembered 'long route marches in service marching order, day and night manoeuvres coupled with arduous physical training' which resulted in his battalion, 11th Battalion South Wales Borderers, becoming a 'fit fighting unit'.[1] The Division was inspected on St David's Day, 1915 by General Henry Mackinnon (General Officer Commanding Western Command), accompanied by Lloyd George. He commented that the sight of the parading Welsh troops was 'one of the most magnificent spectacles' he had ever seen.[2] The London *Daily News* waxed lyrically that St David's Day was:

> Marked by features distinctively expressive of what may be termed the new Welsh nationalism. The newly formed Welsh Guards mounted guard for the first time over the King at Buckingham Palace; Mr

Lloyd George was present at a parade at Llandudno and an address was presented to him at an eisteddfod in the evening; flags were sold in Wales and London on behalf of the national fund for Welsh troops, and the Welsh emblem was flown over the Chancellor's residence in Downing Street.[3]

During August and September 1915, the Division was gradually concentrated at Winchester, allowing training at the operational and tactical level. On 29 November, the Queen (in the absence of the King, who was ill) inspected the Welsh Division on Crawley Down prior to their departure for France. Before this, the most pressing need had been to ensure that all the recruits had undertaken a basic musketry course. The lack of rifles during the training in north Wales meant that most of the men, in the twelve or so months since they had enlisted, had not even fired a rifle on a range, never mind at the enemy. When Emlyn Davies embarked for France he 'felt naked' because of the lack of rifle training and bayonet practice.[4] The perceived glamour of war which had encouraged men to enlist in the autumn of 1914 was not apparent to Ll. Wyn Griffith as his battalion marched from Winchester to Southampton, before embarking for France:

Late afternoon that found us on a wet quayside, staring at a grey ship on a grey sea. Rain in England, rain on the Channel and rain in France; mud on the Hampshire downs and mud in the unfinished horse-standings in Havre where we sheltered from the rain during the hours of waiting for a train. Rain beating against the trucks as we doddered through an unknown land to an unknown destination, and, late at night, as we stood in the mud of a station yard near St Omer, the rain was waiting for us, to drive us along twelve miles of muddy lanes to a sodden hamlet near Aire. Four days out of England, days and nights of fatigue and stiff-limbed weariness, nights of little sleep and days of little rest: a hundred hours of rain.[5]

By 6 December 1915, 639 officers, 18,875 other ranks, 5,087 horses and mules, 979 horse-drawn vehicles, 546 bicycles, 70 lorries, 36 cars and 29 motor-cycles had safely reached the billeting area, ten miles south of St Omer, thirty miles behind the British front line. There were thirteen battalions in total in the three infantry brigades, each with a commanding officer and twenty-eight other officers. There were still concerns that despite over a year's training, the Division needed further instruction in bombing, musketry – especially rapid loading – and engineering work prior to going into the line. Major-General Ivor Philipps issued an order on 12 December that every unit should try and open a firing range, giving special attention to firing at distances of up to 100 yards and sniping practice. Snipers had to be able to hit an envelope, 3½ ins x 4 ins at 100 yards, three times out of four. Lieutenant-General R. Haking, commanding officer of XI Corps, of which the 38th Division was a part, issued an encouraging memo on 19 January 1915 that the Division had 'made more rapid strides towards efficiency than any of the several new formations' that he had under his command.[6]

In January 1916, the 38th Division took over the Neuve Chapelle sector of the line from the 19th Division, remaining in the area around Givenchy until 10 June. During this period the Division gradually got used to life in the trenches:

> Unless something unexpected happened, the pattern was much the same – four days in the front line, four days out. We were fully engaged when out [of] the trenches in various duties, most of which [were] repairing defences, digging new trenches in reserve, erecting barbed wire, and the ever [lasting] job of filling sandbags. Our billets mainly consisted of small barns and outhouses. There was the usual covering of ancient straw, wet, dirty and rat-infested, on which to rest our weary bodies … Over the months located in the area from Laventie to Givenchy there was not what one would call great activity so casualties were few as far as our battalion [11th Battalion South Wales Borderers] was concerned.[7]

This 'live-and-let-live' approach to trench life was also noticed by Ll. Wyn Griffith: 'the enemy rarely shelled this post unless our fires gave out too much smoke during the day … Two days and nights followed, uneventful and uncomfortable, with a drizzle of rain to accentuate the feeling that war was mostly a matter of being wet, of struggling for a temporary mastery over mud'. He still concluded that, 'there were two kinds of men in the world – those who had been in the trenches, and the rest'.[8] The entry in the Welsh Division's war diary on 25 January 1915 recorded that 'the enemy opposed to the Division appear to be a quiet though industrious lot and labouring under the same handicap as ourselves regarding trenches'.

David Lloyd George in Llandudno, with Brigadier-General Owen Thomas on his left.

(Imperial War Museum)

A tactical progress report for 29 January stated: 'the Germans opposite Copse Street-Mole Street [trenches] were heard to shout several times "Who are you?" while those further on our right shouted "You bloody murderers". This is eminently satisfactory if it indicates that our activity has been giving them a thin time'. A further report the following day indicated the relatively mundane level of trench activity at this time:

> A German who was laying sandbags on top of the parapet was shot by our snipers ... Much talking and an accordion were heard in the German trenches. Several Germans were observed in a sap near Boars Head by our listening post. Some were dressed in oilskins and others in light-bluish green uniform. They were of fine physique.[9]

63

This generally quiet introduction to trench warfare was soon to be shattered when orders were received in mid-June 1915 for the Welsh Division to move to St Pol, in preparation for the forthcoming offensive on the Somme. Plans for a major joint French and British offensive had been debated since the Chantilly conference in December 1915. Although Douglas Haig disliked both the timing and location of the proposed assault – he would have preferred an operation in Flanders in mid-August – it was agreed that the area of the front line immediately north and south of the River Somme would be the focal point of an attack in early July 1916. The French Sixth Army held the line to a point just south of Maricourt, where the British Fourth Army took over. The British line ran westwards from Maricourt to Fricourt, then northwards to Thiepval, Serre and Gommecourt. The Germans had learnt that a single line of defence was not sufficient to withstand the increasing strength and volume of the British and French artillery. During 1915 and early 1916, they had constructed a second and third defensive line, roughly two miles apart. The front line trenches were considerably strengthened, with traverses to restrict shell blast, deep dug-outs and wide belts of barbed wire interlaced with iron posts to the front. The town of Mametz lay behind the German front line, mid-way between Fricourt and Montauban. Mametz Wood lay one and a half miles to the north of the town, just in front of the German second line of defence, in generally hilly and woody country. Following seven days of heavy bombardment of the German lines, Haig's objective was to capture the German front along an eleven mile stretch from Maricourt to Serre, then continue eastwards and take the German second line from Pozières to Grandcourt and beyond. This he hoped would allow the cavalry to push through in to open country behind the German lines, then turning northwards taking the enemy's lines from the flank and reverse.

The first day of the battle of the Somme has become symbolic of the apparent futility of the First World War and the blatant devaluation of human life. In a single day, almost 20,000 British soldiers were killed and a further 40,000 became casualties. The gains, such as they were, seemed a paltry reward for the profligate loss of life. At the southernmost point of the British attack, the area around Montauban was captured by the 18th and 30th Divisions, and the 7th and 21st Divisions captured Mametz village and broke up the German front line west of Fricourt. Elsewhere, the carefully prepared German front line had proved impregnable. On the afternoon of 1 July 1916, Haig decided that the situation was still too obscure for any radical change of plan, and that 'the best that could be done for the moment was to keep up the pressure on the enemy, wear out his defence, and, with a view to an attack on his second position, gain possession of those parts of his front position and of the intermediate lines still in his hands'.[10]

The Welsh Division had been in GHQ (General Head Quarters) reserve since 30 June, awaiting orders as to their exact role in the Somme offensive. By the end of 2 July, Fricourt had been taken, establishing the British line between La Boiselle and Montauban, approximately one mile beyond the old German front line and south of Mametz Wood. On 5 July, the 38th Division took over a section of the front line immediately south of Mametz Wood, with orders to prepare for the capture of the Wood. With typical understatement, the history of the 38th Division commented: 'The task that lay before the Division was one of some magnitude'.[11] The capture of Mametz Wood had been thought to be so difficult, that GHQ left it out of their orders for the attack on 1 July, though British troops were to have moved forward to the east and west. Haig attached considerable strategic importance to the capture of this feature, seeing it as the key to an attack on the German second line in the area. Once captured, the attacking force would be able to move eastwards and advance on Longueval, whilst British artillery could be placed in the Wood and target the German second and third lines more effectively.

Mametz Wood occupied an area of approximately 220 acres, covered in thick undergrowth of hawthorn and briar intermingled with fallen trees and branches from previous bombardments, all of which would impede any progress on foot. Also on the floor of the Wood, there was a considerable amount of wire, which had been laid by the enemy during the respite from fighting after 1 July. There were still considerable numbers of standing trees of oak, beech and ash, averaging thirty to forty feet in height. The Wood measured about one mile from north to south and three-quarters of a mile from east to west at its widest point. Mametz Wood was divided transversely by two straight rides and longitudinally by a third. In July 1916, with the trees in full leaf and the depth of undergrowth, these features were not easily recognizable. It lay on a slight spur, with a small

A German observation post in Mametz Wood, 10 August 1916.

(Imperial War Museum)

re-entrant on either side, rising up towards Longueval Ridge behind. Whether the Wood was attacked from the south, east or west, it would involve troops moving down the slope of a valley, then being faced with an uphill slope in open country to reach the enemy. Furthermore, from the south (the most likely direction of a British attack) there was Willow stream to traverse, which had a steep chalk bank varying in height from thirty to fifty feet.

Siegfried Sassoon

Siegfried Sassoon, an officer in the 2nd Battalion Royal Welsh Fusiliers, had been involved in attacks in the area of Mametz Wood between 3-5 July. In his autobiographical work, *Memoirs of an Infantry Officer*, he quotes the rumour which was current in the battalion that, '"we've got to attack some wood or other", which could not fail to cause an uneasy visceral sensation'. He describes moving across the open hillside with Mametz Wood 'looming on the opposite slope ... a dense wood of old trees and undergrowth'.[12] It was 'a menacing wall of gloom'.[13]

66

On 5 July 1916 the Welsh Division took over a section of the front line immediately south of Mametz Wood; they found half-dug trenches and spent most of the first night removing dead German soldiers and deepening the trench system. Siegfried Sassoon was both patronising and insulting about the relieving troops, which is perhaps indicative of the way regular army battalions, such as 2nd Battalion Royal Welsh Fusiliers, viewed the Kitchener battalions: 'unseasoned New Army troops … a jostling company of exclamatory Welshmen … a panicky rabble … mostly undersized men … like a lot of children … [a] forlorn crowd of khaki figures … half trained civilians'.[14] On the morning of 6 July the Division took over took over the defensive positions in the western half of Caterpillar Wood and also Marlborough Wood. Sergeant A.E. Perriman, 11th Battalion South Wales Borderers, was amazed to occupy well-constructed, timber-lined dug outs which had been abandoned by the German troops. Not only did they find bunks, tables and chairs, but also allotments where seasonal vegetables were growing.[15] Orders were then issued for a two-pronged attack on Mametz Wood for the following day, with the 17th Division aiming to capture the western part of the Wood and the 38th Division the eastern section. A heavy bombardment of the Wood, the German second line and surrounding strong points was to precede the attack. Ll. Wyn Griffith recalled that his Brigade-General 'was cursing last night at his orders. He said that only a madman could have issued them. He called the Divisional Staff a lot of plumbers, herring-gutted at that'.[16]

The Welsh Division was to be tested in a major attack for the first time. Major-General Ivor Philipps, commanding officer of the Division, sent a message of encouragement to every man:

> You have worked hard for many months with an energy and zeal beyond praise to fit yourself for the task you have voluntarily undertaken … You have now held for 6 months a section of the British line in France, during which time you have not allowed one of the enemy to enter your trenches except as a prisoner … I always believed that a really Welsh Division would be second to none. You have more than justified that belief. I feel that whatever the future may have in store for us I can rely on you, because you have already given ample proof of your worth … I am confident that the young battalions of the famous Welsh regiments serving in the 38th (Welsh) Division

will maintain the high standard for valour for which all three Welsh regiments have been renowned throughout the war.[17]

Sergeant Perriman was worried about more prosaic matters such as the rations which were issued for his platoon for the day of the forthcoming attack: 'For 52 of us I was allocated 1½ loaves of bread, a piece of boiled bacon weighing about 16 ozs after the Somme mud had been removed, a small quantity of biscuits, some currants & sultanas, and a petrol tin of tea'. Of greater concern was the fact that he had six men in his platoon who had not even reached the age of eighteen.[18]

At 0800 the artillery began its bombardment of the edge of Mametz Wood. Ll. Wyn Griffith feared the German machine-gunners would mow down the men of the Welsh Division as soon as they stood up:

> … scanning the Wood with our glasses, it seemed as thick as a virgin forest. There was no sign of life in it, no one could say whether it concealed ten thousand men or ten machine guns. Its edges were clean cut, as far as the eye could see, and the ground between us and the Wood was bare of any cover. Our men were assembled in trenches above a dip in the ground, and from these they were to advance, descend into the hollow, and cross the bare slope in the teeth of the machine-gunners in the Wood. On their right, as they advanced across the bullet-swept zone, they would be exposed to enfilade fire, for the direction of their advance was nearly parallel to the German trenches … there was a weird stillness in the air, a brooding menace.[19]

At 0830 on 7 July the 16th Battalion Welsh Regiment and the 11th Battalion South Wales Borderers moved out of Caterpillar Wood and began their uphill westward advance towards Mametz Wood. The expected smoke barrage did not materialize, both battalions immediately coming under heavy enemy fire with no protection. The attack floundered in chaos 200-300 yards short of the Wood, with the troops taking cover wherever they could in random shell holes. Ll. Wyn Griffith described the scene:

> Along the bare ridge rising up to Mametz Wood our men were burrowing into the ground with their entrenching tools, seeking whatever cover they might make. A few shells were falling, surprisingly few. Wounded men were crawling back from the ridge,

men were crawling forward with ammunition. No attack could succeed over such ground as this, swept from front and side by machine-guns at short range.[20]

Sergeant Perriman found that initially the ground they were covering was undulating and offered plenty of cover, 'but when the apex was reached some 150 yards from the fringe of the wood, the ground fell away leaving us completely exposed to enemy fire'.[21] They were subjected to 'murderous machine gun fire' from three posts dug deep into the ground, providing 'an ideal target'. Private William Joshua, 16th Battalion Welsh Regiment was in a Lewis machine-gun team:

> We advanced about 50 yards when the German machine guns opened up … One of my gun team gave me the signal to take a casualty's place in the team, and as I struggled on, I felt a severe shock in my thigh and I was down looking for my leg, thinking I had lost it. Another platoon came along and rested for a breather leaving about ten casualties behind … Each wave passing me left its quota of dead behind … Now the German and our own artillery started up, and to add to the horror rain started to fall heavily making the churned up ground into clinging mud. I dumped my equipment and started to crawl back, hugging the ground. Some stretcher bearers found me and took me to a large shell hole. They were members of the Tylorstown Silver Band who had enlisted en bloc in our early recruiting days.[22]

At 1100 after another artillery bombardment, a further attempt was made to enter the Wood but again machine gun fire from the flanks and front made progress impossible. A third attack was then ordered and an artillery bombardment arranged for 1630. The rain had continued to fall, the ground was sodden, telephone wires had been cut and progress was extremely difficult. The divisional war diary recorded that 'the Artillery bombardment was also inaccurate and ineffective, and the Battalions of the 115th Brigade were disorganised'. The decision was made by the commanding officer of the 115th Brigade not to carry out the planned attack. Under the cover of darkness, the bedraggled troops returned to their positions in Caterpillar Wood. Ll. Wyn Griffith bitterly commented, 'It was nearly midnight when we heard that the last of our men had withdrawn from that ridge and valley, leaving the ground empty, save for the bodies of those who had to fall to prove to our command that machine guns can defend a bare slope'.[23]

At the end of 7 July, the Welsh Division was back in exactly the same position as it had been at dawn that morning, the only difference being that 177 men and three officers had lost their lives. The day's fighting was described tersely and without emotion by Lieutenant Henry Apps, 11th Battalion South Wales Borderers:

> Arrival at our destination at 2.0 a.m. I get the men into shell holes. The enemy started shelling us with gas shells. The General addressed the officers at 5 a.m. We attacked at 8.0 [a.m.] All went well till we reached the ridge and then machine-guns opened on us and snipers picked off officers. Hamer [Lieutenant Thomas Pryce Hamer] the Adjutant was killed. I took over his job. B Coy[Company] lost all their officers. I paraded the Coy after the battle. 16 men, 3 Sergeants. Battalion withdrew at 9.0 [pm]. The road out was awful.[24]

The two battalions which had led the attacks bore the brunt of the casualties: the 11th Battalion South Wales Borderers lost thirty men, whilst the 16th Battalion (Cardiff City) Welsh Regiment lost 129 men, with sixty-one of those being residents of Cardiff. The death toll led many to question the wisdom of recruiting pals battalions from one town or city. The death rates also affected the morale of the home population when so many deaths on a single day were from a single locality. One who died was Corporal Frederick Hugh Roberts, a Senghenydd miner, originally from Bethesda, who had enlisted in the 16th Battalion Welsh Regiment early in the war. He had cheated death already once, when a successful bet on a horse had led to a heavy night's drinking and a resultant hangover. This had kept him away from the pit on 17 October 1913 when the worst mining disaster in British history killed 439 of his workmates. Roberts died of his wounds on 10 July and is buried in Heilly Station Cemetery, Méricourt-l'Abbé.[25] His name also appears on the Senghenydd war memorial with sixty-two other men from the town. Two of the officers who died were brothers, Arthur and Leonard Tregaskis. Having emigrated to Canada, they returned to fight in the war, joined up together, were awarded temporary commissions on the same day and died together on 7 July.

The attack on Mametz Wood had failed because of a multitude of reasons, which questions the strategic and tactical awareness of the corps staff that had authorized it. Common sense would dictate that to begin an attack in difficult, open country, with significant exposure to enfilade fire (the German trenches were parallel to the line of advance) and against an enemy of unknown strength, would have a poor chance of success. Furthermore, the artillery bombardment had been a failure, the expected smokescreen had not been laid and communications between front line battalions, the 38th Division and XV Corps headquarters were virtually non-existent. The weather had also played a critical part in day's events. Even though it was mid-summer, the ground was already sodden before very heavy showers set in on the morning of 7 July:

> The trenches became knee-deep, in some places waist-deep, in clinging slime, and under shellfire, collapsed beyond recognition. Movement was often agony: men fainted from sheer exhaustion whilst struggling through deep mud; in some locations a team of fourteen horses was required to bring up a single ammunition wagon. Under such handicaps, the advance of reinforcements and the circulation of orders suffered grave delay.[26]

Haig laid the blame for the failed attack squarely at the door of the Welsh Division. He wrote in his diary on 8 July 1916 that, 'The 38th Welsh Division, which had been ordered to attack Mametz Wood had not advanced with determination to the attack'. His chief of staff commented that the commander-in-chief did not consider the failure of the 38th Division a 'creditable performance'.[27] The first real test of the Welsh Division in battle had ended in ignominy and recrimination. Worse was to follow. During the afternoon of 8 July information had been received that Mametz Wood had been evacuated by the German troops. Patrols were sent out to see if this was the case, but they came under heavy fire. Despite this, plans were made for an isolated attack at 0200 on 9 July on the southern end of Mametz Wood, focusing on Strip Trench. The newly appointed commanding officer of the 14th Battalion Royal Welsh Fusiliers, Lieutenant-Colonel H. Hodson, reported at 0300 that owing to 'congestion in the mud-filled trenches his party had been obliged to take to the open, but even then found it impossible to reach the starting-point in the darkness over ground pitted with shell-holes and littered with loose wire'.[28] The attack never took place.

German soldier's overcoat, hanging from a tree in Mametz Wood, August 1916.

(Imperial War Museum)

This was the last straw for Lieutenant-General H. Horne, commanding XV Corps; the Commanding Officer Major-General Ivor Philipps was held responsible for the failures of 7-9 July and given his marching orders. The Welsh Division was placed under the command of Major-General H. Watts, previously of the 7th Division, a man with no knowledge or understanding of the Welshmen he was to lead. A new man at the top was thought to be vital to restore the morale of the Welsh Division and to bring a decisiveness and edge which had so far been lacking. The divisional war diary blandly noted that Major-General Philipps 'vacated command of the Division and proceeded to England'. He was later appointed as Parliamentary Secretary at the Ministry of Munitions by Lloyd George, and was knighted in 1917.

Major G. Drake-Brockman, writing some years after the war, was 'amazed at the political atmosphere in the division', when he was appointed as a staff officer on 8 July 1916. He wrote that the 38th Division 'suffered from having a number of senior officers who owed their appointment to their political position or to being friends of Mr Lloyd George'. Major-

General Philipps had been 'promoted over the heads of many more senior and meritorious officers. As a divisional commander it is hardly surprising that he was ignorant, lacked experience and failed to inspire confidence'. He was further criticized for making it 'difficult to get rid of officers who were useless, since in nearly every case they were often constituents or political supporters of the divisional commander, who held a high opinion of their capabilities'. As a military strategist Philipps was also found wanting for his lack of vision and decisiveness; attacks were never pressed home because instructions were given that if any enemy machine-gun fire was encountered, troops were to return to their starting point and await a further artillery bombardment.[29] For a staff officer such as Drake-Brockman this was weak leadership; for a more humane man this could have been interpreted as a commanding officer doing his best to protect the lives of his men.

In his diary on 8 July Haig noted that Lieutenant-General Horne 'was very disappointed' with the performance of the Welsh Division. Haig's diary continued:

> [that] although the wood had been most adequately bombarded the division never entered the wood, and in the whole division the total casualties for the 24 hours are under 150! A few bold men entered the wood and found little opposition. Deserters also stated Enemy was greatly demoralised and had very few troops on the ground'.[30]

As often was the case, Haig was wrong on all counts: the bombardment of the Wood had failed, casualties were nearer 400 and there were still sufficient enemy troops in the Wood to man the machine-gun posts.

Major-General Watts took command of the Welsh Division during the afternoon of 9 July, and by 1730 orders had been issued for an attack on Mametz Wood, to begin at 0415 on 10 July. Using two brigades (eight battalions) with the third close at hand, the attack would rely largely on weight of numbers to overrun the German defences. The operational order starkly stated, 'The Division will attack Mametz Wood to-morrow with a view to capturing the whole of it'. The 113th and 114th Brigades would move from White Trench and attack the southern and south-eastern edges of the Wood, which would again necessitate infantrymen covering 400-500 yards of rising, open ground with enemy fire on two sides. Army orders were for the troops to attack in parallel lines or 'waves', four paces between each man and 100 yards between each line. The divisional order, issued from divisional headquarters at Grovetown, six miles from the front line stated:

> All men must be carefully instructed in the compass direction of the advance, and of the necessity for consolidation and reorganisation when the various rides and edges of the Wood are reached. Care must be taken to also instruct in the advantage of working up as close as possible to the edge of our Artillery barrage, and it should be explained to the men that Artillery fire will sound much louder in the Wood than outside. To help the men in knowing which is the main central ride, GOC [General Officer Commanding] 3rd Infantry Brigade will arrange for a party to place red flags along it. 25 flags will be issued.[31]

There was clearly a feeling amongst many in the Welsh Division that they were on trial after the failures of 7/8 July. On 9 July Lieutenant-Colonel J. H. Hayes, commanding officer of the Swansea Pals, addressed the officers of the Battalion: 'Tomorrow at five minutes past four our battalion is going to take that wood, but we shall lose our battalion'.[32] Lieutenant-Colonel R. J. Carden, commanding officer of the 16th Battalion Royal Welsh Fusiliers showed the same resolve, but also the same fears: 'boys make your peace with God! We are going to take that position and some of us won't come back. But we are going to take it'.[33] Corps headquarters had sent what was intended to be a morale-boosting message to be read out to all troops prior to the attack:

> The Commander in Chief has just visited the corps commander and has impressed upon him the great importance of the occupation of Mametz Wood. The corps commander requests that the division and brigade commanders will point out to the troops of the Welsh division the opportunity offered them of serving their King and Country at a critical period and earning for themselves great glory and distinction.[34]

By 0300 on 10 July, the leading battalions of the Welsh Division were in position and at 0330 the artillery began a heavy bombardment of the Wood followed by an effective smoke screen. However, the intended co-ordinated attack of the 113th and 114th Brigades was thrown into disarray when the 13th and 14th Battalions of the Welsh Regiment began their advance six minutes ahead of schedule. The 113th Brigade left their trenches only to find parts of the 114th Brigade already in retreat. After two further false starts, the advance down the hillside and up towards the Wood was finally achieved, despite intense artillery and machine-gun fire. The Divisional war diary recorded that there had been 'a good deal of confusion', with some men in advance of their own barrage. Captain Glynn Jones, 14th Battalion Royal Welsh Fusiliers, at the rear of the attack was able to describe the scene ahead:

> Presently the silent waves of men started moving forward, and I, with my third wave joined in. Machine guns and rifles began to rattle, and there was a general state of pandemonium, little of which I can remember except that I myself was moving down the slope at a rapid rate, with bullet-holes in my pocket and yelling a certain amount. I noticed also that there was no appearance whatsoever of waves of movement at this time, and that the men in advance of us were thoroughly demoralised. Out of the most terrible 'mix-up' I have ever seen I collected all the men I could see and ordered them into the cutting. There appeared to be no one ahead of us, no one following us, and by this time it was broad daylight and the ridge behind us was being subjected to a terrible artillery and machine-gun fire … Meanwhile, men were crawling in from shell-holes to our front, with reports of nothing less than a terrible massacre, and the names of most of our officers and NCOs lying dead in front were mentioned.[35]

Sergeant T.J. Price, 13th Battalion Welsh Regiment was involved in attacking the 'hammerhead' of Mametz Wood:

> We were loaded up with four Mills bombs each in our pockets and four bandoliers of ammunition across our shoulders, which was quite heavy and which made the approach to the wood quite a physical task. As the barrage started we moved off in quite an orderly fashion … The tension and noise cannot be described, what with the traction of shells through the air and the noise of explosions all around us … Men were falling in all directions due to intensive machine gun fire coming against us. How we got to the wood I do not know; but we got there and entered it for a short distance before the Germans came at us – head on.[36]

The 14th Battalion Welsh Regiment attacking in the centre, had some protection from the enfilade fire and crossed the open ground in the prescribed wave formation, reaching the edge of the Wood just as the barrage was lifting. The four Royal Welsh Fusiliers Battalions of the 113th Brigade had also reached the Wood but they were hampered by the thick undergrowth, fallen trees and poor visibility. At 0900, the divisional war diary recorded: 'units much intermingled and lacking officers … 16th Royal Welsh Fusiliers could not be found … at 12.30 p.m. they were however located … Lieutenant-Colonel Pryce found the troops in a somewhat confused state'.[37] As the 14th Battalion reached the Wood, Captain Glynn Jones was confronted by about forty German soldiers coming out with their hands up. He thought it was a trick and warily approached them with covering fire from the Battalion. However, the men were genuinely surrendering, were taken prisoner and sent back to headquarters.[38] Between July 6-11, the Welsh Division captured 352 prisoners of war, including four officers.

For the remainder of the morning fierce fighting, often chaotic, saw the Welsh Division gradually take control of the southern part of the Wood, but suffering heavy casualties in the process. One major problem hampering the success of the attack was the high casualty rate amongst the battalion commanders of the seven battalions originally committed to the attack: five were either killed or seriously wounded. In total, on 10 July five officers from the Royal Welsh Fusiliers were killed, one from the South Wales Borderers and twelve from the Welsh Regiment. Of those from the Welsh Regiment, eight were Temporary 2nd Lieutenants, meaning they were almost certainly new to command in battle and probably far younger than the men they were commanding.

There were numerous individual acts of bravery. Lieutenant-Colonel R.J. Carden, commanding the 16th Battalion Royal Welsh Fusiliers led his men from the front across the exposed terrain of no-man's land, apparently brandishing his swagger stick above his head and encouraging his troops forward. He was shot and wounded by a German sniper, but managed to struggle to the edge of the Wood. Still exhorting his men to even greater efforts he was hit again and killed, becoming a victim of his own eve of battle prediction that, 'some of us won't come back'. Lieutenant Edward Wilson 14th Battalion Welsh Regiment, leading his company in a bayonet charge, reportedly killed a 'burly German' and then shot a sniper in a tree. Lieutenant F.J. Hawkins, 14th Battalion Welsh Regiment, a Welsh international rugby player, charged down two separate machine-gun posts, both of which he successfully captured.

By mid-morning on 10 July the Welsh Division had reached the first cross-ride and during the afternoon, after fierce and unrelenting close-quarter fighting, reached a position within 30-40 yards from the northern edge of Mametz Wood. Throughout the day, the thick undergrowth, poor visibility, well-established machine-gun posts and effective sniper fire had made every yard gained a gargantuan effort. The ferocity of the fighting was described by Emlyn Davies, 17th Battalion Royal Welsh Fusiliers, who had entered Mametz Wood during the afternoon:

> Gory scenes met our gaze. Mangled corpses in khaki and in field-grey; dismembered bodies, severed heads and limbs; lumps of torn flesh half way up the tree trunks; a Welsh Fusilier reclining on a mound, a red trickle oozing from his bayoneted throat; a South Wales Borderer and a German locked in their deadliest embraces – they had simultaneously bayoneted each other. A German gunner with jaws blown off lay against his machine gun, hand still on its trigger.[39]

As nightfall approached, the bedraggled troops found cover where they could, exhausted after fifteen hours of continuous fighting. The night was marked by a great deal of wild firing and false alarms, but the enemy did not make any counter attack. At daybreak on 11 July the Welsh Division was in a state of disarray, scattered throughout the Wood, with many battalions severely depleted. The 13th and 14th Battalions Welsh Regiment had borne the brunt of the attack on the previous day, suffering ninety-six and seventy-five deaths respectively. In addition, each Battalion probably lost another 300 men as casualties. Once again the pals battalions were the most severely affected: of the seventy-five members of the 14th Battalion Welsh Regiment who had died on 10 July, forty-one were living in Swansea on enlistment, many from the St Thomas district of the town. In a close-knit community, with large extended families, forty-one deaths in a single day had a grave effect on the morale of the home front.

For both strategic and technical reasons news did not travel fast in 1916. It would have often been one to two weeks after a soldier died in battle that the news would reach home, and often then only to be told 'missing in action'. For example, it was not until 19 August 1916 that the *Cardiff*

Times reported the deaths of two sets of brothers at Mametz over a month previously. Henry and Charles Morgan had worked at the Blaenavon Steel & Iron Company, joined the 16th Battalion Welsh Regiment in late 1914 and died together in battle on 7 July. Thomas and Henry Hardwidge, both married men from Ferndale working in the local colliery, enlisted together in the 15th Battalion Welsh Regiment. On 11 July, Tom Hardwidge was fatally wounded and as his brother went to his aid, he was shot and killed by a German sniper. The brothers lie buried side by side in Flatiron Copse Cemetery, close to Mametz Wood.

Brigadier-General H.J. Evans (115th Brigade) took over command of all British troops in Mametz Wood early on 11 July, immediately making a reconnaissance of the line. He found that 'the men were tired, and the morale of some units shaken'.[40] His newly appointed Brigade Major was to be Captain Ll. Wyn Griffith, who until a few weeks previously had been a company officer in the 15th Battalion Royal Welsh Fusiliers; such rapid promotions were commonplace. He described the scene confronting him in Mametz Wood:

> Men of my old battalion were lying dead on the ground in great profusion. They wore a yellow badge on their sleeves, and without this distinguishing mark, it would have been impossible to recognize the remains of many of them … My first acquaintance with the stubborn nature of the undergrowth came when I attempted to leave the main ride to escape a heavy shelling. I could not push a way through it, and I had to return to the ride. Years of neglect had turned the Wood into a formidable barrier, a mile deep. Heavy shelling of the Southern end had beaten down some of the young growth, but it had also thrown trees and large branches into a barricade. Equipment, ammunition, rolls of barbed wire, tins of food, gas-helmets and rifles were lying about everywhere. There were more corpses than men, but there were worse sights than corpses. Limbs and mutilated trunks, here and there a detached head, forming splashes of red against the green leaves, and, as an advertisement of the horror of our way of life and death, and of our crucifixion of youth, one tree held in its branches a leg, with its torn flesh hanging down over a spray of leaf.
>
> Each bursting shell reverberated in a roll of thunder echoing through the Wood, and the acid fumes lingered between the trees. The sun was shining strongly overhead, unseen by us, but felt in its effort to pierce through the curtain of leaves. After passing through

that charnel house at the southern end, with its sickly air of corruption, the smell of fresh earth and crushed bark grew into complete domination, as clean to the senses as the other was foul. So tenacious in these matters is memory that I can never encounter the smell of cut green timber without resurrecting the vision of the tree that flaunted a human limb.[41]

Captain Llewelyn Wyn Griffith, Royal Welsh Fusiliers.

It was still uncertain how many German soldiers were left in the Wood. Divisional Commander Major-General Watts, with the certainty of someone six miles back from the front line, thought it impossible that there was any significant German force left. He ordered the 115th Brigade to attack and occupy the northern and western edges of the Wood at the earliest opportunity. Brigadier-General Evans, with the benefit of being actually on the ground, decided to try and take the remainder of the Wood by surprise, with a bayonet attack planned for 1500 hours. Poor communications rendered the plan useless when, at 1445, the British artillery began a bombardment, giving a clear signal of an impending attack. The German artillery responded, with all the battalions in the Wood suffering heavy casualties from the bombardment both fore and aft. Brigadier-General Evans called the British bombardment 'sheer stupidity', reflecting rhetorically, 'How can we attack after our own barrage has ploughed its way through us? What good can a barrage do in a wood like this?'[42] The answer was nothing at all, except to alert the enemy and kill and wound countless British troops.

Despite the chaotic nature of the start of the attack, after fierce attritional fighting, the Welsh Division reached the north-east corner of the Wood by early evening, only to be forced to retreat at around 2120. Progress was desperately slow, with many men exhausted after nearly thirty-six hours of continuous fighting. Throughout the night of 11-12 July the German artillery systematically bombarded the Wood inflicting many casualties. On 11 July eighty men from the 16th Battalion Royal Welsh Fusiliers died and fifty-four from the 15th Battalion Welsh Regiment; on 12 July forty-seven men from the 10th Battalion Welsh Regiment died.

During the afternoon of 11 July the decision had been taken at Divisional Headquarters to withdraw the Welsh Division from the battle area. This began on the evening of 11 July for those battalions outside the Wood and was completed for all remaining battalions by 0630 on 12 July. Later in the day, Emlyn Davies remembers his battalion being ordered to try and replace lost items of kit and equipment:

> So there we were in the shell-pocked arena, under fire, searching the prostrate forms for such necessities as small kit, water bottles, towels, socks, mess tins, forks, knives, spoons. We neither enjoyed, nor unduly prolonged the nauseating role of battlefield scavengers'.[43]

The 38th Division was relieved by the 21st Division, which cleared the remainder of Mametz Wood by midday on 12 July, encountering little

Newly hollowed out shelters for the British reserves at Mametz.   *(Imperial War Museum)*

resistance. The German forces had largely been withdrawn during the previous night at the very time when the Welsh Division was also moving out. While the seizure of Mametz Wood was wholly due the efforts of the Welsh Division, they did not have the satisfaction of finally witnessing its total capture.

The human toll at the battle of Mametz was a high one. Between 7-12 July, 911 NCOs and other ranks from the Welsh Division lost their lives, plus thirty-seven officers. This figure is considerably higher than that generally quoted, erroneously, of around 600 killed (see Table 1).

In addition, many hundreds more men would have been posted missing, their bodies never recovered. The 16th (Cardiff City) Battalion Welsh Regiment suffered the greatest loss with 153 men and five officers killed, 129 of whom (and three officers) died on 7 July. The 14th (Swansea) Battalion Welsh Regiment had entered its first major engagement of the First World War on 10 July with 676 men; by nightfall, seventy-five men and one officer had died, with a further 376 casualties. Over half the Battalion was lost in one day. The attacking strength of the 17th Battalion

Table 1: 7–12 July 1916, deaths in the Welsh Division of NCOs and other ranks, with numbers of officers in brackets.

	July 7	July 8	July 9	July 10	July 11	July 12
113th Brigade						
13 Btn RWF	2	2 (1)	0	36 (1)	8	4 (1)
14 Btn RWF	4	3	16	52 (3)	3 (1)	2
15 Btn RWF	5	1	0	23	6 (2)	0
16 Btn RWF	2	0	0	23	80 (1)	3
114th Brigade						
10 Btn WR	0	1	0	17 (2)	2	47 (2)
13 Btn WR	0	0	0	96 (6)	1	1
14 Btn WR	0	0	0	75 (1)	2	25
15 Btn WR	0	0	0	13 (2)	54	0
115th Brigade						
10 Btn SWB	1 (1)	0	2	26	4	2
11 Btn SWB	30 (1)	1	0	10	13 (3)	1
16 Btn WR	129 (3)	2	0	18 (1)	4	0 (1)
17 Btn RWF	4	0	23	14 (2)	3 (1)	19 (1)

Royal Welsh Fusiliers was recorded as '950 bayonets'; on 12 July Emlyn Davies transmitted a message to 115th Brigade headquarters, 'strength 5 Officers, 142 Other Ranks'.

Although the name of Mametz Wood has come to symbolize the sacrifice and commitment of Welsh troops in the First World War, their actual contribution – and even their bravery – is still wreathed in controversy and debate. Was it a glorious success or a chaotic failure? In the words of the officers of a neighbouring division, the advance of the Welsh Division on 10 July was 'one of the most magnificent sights of the war', as wave after wave of men were seen 'advancing without hesitation and without a break over a distance which in some places was nearly 500 yards'.[44] Colin Hughes, after a painstakingly thorough analysis of the battle concluded that 'the Welsh Division, inexperienced and inadequately trained, pushed the cream of Germany's professional army back about one mile in most difficult conditions, an achievement that should rank with that of any division on the Somme'.[45] Major G.P.L. Drake-Brockman laid the blame with the officers of the Division for any perceived failure: 'the disrepute into which the division fell as a result of the attack on Mametz Wood was not primarily due to any fault of the fighting troops, who were really good material and did very well later in the war'.[46] Others, however, accused the Welsh Division of indiscipline, a failure to follow orders and even cowardice. Brigadier-General L.A.E. Price Davies, commanding officer of the 113 Brigade, was scathing in his criticism of his own troops:

> After the wood was entered however, and certainly by the time the first objective [on 10 July] was reached the sting had gone from the attack and a certain degree of demoralisation set in. The desire to press on had vanished and it was only by the utmost strenuous efforts on the part of a few officers that it was possible to make progress. The demoralisation increased towards evening on the 10th and culminated in a disgraceful panic during which many left the wood whilst others seemed quite incapable of understanding, or unwilling to carry out the simplest order. A few stout-hearted Germans would have stampeded the whole of the troops in the wood. Later in the night, rapid fire was opened on the slightest alarm and several of our men were hit and one officer was killed by this indisciplined action.[47]

Battalion commanders in the 113th Brigade were subsequently told to instil in their men that the word 'retire' was not to be used, and that any man doing so was liable to be shot on the spot. Major Drake-Brockman thought that during the ten months that he served with the Welsh Division, 'the stigma of Mametz Wood stuck to the division and it was common talk in the BEF [British Expeditionary Force] that 38th Division had "bolted"'. He concluded, 'the fact remains that 38th Division was never employed again on the Somme'.[48] Siegfried Sassoon referred to the 'massacre and confusion', which was 'only a prelude to that pandemonium which converted the green thickets of Mametz Wood to a desolation of skeleton trees and blackened bodies'. Tellingly, he concluded that the battle was 'a disastrous muddle with troops stampeding under machine-gun fire'.[49]

The official history of the campaign also damns the efforts of the Welsh Division on 10 July with faint praise:

> Some men pressed forward, others drifted to the rear, and there were wild bursts of firing as the confused struggle continued amid the undergrowth and fallen trees ... attempts to reorganise the confused mass of troops already in the wood had met with little success ... The troops had required much leading to keep them in any sort of formation ... A decision to advance again at 8 p.m. was cancelled owing to the manifest exhaustion of the troops, who were also in dire need of water.[50]

Emlyn Davies, who witnessed the fighting at first hand on 10-11 July, offered a plausible explanation:

> ... numbers of our men were seen tramping to the rear, crowding the wide track. A co-signaller R.T. Evans ... called out to me – "Come on Double Dot, Retire" ... Standing nearby was an officer pointing his revolver at his own men. He dared not fire. Was this to end in tragedy; to lose all the hard won ground involving terrific losses? The silent officer remained silent. Suddenly the loud shout of a sergeant rang out in the wood: "Stick it Welsh!" To a man they stuck it, halted, turned round. Their lines were reformed ... The order had been "Retire two hundred yards". The order in passing along the line was reduced to "Retire". They retired, but tending to crowd into the ride, some confusion arose. There was no sign whatsoever to panic ... Cool as cucumbers.[51]

Between 7–11 July, the 38th (Welsh) Division, yet to see battle, attacked Mametz Wood seven times. It did so on virtually every occasion without support on either flank: no operations were carried out in this period by the 3rd Division on its right, and the few attempts to co-ordinate attacks with the 17th Division on its left largely failed. Attacking forces were subjected to enfilade fire as they made their way towards the Wood, moving uphill on open ground. The bombardments which preceded the attacks failed to knock-out the machine-gun posts in the Wood, while the principles of a creeping barrage were still in their infancy. Troops were often hit by their own artillery because insufficient time had been taken to ascertain their position within the Wood. Orders to attack were received late, meaning that men were still struggling forward to their start lines at zero hour. Command headquarters was situated six miles from the front line, communication was largely dependent on runners as the telephone lines were cut and consequently unrealistic attacks were ordered, with little understanding of the situation facing the troops on the ground. Against all these difficulties, the Welsh Division succeeded in pushing back Germany's professional army about one mile in the most difficult physical conditions experienced on the Somme in this period. Undoubtedly there had also been moments of panic, confusion and lack of resolve which were to taint the reputation of the Welsh Division for the remainder of the war.

In August 1916, the battered 38th Division took over the line just north of Ypres, opposite Pilckem Ridge, where it was to remain until June 1917. This was a relatively quiet sector of the line and most time was spent repairing and improving the previously muddy and disorganised trenches. Following the capture of the Messines Ridge on 7 June 1917, Douglas Haig was determined to press home the advantage with a major counter-offensive on the Ypres salient. This was to become known

For gootness sake go back! Here kom der WELSH

A contemporary postcard.

as the Third Battle of Ypres or the Battle of Passchendaele. The offensive began in the early hours of 31 July, following an artillery bombardment on the German lines, totalling four million shells (four times the number preceding the Somme offensive). In the afternoon of 31 July, torrential rain had begun falling which did not abate for three days. The battlefield became a quagmire, described as 'soupy mud' or 'porridge', sometimes to a depth of eight feet or more. Many soldiers were to suffocate or drown in water-logged shell holes and craters. The 38th Division, despite significant losses, was instrumental in capturing Pilckem village and Pilckem Ridge from the German 3rd Guards Division, including the notorious regiment known as 'The Cockchafers'.

On the eve of the attack, Major General C. Blackader sent a message to the Welsh troops: 'To-morrow the

The 38th (Welsh) Division memorial at Mametz Wood. It was created by the Welsh sculptor and blacksmith, David Petersen and was unveiled on 11 July 1987. The regimental badges of the South Wales Borderers, the Royal Welsh Fusiliers and the Welsh Regiment are sculpted into the plinth.

38th (Welsh) Division will have the honour of being in the front line of what will be the big battle of the war' and a chance to uphold 'gloriously the honour of Wales and the British Empire'.52 That they did so, restored the reputation of the 38th Division following the events at Mametz Wood twelve months previously.

85

View in Mametz Wood after the battle in July 1916.

NOTES

1. IWM, Private papers of A.E. Perriman, 80/43/1.
2. *Western Mail*, 2 March 1915.
3. *Daily News and Leader*, 2 March 1915.
4. Emlyn Davies, *Taffy Went to War* (Knutsford: Knutsford Secretarial Bureau, 1975), p. 6.
5. Ll. Wyn Griffith, *Up to Mametz* (London: Faber and Faber, 1931), p. 12.
6. IWM, WO 95/2539.
7. IWM, Private papers of A.E. Perriman, 80/43/1.
8. Griffith, *Up to Mametz*, p. 21.
9. IWM, WO95/2539.
10. J.E. Edmonds (ed.), *History of the Great War, Military Operations France and Belgium, 1916, Vol. 1* (London: Macmillan, 1938), p. 481.
11. J.E. Munby, *A History of the 38th (Welsh) Division* (London: Hugh Rees, 1920), p. 17.

[12] Siegfried Sassoon, *The Complete Memoirs of George Sherston* (London: Faber and Faber, 1972) p. 337.
[13] Ibid., p. 342.
[14] Ibid., p. 347.
[15] IWM, Private Papers of A.E. Perriman, 80/43/1.
[16] Griffith, *Up to Mametz*, p. 194.
[17] IWM, WO 95/5261.
[18] IWM, Private Papers of A.E. Perriman, 80/43/1.
[19] Griffith, *Up to Mametz*, pp. 195-7.
[20] Ibid., p. 201.
[21] IWM, Private Papers of A.E. Perriman, 80/43/1
[22] Quoted in Colin Hughes, *Mametz – Lloyd George's 'Welsh Army' at the Battle of the Somme* (Gerrards Cross: Orion Press, 1982), pp. 87-8.
[23] Griffith, *Up to Mametz*, p. 206.
[24] Malcolm Brown, *The Imperial War Museum Book of the Somme* (London: Sidgwick & Jackson, 1966), pp. 126-7.
[25] Neil Oliver, *Not Forgotten* (London: Hodder & Stoughton, 2005), pp. 226-7.
[26] J.E. Edmonds (ed.), *History of the Great War, Military Operations France and Belgium, 1916, Vol. 2* (London: Macmillan, 1938), p. 28.
[27] Quoted in Hughes, *Mametz*, p. 94.
[28] Edmonds, *History of the Great War, 1916, Vol. 2*, p. 40.
[29] TNA, CAB/45 188.
[30] Quoted in Peter Hart, *The Somme* (London: Weidenfeld & Nicolson, 2005), p. 254.
[31] TNA, WO95/2539.
[32] Bernard Lewis, *Swansea Pals: A History of 14th (Service) Battalion, Welsh Regiment in the Great War* (Barnsley: Pen & Sword Military, 2004), p. 103.
[33] Ibid.
[34] Hughes, *Mametz*, pp. 100-1.
[35] C.H. Dudley Ward, *Regimental Records of the Royal Welch Fusiliers, Vol. III, 1914–1918* (Uckfield: The Naval & Military Press, 2005), pp. 206-7.
[36] Hughes, *Mametz*, p. 107.
[37] Dudley Ward, *Royal Welch Fusiliers*, p. 208.
[38] Ibid., p. 207.
[39] Davies, *Taffy Went to War*, p32.
[40] Ibid.
[41] Griffith, *Up to Mametz*, pp. 209-10.
[42] Ibid., p. 221.
[43] Davies, *Taffy Went to War*, p. 36.
[44] Munby, *38th Division*, p.18.
[45] Hughes, *Mametz*, p. 151.
[46] TNA, CAB45/188.
[47] TNA, WO95/2552.
[48] TNA, CAB45/189.
[49] Sassoon, *Complete Memoirs*, pp. 348-9.
[50] Edmonds, *History of the Great War, Vol 2, 1916*, p. 52.
[51] Davies, *Taffy Went to War*, p. 34.
[52] Dudley Ward, *Royal Welch Fusiliers*, pp. 327-8.

Chapter 5

'The Gorgeous East'

The Gallipoli campaign and the experiences of two Welshmen

—ᴍ—

A T THE START OF 1915, the war was already reaching a military stalemate on the western front. A new strategic direction was needed, especially one which would bring a military solution to the political aims of the civilian government. In other words, a way to begin to win the war. The Gallipoli campaign was intended to force a passage through the Sea of Marmara, knock Turkey – who was collaborating with Germany – out of the war and open a supply route to beleaguered Russia. Furthermore it was hoped that an 'Eastern' success would offset the growing casualties in France and give the British public a naval success which it had been expecting since August 1914. The Gallipoli peninsula is sixty-two miles long, varying in breadth between four and twelve miles. The terrain is rough and inhospitable, with steep and rocky cliffs leading up from virtually the whole coastline. The few beaches on which any invading force could land are overlooked by hills, giving all the advantages to a defensive force. The Turkish defences of the Dardanelles were substantial in 1915 and much more so than the British rather patronisingly believed.

In March 1915 an allied naval bombardment was largely unsuccessful and it was decided to undertake a combined naval-military operation in April, with the revised aim of securing the peninsula. An enormous amphibious assault may have been strategically correct, but its execution was a military disaster. The allied forces managed to establish themselves at the southern end of the peninsula and also in the area later to be known as Anzac Cove, but they were forced into trench warfare much like that on the western front. Conditions were different but equally appalling: the heat was virtually unbearable, the trenches were like ovens, the troops were besieged by 'corpse flies' and eighty per cent of the allied force was to succumb to dysenteric diarrhoea. To try and break the stalemate, a massive assault was planned for August 1915, which necessitated reinforcements being sent from home, largely comprising Kitchener's New Armies.

Cecil Phillips from Llanelli was training as a solicitor at the outbreak of war, but returned home to join his local territorial battalion, the 4th Battalion Welsh Regiment. His letters home paint a vivid picture of the Gallipoli campaign.[1] The 4th Welsh set sail on 17 July 1915 on HM Transport *Huntsend*, 'a fine large vessel, one captured from the Germans', a fact which Phillips found 'most satisfactory'.[2] There were around 2,500 men on board, with 29 officers and 969 other ranks in the 4th Welsh, plus

British Army camp at Gully Beach, Cape Helles, Gallipoli. Note a mass of horses and mules used for transportation.

(Imperial War Museum)

Os ydych am

YMUNO YN WIRFODDOL

a'r Fyddin
cyn dyfod o Fesur

Y GWASANAETH MILWROL
i rym

PEIDIWCH OEDI
I'R FUNYD OLAF

Canlyniad gohiriad fydd
rhuthr fawr ar y terfyn, yr
hyn a achosa anghyfleustra
i chwi ac i'r Awdurdodau

YMUNWCH DA CHWI
AR UNWAITH

Parliamentary Recruiting Committee poster No 147. (If you want to join up voluntarily, before conscription comes into force, don't delay until the last minute. The results of procrastination will be a great rush at the end which will cause inconvenience to you and the authorities. Come on, enlist at once.)

the 4th Battalion Cheshire Regiment and divisional staff. Phillips clearly saw his embarkation as a time for taking stock: he gave his father clear instructions on how to reclaim some overpaid income tax just in case anything happened to him and a list of bills to be settled. He concluded: 'though I have my faults & weaknesses I have always tried to be unselfish & I can honestly say I have never done anything very bad.'[3] Phillips, like most others on board, suffered from severe sea-sickness (known as 'feeding the fishes') during the first few days of the voyage. However, once they neared Gibraltar, he began to appreciate the beautifully blue sea, and the flying fishes and porpoises. He found that the feeding on board was excellent, 'better than most first class hotels, and we can get anything you can think of, game, fish of all kinds and a simply wonderful selection of fruit'.[4] Days were spent on weapon training, military instruction, in the gymnasium, or even riding. The main danger during the voyage was of a submarine attack which led to frequent boat drills and lifebuoy parades. These were taken particularly seriously, as it was soon realized that there were not nearly enough lifeboats on board for the number of men. With time for reflection, Phillips wanted to wipe the slate clean with his parents:

There is one thing I should like to tell you. I have never mentioned it to a soul before, no one at all ... I took private tuition when in London studying for my Final. I did not work as hard as I should have I know, but I had hoped to get Honours in order to please Dad ... I kept the private tuition absolutely to myself, though I had a heap of friends with me daily who often wondered when I was out for a certain hour, usually from 5 to 6 p.m. I paid nearly £20 for this, so you see what I used to do with my private money.[5]

Another Carmarthenshire man who was to be involved in the Gallipoli campaign was Lieutenant Robert Peel, a regular officer in the 58th Brigade Royal Field Artillery, whose family owned the Taliaris Estate near Llandeilo. He sailed from Liverpool aboard the *Empress of Britain* on 1 July 1915, and spent the early part of the voyage practising morse code and playing bridge. He was put in temporary charge of the Lincoln platoon and had to carry out a foot inspection; he found 'all very dirty and many mis-shapen'.[6] Both Peel and Phillips docked in Malta to re-coal, and both had the opportunity to spend time on shore. Peel visited the military club, had his hair cut, bought a small electric fan and a flask, and hired a boat to tour around the harbour. Phillips watched the coal being loaded on board from barges moored alongside. He was fascinated by 'the ceaseless chatter of the lower class Maltese which likened them to monkeys'.[7] War was living up to its nineteenth-century reputation as an opportunity to travel to exotic places and to experience an adventure. The next port of call was Alexandria, reached by Peel on 12 July, and Phillips on 29 July. The heat and the flies were beginning to affect all the men, and Peel found 'the smell of perspiration on board … becoming very unpleasant'.[8] Phillips found himself running with perspiration all day, 'till my thin outer clothes are soaked through and look as if I had fallen in a bath of water'. The chimney stacks and smoke in one quarter of Alexandra made him 'think of Llanelly'.[9]

The initial attacks on the peninsula took place on the night of 6-7 August on the Helles front, Anzac Cove, and Suvla Bay with the object of seizing a position across the Gallipoli peninsula from Gaba Tepe to Maidos. A total of 20,000 troops were to be disembarked at Suvla Bay to confront an enemy numbering an estimated 2,000. In the event, the landings were chaotic and Turkish resistance was far more dogged than expected. Despite this, on 8 August, against all the odds, the possibility of achieving the military objective was at hand. However, due to delay, prevarication, poor communications and indecision, the golden opportunity had passed. 'Never was there a more striking illustration of the adage that, in war, time is all-important.'[10] Historians ever since have mulled over what might have been. By 8 August Phillips was writing to his parents to say that he was on his way to land on the Gallipoli peninsula and within a few hours would be 'in the thick of it'. It was a time for reflection:

I am sending my watch back as Grannie gave it to me and I would not like it to get lost. Should anything happen, I would like to let you know how I have always appreciated everything you have all done for me, and how proud I have always felt to be the son of my good Father & Mother ... Don't think that because I write in this way that I think I am not coming out if it. I will do my part, you may be sure but I shall be alright and will return safely very shortly ... remember I am only one of millions of sons fighting, somewhere or other for some country.[11]

The 4th Battalion Welsh Regiment completed their disembarkation onto the shores of 'C' Beach, just south of Suvla Bay at daylight on 9 August, suffering some casualties from shell-fire. The Battalion was hardly prepared for a battle such as this. Although the officers had enjoyed an 'exceedingly uneventful & pleasant voyage', with occasional trips ashore, the vast majority of the troops had been at sea for three weeks without landing once.[12] Furthermore, the ship in which they had travelled had not been designed for passenger traffic. The men were physically unfit for operations in the height of the hot weather on a sandy sun-scorched plain.

Peel had written, 'Atmosphere & temperature down in the men's bunks something altogether out of my previous experience. Have seen natives of India huddled together in much the same manner smell nothing like so bad; this I think is because white man eats more meat than native'.[13] Peel spent 8 August watching the battle in Suvla Bay through field glasses from the safety of his ship, noting the heavy firing of the Turkish troops. He landed on 10 August, and his diary entry illustrates the general confusion and disorganization:

Landed from lighters at 4 a.m. on C Beach. Made out horse lines there and got shelled for the 1st time. Major marched all the gunners to Anzac where we found our guns. Horses arrived that night 11.45: we booked in & were directed by a New Zealand guide. He led us wrongly & all today we had to lie low in a dried up river bed. An escort was sent out to us at night and we got clear away having lost 2 horses and one man wounded. [12 August]. Arrived at 'Base' camp at 2-30 a.m. and immediately ordered to take up a position.[14]

Cecil Phillips could not find time to write home until 15 August:

> This is the first opportunity I have had of writing since landing. It is now 10 days since I have had my boots off & no wash. Feeding on ship biscuits, a little jam, tea seldom & bully beef. We have been under fire (both shrapnel & rifle) since landing. The very day we attacked there was a tremendous casualty list but fortunately many more wounded than killed … As I write in a rough trench we have made & have not moved from here for three days, the bullets are passing & I could not put a finger up without getting it; besides this shrapnel is falling all around. However it is wonderful how one gets used to everything, so that now we hardly notice it.[15]

Undoubtedly, Phillips's strong religious conviction helped him during this time: 'I will never as long as I live cease to publicly acknowledge what I owe to God for protecting me as he has done. Never for an instant will I cease to praise His name for ever & ever'.[16] However, he was also sufficiently realistic to see the value of a 'Blighty' injury: 'At times, one prays to be slightly wounded. I know it is awfully wicked, but I always say "Thy Will Be Done", after every prayer'.[17]

Throughout August, the campaign ground on with the allied forces unable to make any real headway against the superior defensive positions of the Turks. On 17 August 1915, the Commander-in-Chief, Sir Ian Hamilton, had requested reinforcements of 95,000 men, to give the campaign any chance of success. After one attack by 5,000 men on 21 August, the official history of the Welsh Regiment concluded that 'prodigies of valour were performed but all in vain, and the end of the day saw our troops

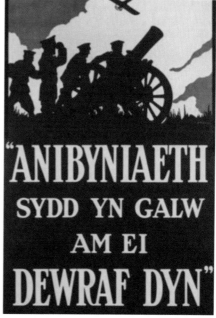

Parliamentary Recruiting Committee poster No 148. (Independence calls for the bravest of men.) When this poster was printed in English, the caption used was a quotation from Lord Kitchener: 'Be honest with yourself. Be certain that your so-called reason is not a selfish excuse'. Enlist today.

back in their original position.'[18] This comment would equally apply to the rest of the campaign. The morale of the troops was extremely low, mainly due to the appalling conditions which the men had to endure, both at the front and in the reserve lines. Although Phillips always tried to put a brave face on things when writing home, even he was becoming dispirited: 'To-day Sunday, a Sabbath Day and here we are in holes in the ground like animals not human beings. Strange that civilisation should have-brought us to this stage'.[19] By the beginning of September, he was further depressed:

> What a cruel disappointment, I heard to-day that the ship carrying our mails, has been sunk. Only two letters from you since I left home nearly two months ago … The heat here is terrible and we have but a little water allotted us per day, as it all has to be brought from the ships. We are now up in the hills and it is hotter than ever. All day lying under a blazing sun with absolutely no shelter but what we carry up, and we must make it invisible, otherwise aeroplanes will sight it and the CO [Commanding Officer] order it down. At night we have a very heavy dew which soaks everything and it is frightfully cold. Every night one longs for the morning and when the light comes one prays for sunset. What a climate. Flies worse than anyone could describe. It is really impossible to eat or drink after about 7 a.m. until 7 p.m. for flies cover everything. We do 48 hours in trenches awake and on duty all the time and then 6 days out. Thank God. Then these 6 days we have fatigue work all night and try to sleep in the day, but the flies do not let one get rest. They settle on the face and hands by the score. The men out here are suffering a great deal for their country, and yet we heard that the Welsh miners are out again. The men are mad about it, and they would soon deal with them if they had the opportunity … Well I must wind up now. If you could only see the way in which my pencil is steering on this paper through dozens and dozens of flies you would shudder.[20]

The loathsome 'corpse flies' were directly responsible for a virulent form of dysenteric diarrhoea, generally known as the 'Gallipoli Gallop' or the 'Gallipoli Trots'. It was impossible to protect food from the swarms of flies, basic hygiene was virtually impossible and consequently the disease spread like wildfire. Latrines were usually a hole in the ground with a pole to hang on to; box latrines with seats were regarded as a great luxury. By the middle of August, it was estimated that the whole force, from the Commander-in-Chief downwards, was affected by this complaint, and the men were so weak from it that few could walk at a quicker pace than a crawl. Phillips suffered, just like the rest of his battalion. He wrote: 'I had frightful pains and sickness, and felt as weak as a cat. However I starved myself all yesterday and lay down the whole day and night and now I am as fit as anything again. It is rotten being ill so far from home.'[21] In a previous letter, Phillips had warned his parents 'not to let anyone know the contents of this letter, in any case it should get to the papers'. His concern was the number of men who were falling ill with dysentery:

> Over 100 of our men [4th Battalion Welsh Regiment] have gone to hospital with diarrhoea. This has given more trouble than anything since coming out. 50 are isolated suffering from scabies, so now we have but 200 in the Batt[alion]. We should have returned to the trenches yesterday but owing to our depleted strength we could not go & do the duty of the Batt[alion] 1000 strong who we were to relieve.[22]

The total number of troops sent to the Gallipoli peninsula during the campaign was estimated to be 410,000. Of this number, 90,000 were evacuated because of sickness at some time; during October 1915, evacuations were averaging 750 per day. Of the 104 men from the 4th Battalion Welsh Regiment who died on the peninsula, 12 died from sickness or disease. After the decision not to send reinforcements to the Dardanelles in August, with the subsequent decision to open up another front in Salonika and with winter weather approaching, the chances of success in Gallipoli were fading into the distance. 'The history of September and October 1915, on the Suvla Front was bare of incident', reported the Welsh Regimental history. 'Work and sickness filled these months'.[23] For Phillips, however, September was to bring great personal honour and achievement for his acts of bravery. He had developed a reputation in the 4th Battalion as being something of a 'mad jack', willing to undertake any mission, whatever the danger. He had written to his parents:

> I have always walked about outside the trench, when the men would
> not show their noses out, just to give the men courage … I was chosen
> out of the Brigade to rush a farm last night with 30 men & though I
> got near enough to see the Turks 10 yds off … the thing could not be
> done. May have another chance soon … I was a 100 yds beyond the
> front line last night & could have shot a few of the enemy with my
> revolver had I cared.[24]

On 4 September 1915, the *Western Mail* reported that 'all the officers
[of the 4th Welsh Battalion] have an excellent reputation among the men,
and what pleases one most is to hear the men relate some of the doings
of young Cecil Phillips, who is the hero of the regiment, and deserves
the V.C. The things he has done are really marvellous, and he seems to
bear a charmed life.' In fact, Cecil Phillips was to receive the Military
Cross for his bravery, when rescuing four wounded men on 14 August
1915. His official citation read: 'For great gallantry in going out almost
70 yards under much heavy shrapnel and rifle fire and assisted by a NCO
bringing in a wounded officer without covering of a trench and again
returning and bringing in 3 other wounded soldiers'.[25] Phillips's reaction
to his decoration was somewhat enigmatic: 'if this recommendation goes
through, I shall be glad because a Phillips has had it & you say we have
come from a good old stock & these things will prove blood is thicker than
water, and who knows perhaps our descendants will come into their own
again, some day'.[26]

As winter approached, a decision had to be made about the viability of
continuing the Gallipoli campaign. Not only was it becoming increasingly
certain that German munitions would be reaching the Turks by early
December, but also the arrival of winter weather might make it impossible
either to land a new army on the peninsula, or to withdraw the existing
force if evacuation were decided upon. Before a final decision could be
made, one of the most cruel and strange events of the campaign was
to take place on the peninsula: a freak storm and blizzard which lasted
three days. Meteorological experts had predicted that November would
be glorious weather, and that though a few southerly storms might be
expected, heavy gales and real winter weather need not be feared until the
latter end of January. Robert Peel's diary, largely written after the storm,
had the following entries for 27, 28 and 29 November 1915:

Thunderstorms, torrential rain, blizzard and frost; great suffering among infantry. During this period all ranks at Suvla Bay went through the greatest hardships. November 27th at 5.30 p.m. a fierce thunderstorm set in with torrential rain. This continued on & off all night till 1 a.m. when the weather turned cold & the 'blizzard' period began. This period lasted till the evening of the 28th when a hard frost luckily dried up the ground and made existence more bearable. The infantry in the lst line trenches were in a most luckless state, many reserve trenches & rest camps were in little better condition, there being no overhead cover available. Winter cover had been repeatedly applied and indented for by all units. The only consolation is that from general observation the condition of the Turkish troops was if anything rather worse than that of ours, a lamentable affair.[27]

The official history of the Gallipoli campaign wrote of 'nights of horrors', with the severe cold proving an unbearable strain to the men whose health had already been undermined by the hardships of the earlier months. 'All over the plain streams of utterly exhausted men were struggling back to the beach, many collapsing on the roadside and freezing to death where they fell'.[28] There were two hundred deaths from frostbite or drowning, and ten thousand men had to be evacuated with frostbite or sickness. Ironically, on 30 November, the wind died away, the frost disappeared, and for the next three weeks there was an almost unbroken spell of perfect autumnal weather. General Sir Charles Munro, the new commander-in-chief, took little time to come to the conclusion that the situation on the peninsula contained the seeds of disaster and he immediately recommended evacuation. The withdrawal of 118,000 officers and men, 300 guns, 2,300 vehicles and 7,200 horses and donkeys from right under the noses of the enemy, showed all the military skill and expertise which had been so patently lacking earlier in the campaign. The Turks had simply not realized what was going on, and there was not a single loss of life on the allied side.

The Gallipoli campaign had shattered many illusions for the largely volunteer units which had served there. War was not the glorious adventure that many had believed it would be. For both Peel and Phillips, the death, disease and hardships of the campaign must have seemed a long way from the heady days of August and September 1914, when they had so eagerly volunteered for overseas service. Peel, after spending some months in Egypt, was posted to the western front as a brigade commander, where he was also to receive the Military Cross. He died of wounds on 3 September 1917, during the 3rd Battle of Ypres. Phillips survived the war and took up his chosen career as a solicitor. Neither would have agreed with Prime Minister Asquith's remark, 'how lucky they are to escape Flanders & the trenches and be sent to the "gorgeous east"'.[29]

The crew of HMS *Tara* recuperating in hospital in Alexandria, Egypt in March 1916. HMS *Tara*, formerly an express passenger steamer, was on patrol along the Egyptian coast when she was sunk by a German torpedo on 5 November 1915. The crew, mostly from Anglesey, was taken captive, marched 250 miles across desert and mountain to Bir-el-Hakim, from where they were rescued in March 1916 and taken to Alexandria. *(Courtesy of the Anglesey Archives, WSP/193)*

NOTES

1. Carmarthenshire Archives Service (CAS), DX/26.
2. Ibid., C. Phillips to his family, undated.
3. Ibid., C. Phillips to his family, undated.
4. Ibid., C. Phillips to his family, 21 July 1915.
5. Ibid., C. Phillips to his family, 22 July 1915.
6. CAS, Taliaris Muniments, Box 428, Diary of Robert Peel (hereafter Peel Diary), 4 July 1915.
7. Ibid., Peel Diary, 6 July 1915.
8. Ibid., Peel Diary, 9 July 1915.
9. CAS, DX/26, C. Phillips to his family, 30 July 1915.
10. T. O. Marden, *History of the Welch Regiment Vol II* (Cardiff: Western Mail, 1932), p. 500.
11. CAS, DX/26, C. Phillips to his family, 8 August 1915.
12. Ibid., 22 July 1915.
13. CAS, Peel Diary, 12 July 1915.
13. CAS, DX/26, C. Phillips to his family, 8 August 1915.
14. CAS, Peel Diary, 12 August 1915.
15. CAS, DX/26, C. Phillips to his family, 16 August 1915.
16. Ibid., C. Phillips to his family, 27 August 1915.
17. Ibid., C. Phillips to his family, 19 August 1915.
18. Marden, *History of the Welch Regiment*, p. 504.
19. CAS, DX/26, C. Phillips to his family, 22 August 1915.
20. Ibid., C. Phillips to his family, 8 September, 1915.
21. Ibid., C. Phillips to his family, 4 September 1915.
22. Ibid., C. Phillips to his family, 1 September 1915.
23. Marden, *History of the Welch Regiment*, p. 505.
24. CAS, DX/26, C. Phillips to his family, 21 August 1915.
25. Ibid., citation of C. Phillips, undated.
26. CAS, DX/26, C. Phillips to his family, 14 September 1915.
27. CAS, Peel Diary, 27-29 November 1915.
28. C. F. Aspinall-Oglander, *History of the Great War, Military Operations Gallipoli, Vol II* (London: William Heinemann, 1932), p. 434.
29. M. and E. Brock, *H. H. Asquith, Letters to Venetia Stanley* (Oxford: Oxford University Press, 1982), p. 449. The letter is dated 26 February 1915.

Chapter 6

'Wild and insubordinate'

The Welsh soldier

—ᜠ—

W ELSHMEN SERVED IN THE armed forces in every theatre of war and in every conceivable regiment, unit and formation. For some, joining battalions of the Welsh Regiment or Royal Welsh Fusiliers, they would have been in a majority. For others, in the Devonshire Regiment or the Scots Guards, they would have been very much in the minority. John Davies has argued that by 'suffering alongside Geordies and Brummies, Cockneys and Scousers, Micks, Jocks and Aussies, the Taffs became part of a new brotherhood; to become a soldier was to assume a new nationality'.[1] However, there is ample evidence to show that for many fighting in the war, their Welsh cultural roots remained an important touchstone in their dislocated lives.

In the year of Dylan Thomas's birth, it was appropriate that the willingness to sing was mentioned frequently as an important feature of Welsh identity. The Welsh were already thanking their Creator for being a very musical nation. Ll. Wyn Griffith, an officer in the 15th Battalion Royal Welsh Fusiliers, remembered an incident when a company was waiting to go to the front line trenches:

> They started singing in harmony … a fine old Welsh hymn in a minor key. The brigadier-general asks me, 'Why do they always sing these mournful hymns? Most depressing – bad for morale. Why can't they sing something cheerful, like other battalions?' I try to explain to

him that what they are singing now is what they sang as children,
as I did, in chapel, in the world to which they really belong. They
are being themselves, not men in uniform. They are back at home,
with their families, in their villages. But he does not understand. Nor
can he with his background … While they sang, they, and I, were in
another country.[2]

This important connection between home life and the familiarity of Welsh
hymns and songs was also commented on in a newspaper report on the
38th Division, prior to their embarkation to France in December 1915:

The Welshmen bring with them into their lonely exile a certain
homely warmth and clannishness which you do not find in
communities more racially mixed. To feel how the Welsh bring their
own atmosphere with them into an alien land you must be there as
I was, when the weary route-marchers swing back into camp, in the
twilight singing 'Sospan Bach' [sic] which may be called the football
national anthem of Wales and which has been heard on many a field
of triumph.[3]

Members of the 6th Battalion, Royal Welsh Fusiliers, outside the cricket pavilion in Rushden,
Northamptonshire, where they were stationed from May 1915 for three months.

Emlyn Davies recollected that marching men, whatever their nationality, often broke into song because this 'tended to shorten the miles and lighten the heavy load borne by the P.B.I. [Poor Bloody Infantry]' He thought that with Welshmen, 'the urge to sing formed part of their nature.' The battalion did not confine itself to Welsh songs because it contained a proportion of Englishmen; favourites were 'Keep the Home Fires Burning', 'Tipperary', 'The March of the Men of Harlech' and 'La Marseillaise'.[4] Robert Graves also refers to the importance of singing in the Welsh regiments, when a new draft of soldiers arrived in France at Béthune Station in June 1916 and had to be marched to the front line trenches in Cambrin: 'None of the draft had been out before, except the sergeant in charge. They began singing. Instead of the usual music-hall songs they sang Welsh hymns, each man taking a part. The Welsh always sang when pretending not to be scared; it kept them steady. And they never sang out of tune.' On the march a salvo of four shells whizzed overhead and 'this broke up "Aberystwyth" in the middle of a verse'.[5] On another occasion, Graves was in hospital in an old chateau near Rouen: 'That evening, I heard a sudden burst of lovely singing in the courtyard where the ambulances pulled up. I recognized the quality of the voices'. He knew immediately that 'the First Battalion have been in it again', which a nurse soon confirmed to him to be correct.[6] An English soldier in the Royal Army Medical Corps wrote to the *Western Mail* praising the 'singing soldiers' who 'often burst into song when the enemy's bullets and shells shriek over them in the trenches'.[7] An army surgeon followed this up saying that the only songs he heard at the front which were not of the music hall type were sung 'by a famous Welsh regiment'. As far as he knew the soldiers were the only ones 'who sang in parts'.[8]

The Welsh language was another aspect of identity which drew attention to the Welsh. The use of the language within the armed forces had sparked off a row between Kitchener and Lloyd George in a cabinet meeting in October 1914. The ostensible cause of the contretemps was an order to the men of the 2/1st Denbighshire Yeomanry not to speak Welsh in their billets. However, the underlying cause was more to do with Kitchener's refusal to allow previously enlisted men in the Welsh regiments to transfer to the newly formed Welsh Army Corps. Furthermore, Lloyd George wanted to ensure that the use of the Welsh language was not going to be in any way hindered in the Welsh Army Corps, as he feared this might affect the willingness of volunteers to come forward. Kitchener immediately tried to calm Lloyd George's fears saying that the banning of Welsh had come from a 'territorial idiot' who thought that 'muttering in Welsh was a means of using insubordinate language'. Kitchener confirmed that the War Office did not endorse the order and was more concerned that Welsh should not be recognised as the language to be spoken on parade.[9] In practice, it seems that the use of Welsh was an accepted fact in the Welsh regiments, especially with the influx of native speakers commented on by Graves in the 2nd Battalion Royal Welsh Fusiliers where 'as much Welsh as English is now talked in the huts'.[10]

In April 1915 Huw Richards from Pontypridd had written to Lord Kitchener complaining about a ban on the use of the Welsh language. His son, serving on the Western Front, had written a postcard home in his native Welsh. He was called before the regimental censor and told to write it in English otherwise it could not be passed. Huw Richards received the following reply from the War Office: 'I am commanded by the Army Council … to inform you that your son must be under a misapprehension

Soldiers on the front line.

(Courtesy of Ceredigion Archives)

Visit of the tank 'Egbert' to Aberbargoed in 1918.   *(Courtesy of Jeff Alden Collection, Gwent Archives)*

in the matter and that he is at liberty to conduct his correspondence in Welsh if he desires to do so'.[11] It may be that the award-winning film *Hedd Wyn* has clouded the historical record by showing an English officer censoring his company's letters and contemplating rejecting Hedd Wyn's correspondence, including his entry for the 1917 National Eisteddfod, because he could not understand the content. There was the occasional bigot, such as Gerard Burgoyne, who wrote in his diary: 'a few days ago among the letters of the Company, which were sent to me for censoring, I found one written in Welsh. I returned it to the writer and said he must re-write it in English'. Burgoyne also recounts how a lance corporal complained to him that 'these two men won't do a thing I tell them'. Both men apparently replied together saying 'please sir, he's a Welshman, sir, and speaks to us in Welsh, and we can't understand him.'[12]

By the end of the war, specific systems were in place allowing the use of the Welsh language in letters from the front, described by 2nd Lieutenant Alexander Stanier, Welsh Guards:

> As I was in a Welsh regiment it was to be expected that a certain number of men would be using their native tongue in their letters home. That presented a problem in so far as few officers could read Welsh and, therefore, could not censor any letters. Letters in Welsh

were marked as such and sent to Divisional HQ for censoring at the base. Of course, no one there would be interested in what Pte Jones thought of his platoon or company officers![13]

The number of Welsh speakers (and monoglot Welsh speakers) who enlisted in the armed forces would have made any attempt to prevent the use of the language, either in everyday life or in letters home, totally impractical. Malcolm Trustram Eve, later Lord Silsoe, was a junior officer in the 6th Battalion Royal Welsh Fusiliers, most of whom were slate quarrymen; the general talk in the battalion was always Welsh. Although the adjutant of the battalion had decreed that training should be conducted in English, Lieutenant Eve thought this the wrong decision as many men did not understand what was being taught.[14] He further supported the Welsh language when as a more senior officer dealing with soldiers on court martial, Eve insisted that the hearing should be conducted through the medium of Welsh if that was what the accused man requested, even if he spoke good English.

Ll. Wyn Griffith also considered the Welsh language as being vitally important as a buffer against the 'English' army life:

> But if, as I do, you belong to a small nation, with its own language, Welsh, surrounded by a large nation speaking English, you enter into a double life. English is the language of the Army, Welsh the language of friendship and companionship, 'ours' against 'theirs'. There is, inside you, a citadel which cannot be stormed by force, but which can be entered with the key of language. And when you find yourself in the company of your fellow countrymen, private soldiers with a private language with which to escape from this new world of drill and parade and discipline, a language belonging exclusively to a way of life in which you were nurtured and from which you are now exiled, companionship brings a new kind of intimacy. A new bond is created, a sense of being a community within a community, which intensifies the very meaning of comradeship.[15]

While it is impossible to generalize about specific character traits of 'the Welsh soldier', many have described how Welshmen reacted to incidents of perceived unfairness or heavy-handedness. Captain J. Dunn, a company commander in 2nd Battalion Royal Welsh Fusiliers recalled:

These Welshmen are peculiar. They won't stand being shouted at. They'll do anything if you explain the reason for it – do and die, but they have to know their reason why. The best way to make them behave is not to give them too much time to think. Work them off their feet. They are good workmen, too. But officers must work with them, not only direct the work.[16]

'G.J.', writing in the *Welsh Outlook*, saw similar characteristics:

The ordinary Welsh recruit, if not dealt with sympathetically, is a most difficult man to deal with ... because [b]eing very self-conscious and easily offended he seems to carry with him a sort of shell; and when an officer or instructor is unnecessarily harsh with him he disappears into this shell. And whilst he is there nothing on earth can move him, and no more useless person lives ... But [b]e patient with him and you have a plodder ... a man who is always reliable.[17]

There were ex-miners who 'commented with extraordinary fluency upon the unfair division of labour in the battalion' and engineers who presented their commanding officer with a strike note following a dispute over pay differentials'. One officer 'put it down to the years of tuition they have received in Trades Unions and socialistic principles in the South

A temporary barber's shop at Hell-Fire corner on the Menin Road, October 1914.

Wales Coalfields'.[18] At a training camp in Litherland near Liverpool, Robert Graves had received a deputation of soldiers from Harlech and the surrounding area: 'Captain Graves, sir, we do not like our sergeant-major. He do curse, and he do swear, and he do drink, and he do smoke, and he is a man of lowly origins too'. Graves told them to make their complaint in a proper form under the escort of a non-commissioned officer. They did not return.[19] A.E. Perriman, 11th Battalion South Wales Borderers, remembers being on Salisbury Plain in November 1915, prior to embarkation to France: 'two companies arrived late at night, following a heavy storm, which had brought down the canteen marquee. No rations, and no breakfast either. When ordered to fall in for shooting practice they refused. A sgt [sergeant], a cpl [corporal] and 6 privates all arrested and then remanded for a district court martial.' The sergeant and corporal were stripped of their rank and they were all sentenced to two years' detention.[20]

On 11 September 1914 in Preston, a group of aggrieved Welshmen led what was almost a mutiny. About two hundred and fifty men marched through the town to Preston Station carrying a banner stating 'No food, no shelter, no money', demanding to be allowed to return home to south Wales immediately. The men, mostly miners from the Tonypandy area, had been in the town for two weeks with 'nothing to do but walk about the streets in the rainy weather in old boots, down at the heel, and with no money in their pockets'. They had been used to good wages, but had nothing to send home to their families because the administrative system to pay allowances had been totally swamped by the numbers of recruits. The men refused to return to the barracks unless their pay was secured: 'We are Welshmen … when we say a thing we mean it'. Eventually it was agreed that, notwithstanding the regulations, the men would receive a payment on account the following morning. The Mayor of Preston, Harry Cartmell, who had been involved in the negotiations, supposed that 'according to all the rules there had been a very serious infraction of military law, and I am afraid that technically someone had been aiding and abetting a mutiny'.[21]

There is, of course, a danger in thinking that there was a stereotypical 'Welsh soldier' any more than there was a definitive Scottish, French or German soldier. However, it can be argued that the hardships and suffering of everyday life at the front and the shared experience of a long confrontation with death, created a distinct 'war culture' which affected soldiers whatever their background or nationality. Any attempt to try and determine the geographic, linguistic, religious and social background of Welsh volunteers to the armed forces is fraught with difficulty, due to the limited – and sometimes contradictory – nature of the evidence available. Two researchers have made attempts to do so, using individual soldiers' service files (often known as the 'Burnt Documents' and '1914–1920' Collations) now housed in the National Archives, which include both volunteers and conscripts. At the time of their studies, only limited access to the files was available, necessitating somewhat arbitrary sampling. Doron Lamm examined the files of 6,700 men, of which 4.12 per cent were from Wales.[22] Gervase Phillips attempted to gain a picture of the Welsh soldier, using the rather crude method of only selecting the files of those with a typically Welsh surname, such as Jones or Williams, which gave a sample of 202 files.[23]

Lamm's study supports the widely held claim that men from rural counties were proportionately less likely to join the armed forces than men from the more urbanized counties, and this was true not only of Wales, but also for the whole of Britain. Lamm compared the number of men from each county in his sample with the 1911 census figures. This shows that it was only Montgomeryshire and Anglesey which actually supplied more men than would have been expected according to the census figures. All the remaining counties of Wales supplied fewer men than would have been expected. The rural counties such as Cardiganshire, Carmarthenshire and Pembrokeshire supplied fewer than 50 per cent of their notional number, whilst the urbanized counties of Glamorgan and Monmouthshire still only supplied 83 per cent of the number expected according to the census. Lamm found that rural counties in England, such as Devon, Lincolnshire and Cornwall, were similarly under-represented, as were the rural counties of northern Scotland. An in-depth study of Carmarthenshire, which has both rural and industrial areas, reached a similar conclusion.[24]

A second point of contention was that the Nonconformist denominations were not supporting the war in the same numbers as those from the established church. Here the evidence is a little less clear-cut. In Gervase Phillips's study, of the 202 individual files he examined, only 113 men stated their religious denomination:

Religious denomination of men in sample	(%)
Baptist	10.0
Calvinistic Methodist	7.4
Congregationalist	4.5
Wesleyan Methodist	4.5
Other non-conformist	4.5
Anglican	26.0
Not known	44.0

Temporary grave of Private Alcwyn
Evans, 24th Battalion Welsh regiment, in
Kantara, Egypt. He died of sickness on 12
May 1917 aged 23.

(NLW, D. C. Harries Collection)

Kantara War
Memorial Cemetery,
Egypt burial place
of Private Alcwyn
Evans, 24th Battalion
Welsh Regiment.
Evans was originally
from Llanarthney,
Carmarthenshire.

Phillips explains this large proportion of 'not knowns' by two factors. Firstly, the attestation forms used for recruits in 1914 and 1915 simply did not require religious denomination to be specified, and secondly, the collection of such information on enlistment was not considered particularly important. This is certainly correct, because the standard forms for attestation, (Army Forms E.501 and B.2512) asked for address, occupation, age, etc, but did not request religious denomination. Secondly, the failure to ask for denomination is unwitting testimony on the part of the army, which seems only to have recognized Anglicanism and Roman Catholicism. Phillips argues that Kitchener's hostile attitude to Nonconformity extended down the chain of command to certain recruiting officers, and some Nonconformists gave their denomination as Church of England to avoid confrontation. Phillips cites the examples of two particular recruits: firstly, an Aberdare soldier who originally gave his denomination as Church of England, but subsequently married in a Baptist chapel; and secondly, a soldier described as Anglican in 1914, later gives his denomination as Methodist in a form inserted into his service record following medical treatment for a wound. Phillips concludes that 'It could at least be suggested that non-conformists were not reluctant to enlist'. However, his own statistics do not really bear this out, even allowing for a slight over-representation of Anglicans, as explained above. Of those who did state their religious denomination, approximately 46 per cent were Anglicans and 56 per cent were Nonconformists. If we compare these figures with those cited in the *Royal Commission on the Church of England and other religious bodies in Wales and Monmouthshire*, published in 1910, but relating to communicants in 1905, we find that only 26 per cent were from the Church of England, but 71 per cent from the Nonconformist denominations.

Communicants by denomination, Wales, 1905		
Communicants	Number	% of total
Baptists	142,551	19.06
Calvinistic Methodists	170,348	22.77
Congregationalists	175,097	23.40
Wesleyans	43,358	5.79
Church of England	195,004	26.06
Others	21,876	2.92

This reluctance on the part of Nonconformists in Wales to enlist is further illustrated by an examination of the Roll Book of E Company, 16th Battalion Royal Welsh Fusiliers.[25] This give details of 333 soldiers, all of whom were volunteers, with a significant number from north Wales. Only twenty-four do not state their religious denomination, which is in sharp contrast to the information taken from the attestation forms sampled by Phillips.

| Religious denomination of E Company, 16th Battalion RWF ||
Denomination	% of total listing religious denomination
Baptists	12.50
Methodists	13.49
Congregationalists	3.95
Wesleyans	8.55
Church of England	54.93
Others (including Roman Catholics)	6.58

Officers and Sergeants of the 130th (St John) Field Ambulance, part of the 38th (Welsh), taken whilst in training in north Wales in 1915.

Comparing the 1905 figures from the Royal Commission with those of the volunteers in E Company again clearly indicates that Nonconformists in Wales were proportionately less likely to join up than their counterparts in the Church of England. Only 38.49 per cent of those stating their religious denomination were Nonconformists, whereas we might have expected this figure to have been around 50–70 per cent, given the natural recruiting ground of the battalion. Similarly one might have expected around a quarter of E Company to have been members of the Church of England, but there was over double this number. Even allowing for the fact that the whole battalion was not recruited from Wales, these are still telling statistics.

While using evidence from 1905 is not a perfect comparator for the wartime statistics, it is the best available. Furthermore, for a recruit to have given his religious denomination for an army roll book, did not mean that he was necessarily a member or communicant member of that denomination. However, even with these qualifications, it would seem that the balance of evidence supports the assertion that Nonconformists were proportionately less likely to volunteer than their Church of England counterparts. One can argue that this was entirely likely, because the established church gave significantly greater support to the war, both in the pulpit and in recruiting meetings, than did Nonconformist ministers. Opposition to the war in the period 1914-15, such as it was, was almost entirely centred on the work of the Nonconformist ministers, writers and teachers.

To move now to the occupational background of those enlisting from Wales, it is immediately clear that recruiting, both before and after the introduction of conscription, differed widely in its impact on different industries. The roll book of E Company, 16th Battalion Royal Welsh Fusiliers states the occupations of 271 volunteers of the roll of 333 listed. While it is difficult to neatly categorize the occupations, the wide range is striking: there was a baritone vocalist, a soda water worker, a butcher and footballer, a cap packer, a gas maker, a billiard marker, a chauffeur, a jeweller and a foreign correspondent, plus the more prosaic policemen, teachers, colliers, labourers, clerks, hauliers and quarrymen.

The 1911 census showed that 12 per cent of the male working population in Wales was engaged in agriculture, and therefore the

Occupations of those in E Company, 16ᵗʰ Battalion RWF	
	% of total
Agricultural workers, farmers	6
Clerks, salesmen	11
Hauliers, carters	3
Labourers, un-skilled manual	16
Metal workers	4
Miners	22
Professional	3
Quarrymen	4
Shopworkers/keepers	9
Skilled manual	15
Other	7

evidence of E Company, with only 6 per cent of volunteers coming from this sector, shows an under-representation. Similarly, clerks made up 7 per cent of the working population in 1911, but were 11 per cent of the volunteers. Although mining and quarrying accounted for nearly 32 per cent of the workforce in Wales, as far as mining was concerned, this would have been heavily concentrated in south and west Wales, with quarrying concentrated in north Wales. The 16th Battalion was a predominantly north Wales battalion, thus to have had 22 per cent of volunteers from this industry shows over representation. On the other hand, quarrymen were under represented, making up only 4 per cent of volunteers.

Clive Hughes argues that the poor response of slate quarrymen in the north Wales counties was indicative of the attitudes of this group of workers, whose grievances were local rather than being symptomatic of an anti-war stance. Trade had slumped on the outbreak of war: in January 1915 it was calculated that of 8,400 quarrymen in July 1914, only 700 were in full-time employment, with 4,900 others working only a three-day or four-day week; even those still working had often accepted a pay cut. Economic necessity often stimulated men to volunteer, but this was not the case in north Wales. Apathy was blamed on Nonconformist teaching, family ties and hostility towards quarry owners such as Lord Penrhyn, who in August 1914 promised to keep open the places of all the quarrymen who enlisted. In other quarries men were threatened with dismissal if they did not enlist, which meant that increasing numbers left to fill posts vacated by volunteers from the railways, docks and coal mines.[26]

In Phillips's study, he found the biggest mismatch was with those in professional occupations, who made up 10.4 per cent of his sample, but only 2.8 per cent of the male working population in Wales in 1911. He felt that this could reflect the high number of educated, middle-class soldiers serving in the army. Furthermore, he found that the vast majority of those in this occupational category (80 per cent) were volunteers. In all other occupational categories, including agriculture and mines and quarries, Phillips found that his sample closely matched the male workforce in Wales in 1911 according to the census returns. Phillips also highlights the varied socio-economic backgrounds of those serving together in the army, a social mix of collier, teacher, clerk

Royal Welsh Fusiliers at Kinmel Park training camp, Bodelwyddan in 1916.

and railwayman unheard of before 1914. This evidence was supported by contemporary accounts. Captain J.C. Dunn, 2nd Battalion Royal Welsh Fusiliers, described a draft of north Welshmen as 'mostly clerks, small tradesmen and assistants, farmhands, schoolmasters and such like'. Phillips maintains that this accurately reflects the occupations of the men from north Wales in his sample. Anglesey provided four farm labourers, one slaughterman, three transport workers, a butcher and a solicitor. Caernarfonshire provided seven labourers, four quarrymen, a plumber, a clerk, a butcher and a chemist. Merioneth was represented by a farmer, a surveyor, a schoolteacher, a miner, a carter, a joiner and a student. Phillips concluded that 'the sample clearly demonstrates the presence of the emerging Welsh middle class in the ranks of the wartime army'.

In the study of Carmarthenshire, there is further evidence that recruitment was not evenly spread across all industries and occupations. In 1911, 21.2 per cent of the male working population of the county was involved in agriculture, yet only 8 per cent of the sample was so employed. Given the comments in the press in the autumn of 1914 about the reluctance of those from rural areas to enlist, this statistic is not surprising. However, it is harder to explain why the sample showed 14 per cent employed in mines and quarries, compared to 21.3 per cent so employed in the county. Those employed in professional and commercial occupations were proportionately more likely to enlist, which supports the findings of Phillips.

As far as the proportion of Welsh speakers and non-Welsh speakers is concerned, finding reliable evidence is more difficult because linguistic abilities were not asked for on any enlistment forms. We do know from the 1911 census that in some counties over 80 per cent of their population spoke Welsh, while in others it was below 40 per cent.

If these figures are compared with the numbers of men who enlisted from each county, compared to their population, it can be seen that the predominantly Welsh speaking counties (Caernarfonshire, Cardiganshire, Carmarthenshire, Merionethshire and Anglesey) were less likely to volunteer than those from predominantly English speaking counties (Breconshire, Glamorgan, Monmouthshire, Pembrokeshire and Radnorshire).

Total Welsh speakers by county, 1911	
	%
Anglesey	88.7
Brecon	41.5
Caernarfon	85.6
Cardigan	89.6
Carmarthen	84.9
Denbigh	56.7
Flint	42.2
Glamorgan	38.1
Merioneth	90.3
Monmouth	9.6
Montgomery	44.8
Pembroke	32.8
Radnor	5.4
WALES	43.5

Recruits in training in Pembrokeshire.　　　　*(Courtesy of the Roger J. C. Thomas Collection)*

The overall conclusion is that service in the armed forces was not equally shared amongst all Welshmen; county of residence, occupation, religion and language all played their part. The army of the First World War was a social and cultural melting pot. Possibly for first time, those from the middle and upper classes serving in the ranks were sharing an occupational and social experience with those of the working class, whether it was in a tent, army hut or trench. The mutual respect (and sometimes antipathy) which resulted was firmly rooted in this unique period.

NOTES

[1] John Davies, *A History of Wales* (London: Allen Lane, 1993), p. 499.
[2] Ll. Wyn Griffith, 'The Pattern of One Man's Remembering', in George A. Panichas (ed.), in *Promise of Greatness* (London: Cassell, 1968), p. 288.
[3] *Denbigh Herald*, 3 December 1915.
[4] Emlyn Davies, *Taffy Went to War* (Knutsford: Knutsford Secretarial Bureau, 1975), p. 3.
[5] Robert Graves, *Goodbye to All That* (Penguin Books: London, 1960), p. 96.
[6] Ibid., p. 235.
[7] *Western Mail*, 23 March 1915.
[8] *Western Mail*, 24 March 1915.
[9] Peter Simkins, *Kitchener's Army: the Raising of the New Armies, 1914–1916* (Manchester: Manchester University Press, 1988), pp. 98-9.
[10] Graves, *Goodbye to All That*, p. 213.
[11] *Western Mail*, 30 April 1915.
[12] Gerard Burgoyne, *The Burgoyne Diaries* (London: Thomas Harmsworth, 1985), p. 119.
[13] Sir Alexander Stanier, 'A Second Lieutenant at War', *Stand To! The Journal of the Western Front Association*, 31 (1991), 8-11.
[14] Lord Silsoe, *Sixty Years a Welsh Territorial* (Llandysul: Gomer Press, 1976), p. 19.
[15] Griffith, 'Pattern of One Man's Remembering', p. 287.
[16] Quoted in Graves, *Goodbye to All That*, p. 102.
[17] *The Welsh Outlook*, April 1918.
[18] See Gervase Phillips, 'Dai Bach y Soldiwr', *Llafur*, 6/2 (1993), 94-105.
[19] Graves, *Goodbye to All That*, p. 203.
[20] IWM, Papers of A.E. Perriman, 80/43/1.
[21] Harry Cartmell, *For Remembrance* (Preston: George Toumlin & Sons, 1919), pp. 33-5.
[22] Doron Lamm, 'British Soldiers of the First World War: Creation of a representative Sample', *Historical Social Research*, XIII, 4 (1988), 55-98.
[23] Phillips, 'Dai Bach y Soldiwr'.
[24] Robin Barlow, 'Apects of the First World War in Carmarthenshire' (unpublished Ph.D. thesis, University of Wales, Lampeter, 2001).
[25] NLW, MS 6080A.
[26] Clive Hughes, 'The New Armies', in Ian Becket and Keith Simpson (eds), *A Nation in Arms: A Social Study of the British Army in the First World War* (Manchester: Manchester University Press, 1985), pp. 99-126.

Chapter 7

'I am condemning a far better man than myself'

Opposition to the war

—⟋⟋⟍—

IN THE NINETEENTH CENTURY, Wales was the torch-bearer for pacifism. Welshmen such as the Neath Quaker industrialist, Joseph Tregelles Price, and his fellow Quaker, Evan Rees, were instrumental in the formation of the Peace Society in London in 1816. William Rees (Gwilym Hiraethog) and Samuel Roberts of Llanbrynmair ('S.R.'), editors of *Yr Amserau* and *Y Cronicl* respectively, were prominent in campaigning for international peace in the years following the revolutionary upheaval in Europe after 1848. Henry Richard of Tregaron, elected as MP for Merthyr in 1868, had been Secretary of the Peace Society from 1848 and was universally known as the 'apostle of peace'. However, this is not to deny the equally strong militarist sentiment which existed in Wales, dating back to Crécy and Agincourt. The attitudes in Wales to the South African war at the turn of the twentieth century had neatly illustrated a divide between the militarist and pacifist traditions of the nation.

Despite Wales's reputation as a predominantly peace-loving and pacifist nation, opposition to the First World War tended to be localised, limited and largely *ad hoc*, only gaining momentum and wider support from 1916 onwards. There was no significant or overt opposition either to the prospect of war, or its outbreak. What opposition existed was largely based on the actions of committed individuals either from the Nonconformist denominations or the socialist political organizations. Attempts to co-ordinate opposition to the war did not meet with great success. The Fellowship of Reconciliation, basing its opposition to the war on religious grounds, was founded in Cambridge at the end of December 1914. Its first secretary was the Welsh-speaking Revd Richard Roberts, originally from Blaenau Ffestiniog, the minister of Crouch Hill Presbyterian chapel in north London. The assistant secretary was George Maitland Lloyd Davies, born in Liverpool of Welsh parents and a former bank manager in Wrexham. The first branch of the Fellowship of Reconciliation in Wales was set up in Bangor in June 1915, followed by a second in Wrexham. Although public meetings were organised, the Fellowship never gained any widespread support in Wales and indeed there were only around 5,000 members throughout Britain. However, the north Wales branches of the Fellowship of

George Maitland Lloyd Davies, pacifist and campaigner, imprisoned in 1918.

Reconciliation did act as a focal point for those who were disenchanted with the church's attitude to the war, providing a platform from which the pacifist viewpoint could be argued and developed.

In 1913, the students of University College Aberystwyth had founded a Welsh-language journal, *Y Wawr*, which was to become an important mouthpiece for anti-war views. Although only thirteen issues were published between 1913 and its enforced closure by the University authorities in 1917, its influence was widespread owing to the quality and eminence of its contributors. The poets T. Gwynn Jones, T.H. Parry-Williams and G.J. Williams all wrote broadly anti-war articles, albeit in an indirect and allusive style. T. Gwynn Jones claimed that all wars were the result of a clash of imperialisms; Germany was doing what other imperial powers had done, namely expanding its influence by force. Jones did his best to combat the rabid anti-German hysteria with a clear analysis of German cultural traditions. Writing in 1915, he stated: 'I am surer than ever in my opinion that there should only be one Christian Church, and that it should condemn every war without favour. Today the god of

Europe is nothing more than a row of tribal deities'.[1] Jones was a member
of Tabernacle Calvinistic Methodist chapel in Aberystwyth; he regularly
attended, until one evening in September 1915, the minister, Revd R.J.
Rees, in his prayers made a 'barbarous appeal to the God of the tribe'
calling for a British victory.[2] Jones left the chapel and never returned. *Y
Wawr* also sought to challenge and dispel some of the widespread rumours
of German atrocities which had been supposedly perpetrated against
women and babies, and also to debunk the mythical margarine factory
which was dependent on the dead bodies of French and British soldiers.
K.O. Morgan concluded that the anti-war tone of *Y Wawr* was 'largely
cultural and unpolitical' and 'many of its contributions were distinctly
rarefied.'[3]

Thomas Rees, Principal of Bala Bangor Independent College was
to become one of the most tireless and influential critics of the war. In
September 1914, *Y Tyst* published a forthright letter from Rees which

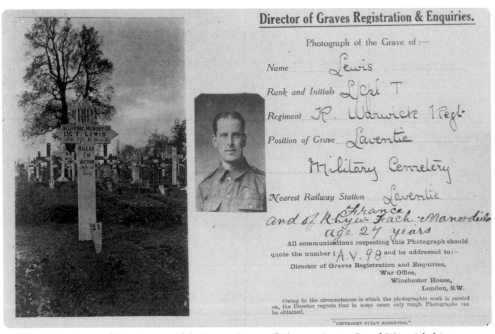

Grave Registration and Enquiries card for Lance Corporal Thomas Lewis, Royal Warwickshire
Regiment, killed in action 16 July 1916, aged 27. He was originally from Manordeilo, Carmarthenshire.
This temporary grave and headstone were replaced in the 1920s.

(NLW, D. C. Harries Collection)

Laventie Military Cemetery, La Gorgue, maintained by the Commonwealth War Graves Commission, burial place of Lance Corporal Thomas Lewis, Royal Warwickshire Regiment.

expressed his 'shame that the Christianity of Europe had not been a sufficient buttress against the tempest of destruction'. The fighting would not put an end to war, he argued, but would instead sow the seeds of more terrible wars in the future.[4] This was to unleash a torrent of opposition. The editor of *Y Tyst*, Revd H.M. Hughes of Ebenezer Chapel, Cardiff. completely dissociated himself from Rees's contribution. The editor of *Y Llan* maintained that Rees was guilty of treason, while the *Western Mail* accused him of a 'gross and unpardonable act of disloyalty', in suggesting that Britain may not have been totally guiltless in the outbreak of war. It continued, in a typically affronted tone, 'If his statements are not publicly repudiated by those who can speak in the name of Welsh Nonconformity serious harm may be done to the national and patriotic movement in Wales initiated by Mr Lloyd George and Mr Asquith'.[5] In a typically small-minded gesture, Rees was famously expelled from Bangor golf club for daring to challenge the pro-war consensus.

The greatest contribution Rees made to the promotion of an anti-war voice was in his editorship of *Y Deyrnas,* a publication which started life in October 1916 and was to continue to be published on a monthly basis until November 1919. Typically, Rees wrote over a third of each edition himself, but other contributors included Wil Ifan, David Thomas (Talysarn), Revd T.E. Nicholas (Niclas y Glais), J. Ellis Jones and D. Stanley Jones. In addition, original poems by T. Gwynn Jones and T.H. Parry-Williams were published. *Y Deyrnas* adopted a broad-based anti-war position which encompassed both the strict Christian pacifists who oppose all war, and the more politically-minded pacifists who opposed the particular war being fought. This approach drew in politicians, poets, ministers of religion, Independent Labour Party (ILP) members and those from the Union of Democratic Control, but the journal never acted as a real unifying, focal point for anti-war and pacifist views. This was largely due to the limited circulation which averaged only 2,500-3,000 copies and was highly localised. Although copies were sold (cost 2d) in newsagents, it was the efforts of strong-minded individuals in such places as Trawsfynydd (96 copies per month), Tumble (96), Blaenau Ffestiniog (79), Clunderwen (46), Llanwrst (49), Cwmtwrch (40), Llangoed (37) and Aberdare (36), which were vital in maintaining circulation.[6] The fact that it was published in the Welsh language would also have had an effect on its circulation, especially in the industrial heartlands of south Wales. The tightrope of economic existence was precarious for *Y Deyrnas,* because it was entirely dependent on its cover price and voluntary subscriptions to remain solvent, refusing to take any advertisements. While the circulation of *Y Deyrnas* was limited, its influence was perhaps greater. It was certainly important to W.J. Gruffydd. He read it while on naval service and believed it was 'one of the strongest reasons why Wales did not completely lose its soul at the time of the great madness'. K.O. Morgan argues that the most influential theme pursued in *Y Deyrnas* was the harmful impact the war was having on Welsh life, from the war profiteers, to the erosion of civil liberties, restrictions on free speech and press censorship.[7] The Revd E.K. Jones, a Baptist minister from Cefnmawr near Wrexham, was to contribute a regular column to *Y Deyrnas* recording the harsh treatment suffered by many conscientious objectors in prison or elsewhere, as a result of their refusal to accept conscription.

In 1916, the extent and depth of opposition to the war was to change; the catalysts were the passing of the Military Service Acts on the home front and the nature of warfare on the Western Front. The Military Service Acts brought into force the machinery which allowed exemption from military service on grounds of conscience. During the period 1916-18 some 16,500 conscientious objectors were granted exemption either on Christian pacifist grounds or political, usually socialist, ones. Historians have argued that a significant proportion of the conscientious objectors were from Wales, although there is no firm evidence for this.[8] Conscientious objectors have often occupied a place in history which is totally at variance with their numerical significance: they made up only 0.66% of those who were compulsorily enlisted. Most conscientious objectors agreed to undertake non-combatant service, but there were approximately 1,500 absolutists who refused to have anything to do with the war. Lloyd George promised that they would 'have a very hard path', which drove a further wedge between him and his Liberal colleagues. Ithel Davies, a farm labourer from Montgomeryshire, described in his autobiography the brutal treatment meted out to try and break the spirit of the absolutists; forty of them came close to being shot for disobedience and nine died, largely as a result of the conditions under which they were held. He was badly beaten by prison officers and placed in a straitjacket while held in custody in Mold.[9]

Rhys Edwards's father was imprisoned in Princetown prison on Dartmoor for his pacifist views; he recalled that on arrival 'all the conchies were stoned by the local children'. The living conditions were deliberately spartan:

> Each had a cell 8 feet by 7 feet on the top landing of the main building where the lunatics were kept ... During the fine weather prisoners were required to go to the quarries on the moor, and remove stone for building purposes. They were required to drag the drams which contained the stone with harnesses attached to their bodies. The criminals were allowed ponies to pull their drams, the conchies were treated as ponies. On wet days they spent their time picking oakum. Each weekend all the conchies were locked in their

cells at 5 pm on Friday and not released until Monday morning in time to go to work. The only thing they were allowed to have in the cells was a Bible. The food was pushed through a vent in the cell door. While on the moor, conchies were not allowed contact with their families, and it was impossible for any member of his family to go to the prison, they were unable to afford the train fare [from Wales]. Everything was done by the Authorities to break my father's spirit.[10]

The torch of pacifism was kept alight in Wales by a number of prominent individuals, whose plight was faithfully recorded in *Y Deyrnas*. George Maitland Lloyd Davies, who was to gain a reputation as a 'saintly' peacemaker, had once held a commission in the Territorial Army. In 1913, following a mental breakdown and a realisation that he could never kill another person, he resigned his commission. When conscription was

Battle of Estaires. A line of British troops blinded by tear gas, reaching an Advanced Dressing Station near Bethune, 10 April 1918. *(Imperial War Museum)*

introduced he refused military service on pacifist grounds. He was first sent to work as a shepherd in north Wales and then in January 1918, he was imprisoned in Wormwood Scrubs, spending much time in solitary confinement. He was then moved to Princetown prison on Dartmoor, followed by Knutsford work camp in Cheshire, before his release in June 1919. The Lieutenant-Colonel in Chester who sentenced Davies to prison acknowledged 'I am condemning a far better man than myself'.[11] Davies was elected to Parliament as an independent Christian Pacifist candidate for the University of Wales constituency in 1923, but lost his seat a year later. He literally refashioned a sword given to him as an officer with the Royal Welsh Fusiliers into a sickle, which he displayed in his office at the Fellowship of Reconciliation. In 1926 he was ordained as a minister in the Calvinistic Methodist church and published widely on the themes of peace and reconciliation. In 1937 he became President of the Welsh National Pacifist Society (Heddychwyr Cymru). He suffered from depression throughout his life and committed suicide in 1949.

Emrys Hughes, another noted pacifist, was also imprisoned for his refusal to serve in the armed forces. Originally from Abercynon, he completed his teacher training in Leeds before taking up a post in Trehafod School near Pontypridd in September 1915. Hughes felt that the Rhondda did not exhibit overt militarism and, 'a young man of military age was still left unmolested and escaped the inconvenience and insult which were now the rule in most parts of the country'. In March 1916, when Hughes was conscripted for service, he immediately appealed to his local military tribunal in Mountain Ash for total military exemption on grounds of conscientious objection. This was rejected as was his appeal to the Glamorgan county tribunal. As an absolutist, Hughes refused to perform any compulsory work, whether of a civil or military nature, but ironically the law still considered him to be a soldier. In April 1916 he was arrested as an absentee and brought before the Mountain Ash Magistrates' Court. He was fined 40s, given over to a military escort, taken to Cardiff barracks and imprisoned, awaiting court martial. He was sentenced to two years' hard labour, reduced to nine months detention. Hughes was initially imprisoned in Devizes military prison, followed by spells in the civilian prisons of Shepton Mallet, Wormwood Scrubs, Caernarfon and Redcar. He continued to refuse to obey all military orders and faced two further courts martial. He was finally released from prison in April 1919, becoming a full-time employee of the ILP and later, MP for South Ayrshire.[12]

Arthur Horner, the trade unionist and communist from Merthyr Tydfil known as the 'Welsh boy preacher', found his chapel deacons trying to censor his sermons for being too political and pacifist.[13] Horner opposed the war on political and religious grounds, adopting an increasingly revolutionary position through his membership of the Rhondda Socialist Society. In August 1917, Horner organised an anti-war meeting in Ynyshir Workmen's Hall and over 1,000 attended adopting a resolution calling for the immediate cessation of hostilities. Despite working as a collier, Horner was called for military service; he adopted an assumed identity and moved from Ynyshir ten miles up the Rhondda Fach to Maerdy. Although he was able to work, he resented not being able to take part in local politics. He consequently took the assumed name 'Jack O'Brien' and like many of those avoiding conscription, he fled to Ireland. He worked as a packer in a wholesale chemist's in Dublin, where also he joined the Irish Citizen's Army. In January 1918, his wife gave birth to a daughter in Ynyshir and homesickness eventually drove Horner back to Wales. On his return in August 1918 he was arrested in Holyhead, taken to the Royal Welsh Fusiliers barracks in Wrexham and court-martialled for evading conscription. He declared to the court-martial, 'I have no intention either now or in the future, of becoming a soldier in any army whose sole object is to carry out the behests of a privileged and exploiting class.'[14] He was sentenced to six months hard labour, serving his sentence in Wormwood Scrubs. On the signing of the Armistice, nearly all those who had evaded conscription were released from prison. However, Horner was sentenced to two further years' imprisonment for continuing to refuse to carry out military service. At the end of April 1919, he went on hunger strike and also refused to take water, demanding his immediate release. On the sixth day of his protest, Horner's wife and parents were sent for and funeral arrangements were made. At the last minute, and without explanation, Horner was released from his cell in Carmarthen Gaol. Six weeks later he received an official discharge from the armed forces for 'incorrigible misconduct'. If nothing else, this provided him with the title of his autobiography, *Incorrigible Rebel*.[15]

For other individuals, their personal beliefs and convictions led them to oppose the war in different but singular ways. T.W. ('Tom') Jones, later to become a Labour MP and life peer, was a pupil-teacher in 1914. As a conscientious objector he joined the Non-Combatant Corps in 1917 but as a result of his refusal to obey an order, he was court-martialled and imprisoned until May 1919, including six months' hard labour. Morgan Jones was to become the first conscientious objector to be returned to the House of Commons (for the Caerphilly constituency) after the end of the war. In 1914 Jones was employed as a teacher. He joined the No-Conscription Fellowship and became chairman of the South Wales Anti-Conscription Council before being conscripted himself in 1916. He refused to serve and was imprisoned for most of the subsequent three years. Long spells of hard labour and solitary confinement combined with an inadequate diet, left Jones in poor health for the rest of his life. He was dismissed from his teaching post as a result of his war-time imprisonment.

Edward Stanton Roberts, headmaster of Pentrellyncymer school in 1916, also found his career in education hampered by his exemption from military service as a conscientious objector. The poet and scholar T.H. Parry-Williams managed to continue with his professional life, although he was originally denied a chair at University College Aberystwyth in 1919, because of his stance as a conscientious objector. Nonconformist ministers such as Henry Morgan Stafford Thomas from Porthmadog and John Thomas Jones from Llanegwad, were also imprisoned for being conscientious objectors.

Philip Snowden, the prominent English pacifist visited Wales in 1917 to undertake various speaking engagements. He described addressing a 'wonderfully enthusiastic meeting' in Merthyr Tydfil when he vigorously denounced the prosecutions which were taking place under the Defence of the Realm Act. A miner had recently been prosecuted for declaring that the Military Service Act contained the possibility of industrial conscription. In a deliberately provocative act, Snowden repeated the words of the miner, concluding with the challenge 'Let them prosecute me!' At the end of the meeting, Snowden recounted that the Chief Constable was anxious to see him: 'he entered the room, shook hands with me very cordially, said he was glad to meet me, and congratulated us on a very successful meeting'. Snowden heard no more of his defiance of the Defence of the Realm Act.[16] Richard Wallhead, who later became the Labour MP for Merthyr in 1922, was not so fortunate with the Glamorgan County police. He was prosecuted under the Defence of the Realm Act in 1918 for a speech he had made in Briton Ferry and was sentenced to four months' imprisonment. His crime was to claim that the government intended to keep young conscripts after the war to form the nucleus of the future army. Due to ill-health, Wallhead was released after one month.

As the war progressed, many people in Wales began to question their pro-war sentiments, or at least their tacit support for the war. As the casualty lists on the Western Front inexorably lengthened and with no end to the war in sight, more organised opposition began to emerge, rather than individual protests. On 11 November 1916 the National Council for Civil Liberties organised a peace conference at the Cory Hall in Cardiff. Prominent speakers were due to put forward various motions: J.H. Thomas MP was to propose that 'military compulsion has already involved industrial compulsion and endangered industrial conditions'; Revd Dr Walter Walsh supporting that 'the administration and effects of Conscription … have proved a national disaster, and calls on the Government to review and correct the administration of the Act in regards to conscientious objection'; J. Ramsay MacDonald MP was to argue that there had been 'progressive invasions of liberty of person, speech and opinion' and he demanded 'the immediate restoration of the traditional rights of British Citizens'; finally, and most controversially, Revd J. Morgan Jones was to propose that 'this Conference is of the opinion that the time has arrived when the objects for which this nation entered upon this war may be secured by negotiation … to bring this war to a satisfactory and honourable end'.[17]

Once the agenda of the peace conference had been publicised in November 1916, the British Empire Union and the British Workers' National League organised a 'great patriotic citizens' demonstration' to protest against 'false peace agitators'. A meeting was arranged for the evening of 10 November, in Wood Street Congregational church in Cardiff, under the chairmanship of Major-General Sir Ivor Herbert MP, with speakers such as the Earl of Plymouth, the Earl of Dunraven,

British casualties of the gas attack on Hill 60 (near Ypres), receiving treatment at No 8 Casualty Clearing Station, Bailleul, May 1915.

(Imperial War Museum)

D. A. Thomas, Lord Merthyr, Ellis J. Griffith MP, J. Herbert Cory MP, Lewis Haslam MP, John Hinds MP and Charles B. Stanton. Cardiffians were urged to 'come in your thousands and prove that you are True Britishers'. More confrontationally, 'a monster open-air demonstration' was to be organised for the afternoon of 11 November in Cathays Park, starting at 2.00 p.m., just thirty minutes prior to the start of the nearby peace conference. Attempts had been made to prohibit the peace conference, most notably by Captain Edward Tupper, national organizer of the Seamen's Union. On the morning of 11 November, he had sent a telegram to the Home Secretary stating:

> As you have not seen fit to prohibit the pacifist meeting to be held
> at 2.30 the seamen and dockers of this port are taking matters into
> their own hands and you must accept full responsibility for what will
> undoubtedly occur if the meeting is held.[18]

It was reported that 'patriots' stormed the Cory Hall, forcing the speakers off the stage. A free fight took place and James Winstone was pelted with tomatoes when he escaped down a side street. Prominent amongst those disrupting the meeting was Charles B. Stanton. A new motion was then tabled, calling for the war to be prosecuted 'to the bitter end.'[19] The Conference was subsequently held in Merthyr Tydfil on 8 December, attracting a crowd of 3,000. It passed off without incident and was dubbed by the *Merthyr Pioneer* as 'the most remarkable meeting of the war'.[20]

Throughout 1917, various organizations began to attract increasingly large audiences to meetings and rallies. Sylvia Pankhurst, of the Women's Socialist Federation was a frequent visitor to south Wales. On 8 July 1917, she addressed an audience of 2,000 people in Ammanford which passed a resolution demanding 'an immediate peace on the basis of no annexations, no indemnities'. On the same visit to Wales she spoke at large gatherings in Gwauncaegurwen and Blaenau. On 28 and 30 September, Pankhurst spoke at meetings in Wattstown, Ynyshir and Porth under the banner of 'Peace and Socialism'.

One of the most prominent and well-known pacifists in Britain, Bertrand Russell, undertook a speaking tour on behalf of the No-Conscription Fellowship between 2-16 July 1916. Large audiences turned out to hear him and Russell reported that 'intense enthusiasm' greeted his attacks on conscription and on the war more generally. In his autobiography, Russell commented that, 'I never had an interrupted meeting, and always found the majority of the audience sympathetic'.[21] He reflected later that he should have visited more hostile districts of Britain, but he described speaking in the industrial areas of south Wales as 'merely a picnic'.[22]

The most brutal and bloody encounter between pacifists and patriots occurred at the Conference of the British Council of Soldiers' and Workers' Delegates, held in Swansea on 29 July 1917. While the 200 or so delegates who attended the Conference were there primarily to set up 'soviets' and to co-ordinate working class activity, there was also an implied anti-war sub-agenda. A crowd of 500 demonstrators gathered outside the Swansea Elysium, largely consisting of munitions workers and members of the Naval and Military Pensions and Welfare League (also known as 'bit-badge' men, because of the small silver badges they wore). Armed with sticks, flag-poles, spikes and other assorted weapons, the bit-badge men stormed the Elysium, attacked the delegates and prevented the Conference ever starting. Arthur Horner lost his front teeth to a punch, Ted Ascott of the Merthyr Tydfil ILP was cut about the head and lost a pint of blood, whilst Ted Davies of Aberdare suffered nine puncture wounds in his neck.[23]

Welsh Guards in a reserve trench at Guillemont. Battle of Guillemont 3-6 September 1916.

(Imperial War Museum)

The *Cambria Daily Leader* reported the following day under the headline, 'A oes heddwch? Swansea's answer to Peace Cranks'. The delegates were 'bleeding profusely and half-stunned' and when fire extinguishers were turned on them, 'with their faces covered with blood, and the water streaming down their clothes, they appeared deplorable specimens'.[24] The bit-badge men then began their own meeting, preceded by the singing of the 'National Anthem', 'Rule Britannia' and 'Tipperary'. A resolution was passed supporting the government in any necessary action in the future to prevent 'pacifist conferences'. Throughout the day, the Swansea police were never seen. Whilst the fact that the Conference was taking place at all showed that anti-war feelings were becoming more evident, especially amongst the rank-and-file members of the South Wales Miners' Federation, events also showed the extent of pro-war support that could be mobilised backed by a sympathetic press.

There is little agreement amongst historians about the strength and efficacy of the opposition to the war in Wales, except perhaps to say that there was never a coherent and unified anti-war movement. There were many brave, committed individuals who had deeply held convictions about why the war was wrong and they were quite prepared to go to prison as a consequence of their views. However, the arguments put forward by a Nonconformist minister for not fighting in the war on grounds of conscience would have had little in common with those of a member of the Independent Labour Party or the South Wales Miners' Federation. The frequent outcome of a prison sentence was their only common ground.

NOTES

[1] Quoted in D. Densil Morgan, *Span of the Cross: Christian Religion and Society in Wales, 1914-2000* (Cardiff: University of Wales Press, 1999), p. 43. See also, David Jenkins, *Thomas Gwynn Jones* (Dinbych: Gwasg Gee, 1994).

[2] John Davies, *A History of Wales* (London: Penguin Books, 2007) p. 499.

[3] Kenneth O. Morgan, 'Peace Movements in Wales, 1899-1945' in *Modern Wales: Politics, Places and People* (Cardiff: University of Wales Press, 1995), p. 95.

[4] *Y Tyst*, 30 September 1914.

[5] *Western Mail*, 7 October 1914.

[6] Aled Eirug, 'Agweddau ar y gwrthwynebiad i'r Rhyfel Byd Cyntaf yng Nghymru', *Llafur* 4 (1986), pp. 59-68.

[7] Morgan, 'Peace Movements in Wales', p. 97.

[8] Davies, *A History of Wales*, p. 500.

[9] Geraint H. Jenkins, *A Concise History of Wales* (Cambridge: Cambridge University Press, 2007), p. 251.

[10] Keith Strange, *Wales and the First World War* (Cardiff: Mid Glamorgan County Council, 1989), p. 66.

[11] Kenneth O. Morgan, *Rebirth of a Nation: Wales 1880-1980* (Oxford: Oxford University Press, 1982), p.164.

[12] See Anthony Mòr O-Brien, '"Conchie": Emrys Hughes and the First World War', *The Welsh History Review*, 13, (1986-7), 328-352.

[13] See Nina Fishman, *Arthur Horner: A Political Biography, Vol 1 1894-1944* (London: Lawrence and Wishart, 2010), pp. 56-66.

[14] Ibid, p. 62.

[15] Arthur Horner, *Incorrigible Rebel* (London: MacGibbon & Kee, 1960).

[16] Philip Snowden, *An Autobiography, Vol I 1864-1919* (London: Ivor Nicholson and Watson, 1934), pp. 425-6.

[17] TNA, HO 45/10810/311932; see also Brock Millman, 'The Battle of Cory Hall, November 1916: Patriots meet Dissenters in Wartime Cardiff', *Canadian Journal of History*, April 2000.

[18] Anthony Mòr O-Brien, 'Keir Hardie, C.B. Stanton, and the First World War', *Llafur*, 4/3 (1986), 31-42.

[19] TNA, HO 45/10810/311932.

[20] I am grateful to Aled Eirug for this information.

[21] Bertrand Russell, *The Autobiography of Bertrand Russell, 1914-1944, Vol II* (London: George Allen & Unwin, 1968), pp. 24-5.

[22] Ibid, p. 67.

[23] David Egan, 'The Swansea Conference of the British Council of Soldiers' and Workers' Delegates, July 1917: Reactions to the Russian Revolution of February, 1917, and the Anti-war Movement in South Wales', *Llafur*, 1/4 (1975), 12-37.

[24] *Cambria Daily Leader*, 30 July 1917.

Chapter 8

'The Unknown Army'

Conscription and the military service tribunals

—⁓ɯ⁓—

FOLLOWING THE FORMATION of the Coalition Government in May 1915, the issue of conscription became ever more prominent at a national level. The Cabinet was split on the issue, but not on strictly party political lines. Broadly, the Conservatives (with eight seats in the Cabinet) and Winston Churchill, supported conscription, and they were joined on 3 June 1915 by Lloyd George. He had strongly supported conscription from the time it became clear that the number of volunteers coming forward was going to seriously hamper the war effort. This caused an increasing rift with his Liberal colleagues both in the War Cabinet and more widely in the House of Commons. The question of conscription was an emotive and contentious one for many Liberals, who saw the principle of military compulsion as being an assault on individual liberty and thus undermining one of the core beliefs of liberalism. John Davies argues that Lloyd George's eagerness to abandon the principle of voluntarism shows 'that he had little loyalty to Liberal ideology'.[1] His defection left ten Liberals in the Cabinet fighting a rear-guard action against conscription.

The declining recruitment figures for 1915 meant that something had to be done to provide the necessary manpower to fight and win the war. Before any form of compulsion could be introduced, every effort had to be made to show that voluntary recruitment was not going to solve the problem. The first step in this process was the introduction of the National Registration Act which was passed in July 1915. For Asquith, this was the lesser of two evils: conscription had been delayed for the time being at least. The National Register of all males aged 15-65 was taken on 15 August 1915, with the work largely carried out by volunteers such as school teachers and county council employees. The aim of the survey was to ensure that the central industries were not going to be depleted of their workforce, while still ensuring that the armed forces were supplied with their requirements. Details of eligible men were passed to the recruiting authorities, who then undertook to canvass them. It was calculated that 1,489,043 single men were available for immediate military service.

It had been estimated that the infantry alone required 30,000 recruits per week, however the monthly figures for the whole regular army and territorial force were falling well below this figure. While there had been calls for compulsory military service from the very start of the war (and before it), it became increasingly likely that this was the only solution.

German prisoners of war with quarryworkers at the Llandybie Limeworks, Carmarthenshire c1917.   (NLW)

On 5 October 1915 Lord Derby, after his successes in raising units in Lancashire, was appointed Director-General of Recruiting. Although he had become a supporter of conscription by this time, he felt it necessary to explore all possible avenues of voluntary enlistment first. The so-called 'Derby Plan' resulted, which called for a canvass of all those men on the National Register, asking for them either to join up at once or to attest a willingness to serve when summoned. They were to be placed in forty-six groups and called up as and when needed. Prime Minister Asquith gave a pledge that married men would not be called up until after all the unmarried men had been drawn in, which caused immense confusion and uncertainty. The Derby Plan had originally envisaged closing the lists at the end of November 1915, but in view of the poor response the closing date was delayed by a further two weeks to 15 December. When the national figures were published they proved a keen disappointment to those who still hoped to cling to a purely voluntary system. Only 1.2 million men had enlisted or promised to enlist, out of an original canvass of over three million men, with no significant differences for married and unmarried men. Over 620,000 men were deemed physically unfit for service.

The failure of the Derby Plan, coinciding as it did with heavy casualties at the Battle of Loos and the need to obtain reinforcements in time for the spring campaign on the Western Front gave further weight to the case for conscription. The Military Service Bill, which would compel single men aged 18-41 to enlist in the armed forces, was introduced in the House of Commons on 6 January 1916. Welsh Liberal politicians were faced with an agonising crisis of conscience. At the first reading of the Bill 30 Liberal MPs voted against it, including three from Welsh constituencies: E.T. John (East Denbigh), G. Caradoc Rees (Caernarfonshire Arfon) and W. Llewelyn Williams (Carmarthen Boroughs). Williams, a reluctant supporter of entry into the war, viewed conscription as a betrayal of the liberal belief in the right of the individual to freedom of conscience. He feared that conscription would, 'Prussianize proud and freedom loving Britain'. For standing by his principles he was dubbed 'The Slackers' Friend' by the local newspaper *The Llanelly Guardian*. From 1916 until his death in 1922, Williams was to be an arch enemy of Lloyd George.[2]

At the second reading on 12 January 1916, only 3 Welsh MPs voted against of the Bill: E.T. John, Thomas Richards (Monmouthshire West) and William Abraham (Glamorgan Rhondda). Five Welsh MPs who had abstained on the First Reading now voted with the government: John Hinds (Carmarthenshire West), Henry Haydon Jones (Merioneth), Ellis W. Davies (Caernarfonshire South), Revd J. Towyn Jones (Carmarthenshire East) and J. Hugh Edwards (Mid Glamorgan). The Bill was passed by the huge majority of 431 to 39. C.B. Stanton, writing in the *Aberdare Leader*, thought 'the compulsion of able-bodied young men was a worthy policy in contrast to the majority of our people becoming the serfs of the Germans'.[3] Surprisingly, the Welsh-language socialist newspaper, *Llais Llafur*, supported conscription:

> We have to defeat Germany, and that we shall do if many other liberties, far more vital to British institutions than the voluntary system, have to go into the melting pot ... neither the Labour party nor trade unions will oppose the compulsion of single laggards ... the great bulk of the working classes realise that compulsion is only one of the disagreeable things we have to suffer as the price of beating Germany.[4]

The main opposition to conscription outside Parliament came from the South Wales Miners' Federation (SWMF) and particularly from Vernon Hartshorn. Both man and union argued that voluntaryism had been successful but were more concerned that military compulsion would lead to industrial compulsion, which would not end with the war. On 13 January 1916 the SWMF Executive passed a resolution supporting the idea of a national strike in opposition to the Military Service Bill. However, the Miners' Federation of Great Britain had decided to support the Bill and no action was taken.

Welsh Nonconformists in general could not see the logic in fighting a war against militarism in the name of freedom and then allowing the state to introduce compulsion in the form of conscription. E. Morgan Humphreys wrote, 'Nonconformity was built on the rights of conscience and once authority is granted to a State or an army or an official to trample those rights underfoot, the foundations of Nonconformity will crumble'.[5] The Baptist Ungoed Thomas thought that 'the acknowledgement of the state's right to force its young citizens, against their own reason, conscience and inclination, to maim and kill their fellow men, indicates the extent to which the Kingdom's morals have deteriorated'. The government trampled on such Nonconformist convictions. Robert Pope argues that 'this was the time when the "Nonconformist Conscience" fizzled out as a force in British politics.'[6]

In May 1916 compulsion was extended to include married men. It is frequently overlooked that 2,504,183 men were enlisted into the British army after January 1916, representing 50.3 per cent of all wartime enlistments and 43.8 per cent of the wartime army as a whole. This calls into question the portrait of a unified nation, eager to enlist. Half those who fought in the First World War only did so because they had to. Perhaps accurately, conscripts have been described as the 'unknown army'.[7]

The Military Service Acts necessitated a system for dealing with those men who wished to obtain exemption from service, whatever the reasons. The Derby Plan had introduced a system of tribunals and whether for reasons of expediency, efficiency or convenience, this machinery was adopted for the purposes of the Military Service Acts. Local tribunals were to be appointed by the local registration authorities, and in practice these were the same tribunals as under the Derby scheme, with an increased membership from an average of five members to perhaps ten or more. In general, across England and Wales, the tribunals corresponded to the urban and rural districts of the county. In all 1,805 tribunals were set up, and in most cases councillors formed the majority group on the tribunals. It was also intended that local citizens with legal experience and representatives of organised labour would be included. The town clerk or council clerk usually became the tribunal clerk. In addition, a military representative was appointed to each tribunal, who was often a retired or serving military officer but this was not always the case. His purpose was simply to obtain as many men as possible for the armed forces and his official position gave him the right to question applicants and to appeal against any decisions of the tribunal. Sixty-eight appeal tribunals were also set up, largely corresponding to the administrative counties. Finally, there was a central tribunal, to hear appeals referred to it by the individual appeal tribunals.[8]

In February 1916, the Local Government Board (LGB) had issued instructions for the guidance of tribunals when dealing with applications for exemption. There were four main grounds for such a ruling: firstly,

Men of the 15th Battalion Royal Welsh Fusiliers (London Welsh) filling sandbags with the earth excavated from of a dug-out in their trenches at Fleurbaix, 28 December 1917.

(Imperial War Museum)

that it was in the national interests to retain the man concerned in civilian employment; secondly, serious hardship would ensue if the man were called up; thirdly, ill-health or infirmity; and fourthly, on grounds of conscientious objection. When Asquith had introduced the Military Service Bill in Parliament and presented the fourth ground for exemption, he was interrupted by 'a considerable volume of groans, catcalls and laughter'.[9]

Despite the lack of documentary evidence, tribunals continue to be perceived as bodies which co-operated with the military authorities in order to maintain a supply of men for the army and which were largely unsympathetic to the local population. As Grieves has noted, the 'historical record has remained highly coloured by assessments which were produced by arch-opponents of the tribunal system'.[10] For example,

Beatrice Webb criticised the tribunals at an early stage in their history: 'The most biased judge on the bench could not have equalled, in malicious bias, the old gentlemen who are now sitting on the claims for exemption'.[11] John Graham, a Quaker chaplain and Chairman of the Friends' Peace Committee during the war, wrote that tribunals were 'groping about with a lack of evidence' and consequently 'fell back on their prejudices'. When the result was in doubt, 'the verdict of the Tribunals generally went against the applicant ... Whilst success was impossible, they need not have failed as badly as they did. In few cases did they obtain the confidence of those whose destiny they decided.'[12]

K.O. Morgan has written dismissively that 'tribunals were loaded in favour of privilege and position, with not a labourer or working man in sight on the bench'.[13] The reality was often quite different, as the experience of the tribunals in one Welsh town suggests. In the case of the Kidwelly Municipal Borough tribunal, two members were both named as 'labour representatives': Edmund Cole, a colliery carpenter and David Rowlands, a tinplate worker. The chairman was Thomas Reynolds, mayor and an alderman of the borough, who was an overseer at the munitions factory at Pembrey. The other members were David Anthony, a farmer and an alderman of the borough; Thomas Griffiths, a doctor and also the medical officer of health for the borough; John Morgan, another farmer and a councillor; and David Thomas, a schoolmaster and councillor. As one would expect, all seven members of the tribunal were resident in the town of Kidwelly and their ages varied from forty-four to sixty-two. The picture sometimes drawn of applicants pleading their case before a battery of elderly colonels had little basis in fact. As Rae has commented, 'the gulf between the applicants and the tribunal members was essentially one of age'.[14] The average age of the Kidwelly tribunal was fifty, which was slightly younger than the average age of two other tribunals of which studies have been made: the average age of the Leeds tribunal was fifty-five, and the York tribunal was fifty-two.[15]

The workload of the tribunals was heavy and there is little doubt that they worked extremely hard. The Cardiganshire appeal tribunal met weekly or sometimes twice weekly from 15 March 1916 until 24 Sept 1918. It criss-crossed the county sitting in Aberystwyth, Lampeter, Newcastle Emlyn, Cardigan and Aberaeron. The papers of the tribunal are littered with claims for overnight accommodation and travelling expenses for the members, and for most it would have been at least a two-day commitment every week.[16] It must be remembered that members of the appeal tribunal would also have been members of their local tribunal (and probably chairman), their local district council and also Cardiganshire county council.

The situation was the same in another rural county. By 23 February 1916 it was reported that Carmarthen Rural District tribunal already had over 500 cases to deal with. One applicant from St Clears said, 'everyone in his parish was appealing and he thought he would follow suit'.[17] Llandovery Rural District tribunal dealt with 88 cases at its meeting on 2 March 1916[18], and Llanelli Borough tribunal dealt with over 150 cases on the same date.[19] By 28 September 1916, the workload had increased to such an extent that the Llanelli tribunal had to be split in to two to hear over 200 appeals simultaneously; each tribunal sat with only four members and a clerk.[20] On 5 October 1916, the same tribunal was again split to hear over 300 cases.[21] One member wrote, 'I have been sentenced to twelve months' hard labour at the tribunal'.[22]

The atmosphere at individual tribunal hearings was very revealing, giving a good indication of the prevailing local attitudes both towards the tribunals and also the war generally. For example, on 9 March 1916, the Llanelli tribunal heard the case of J.O. Thomas, who was appealing for exemption on the grounds of conscientious objection. Thomas was employed as a baker's vanman and he was asked by alderman Nathan Griffiths, a member of the tribunal, whether it was 'consistent to deliver bread to soldiers'. He replied, 'I am not killing the soldiers by giving them bread'. This brought 'laughter and loud applause' from those present, prompting the chairman to say, 'If there is any demonstration again, the court will be cleared, and it will not be open to the public. We are not going to allow any section to applaud in that way'. After further questioning, alderman Griffiths said, 'It's no use arguing with this man', which brought 'laughter' from the public, one of whom called out, 'because he is a better man than you', prompting 'more laughter'.[23] One might have expected the applicants to have been seen as shirkers who should have been sent off to the war, but the opposite was the case; sympathy often lay with the appellant, not the tribunal.

Daniel Harton Davies (bottom left, seated) in a prisoner of war camp in Germany.

(Courtesy of Ceredigion Archives)

This is also confirmed by the actual decisions of the tribunals where applicants were treated with a fair degree of leniency and exemptions were

Recruiting headquarters, Queen Street, Cardiff.

the rule rather than the exception. Of the first 70 cases dealt with by the Kidwelly Borough tribunal only 3 applicants were refused exemption: a carpenter's labourer and 2 herdsmen. Those who were successful included a shopkeeper, a bricklayer's labourer, a flannel merchant, a postman, a blacksmith and an hotel proprietor. On 8 December 1916, the Kidwelly tribunal dealt with 37 cases and all were granted conditional or temporary exemptions. It was deemed 'expedient and in the national interests' that instead of being employed in military service, men should remain employed as a chauffeur/groom, painter/decorator, boot dealer and draper, saddler, jobbing builder and plasterer, fisherman and bill-poster/glazier/rural postman.[24] Llandovery Rural tribunal met on 15 March 1916 and dealt with 35 cases, granting exemptions in 32 of them. The vast majority were agriculturalists and of those refused one was a timber haulier, one a farmer's son with three brothers working on the 450 acre farm and one was an unemployed collier.[25] On 14 April 1916 there were 5 cases and 4 exemptions, and on 26 May 1916 26 cases and 24 exemptions.[26] On 27 June 1916, 82 cases were heard, and in only one case was an exemption not granted.[27] On 26 September 1916 a further 17 farmers, farmers' sons and farm servants were all granted exemptions and in other cases, a bootmaker from Llanddeusant (an isolated village of approximately thirty inhabitants), and a gardener from Gwynfe, were granted exemptions, with the chairman commenting, 'gardeners are scarce in that district'.[28] On 13 October 1916, all 17 applicants were granted exemptions including men in varied occupations such as postman, mason, timber haulier, wheelwright, motor driver and gardener.[29] The one divergence from this pattern of exemptions occurred on 27 October 1916, when 68 cases were heard, and 9 were dismissed, including 3 farmers, a wheelwright from Llansadwrn, a tailor from Caio, a timber-feller from Llangadog, and a grocer from the same village.[30] On 7 November 1916, there were 27 cases heard from agriculturalists, and all were granted conditional or temporary exemptions.[31]

Prisoner of war camp in Germany where Daniel Harton Davies of Cardigan was held.

(Courtesy of Ceredigion Archives)

At a national level, between 1 March 1916 and 31 March 1917, 371,500 men were compulsorily enlisted. However, up to 30 April 1917, 779,936 men had been exempted from service by the tribunals, meaning that approximately one man was compulsorily enlisted for every two men granted an exemption by a tribunal.[32] The statistics for Carmarthenshire show a much greater propensity to exempt applicants where approximately one man was enlisted for every nine men exempted. The situation in west Wales was deemed to be so bad that the matter was actually raised in parliament by Stuart Wortley MP on 16 March 1916:

> I have been in Carmarthenshire, Pembrokeshire, and Cardiganshire for ten days, and I am thoroughly disgusted with what I have seen and heard of the recruiting. They are exempting everybody. I cannot mention names, but one public character who attests people and pays them 2s 9d tells everyone to 'get an appeal paper at once and see So-and-so, and he will help you to fill it in'. You would think it was an election day to see them running about looking for influence to get out of serving their country … the whole of the Nonconformist

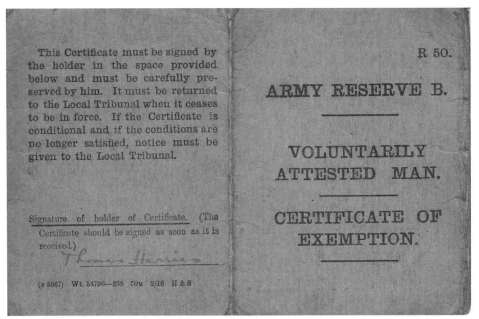

Certificate of exemption from military service issued by the St Dogmaels Rural District Military Service Tribunal. Thomas Harries was granted conditional exemption providing that he remained in his occupation as the proprietor and manager of a jeweller's business.

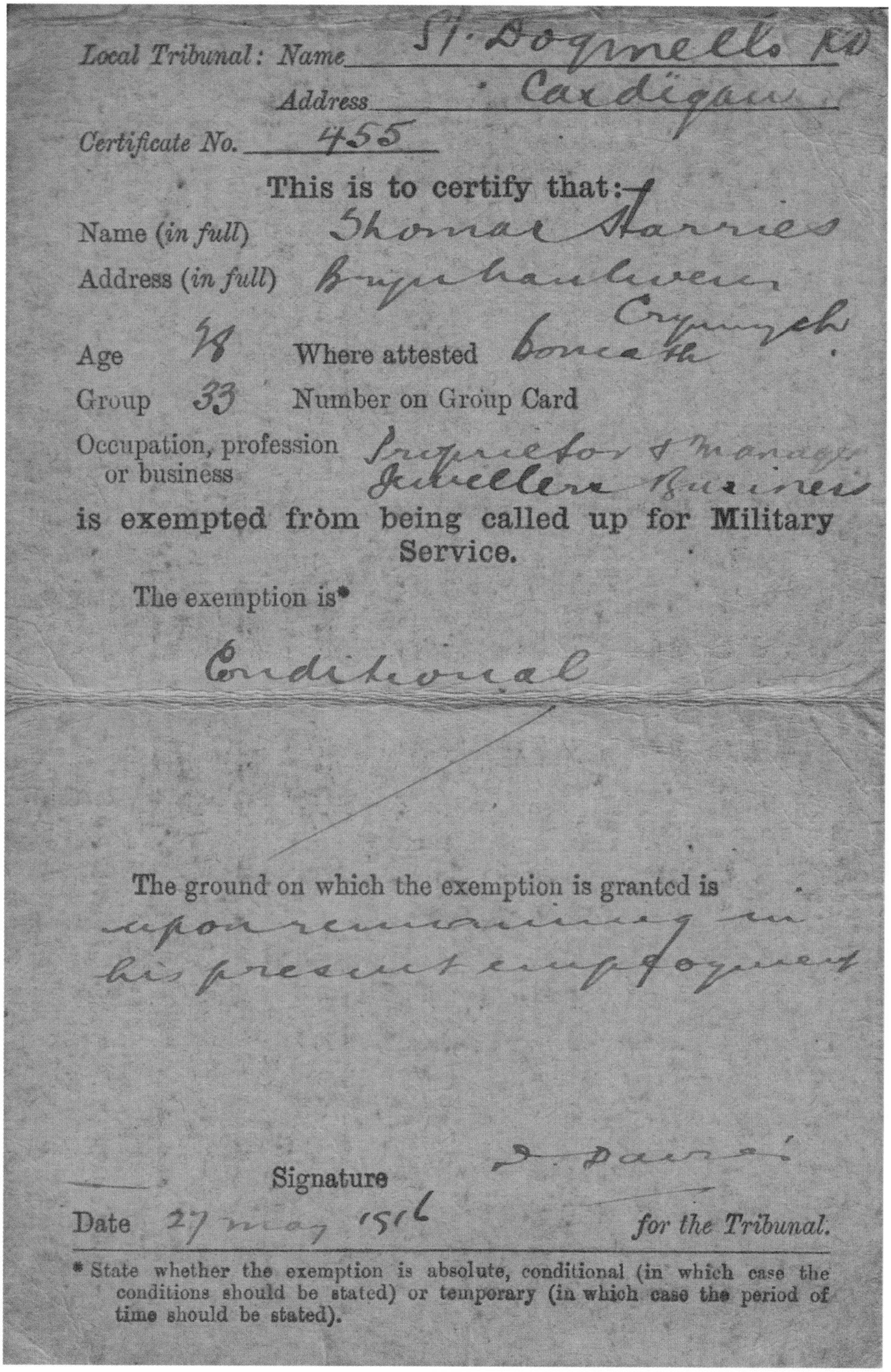

Local Tribunal: Name _St. Dogmell Rd_

Address _Cardigan_

Certificate No. _455_

This is to certify that:—

Name (*in full*) _Thomas Harries_

Address (*in full*) _Bryn hawlwen_

Cryngych

Age _38_   Where attested _Boncath_

Group _33_   Number on Group Card

Occupation, profession or business _Proprietor & Manager Jewellers Business_

is exempted from being called up for Military Service.

The exemption is*

Conditional

The ground on which the exemption is granted is

upon remaining in his present employment

Signature _J. Davies_

Date _27 may 1916_   for the Tribunal.

* State whether the exemption is absolute, conditional (in which case the conditions should be stated) or temporary (in which case the period of time should be stated).

ministers are working against the Act, and, if attested, using influence to get exemption.[33]

If we turn now to those who applied for exemption on grounds of conscience, a different picture emerges. Although conscientious objectors numbered only 16,500 (well under one per cent of all those who were conscripted) the attention given to their cases far outweighs their numerical strength.[34] John Davies estimated that there were at least a thousand conscientious objectors in Wales, a proportionately greater number than the rest of the United Kingdom, although he does not cite any evidence for this.[35] The Military Service Act had stated that any certificate of exemption on conscientious grounds could take the form of 'an exemption from combatant service only, or may be conditional on the applicant being engaged in some work which in the opinion of the tribunal

A Welsh unit of the Bicycle Corps. *(Imperial War Museum)*

dealing with the case is of national importance'. Although the ambiguity of the wording of the Act led to some tribunals being reluctant to grant absolute exemptions to conscientious objectors, John Rae estimated that tribunals granted some form of exemption to 80 per cent of all such applicants.[36] From the evidence of the local press in Carmarthenshire, the percentage of exemptions in the county seems to be far less. For example, between 3 March 1916 and 3 August 1916, of 21 reported cases where applicants applied for exemptions as conscientious objectors only four were granted, and 17 were rejected. This also accords with the situation in neighbouring Cardiganshire; K.O. Morgan concluded that 'prosperous farmers and solicitors, and former high sheriffs in Cardiganshire, acted rigorously to suppress or imprison those who adopted an anti-war stand on grounds of conscience'.[37]

In conclusion, the decisions of the rural tribunals in Wales indicate a reluctance to send men to the war. The tribunals were not dominated by the military representatives, nor did they act as agents of the armed forces. Applicants were treated sympathetically by most tribunal members and exemptions from military service were granted with a readiness which reflected the prevailing attitudes of the locality. Those who appeared before the tribunals were often accorded public support rather than being labelled as shirkers or cowards, as they were in some other parts of Britain. The one group which was treated harshly by the tribunals – whether because of lack of understanding or lack of sympathy – was the conscientious objectors.

NOTES

1 John Davies, *A History of Wales* (London: Allen Lane, 1993), p. 500.
2 J. Graham Jones, 'Lloyd George, W. Llewelyn Williams MP and the 1916 Conscription Bill', *The National Library of Wales Journal*, 31/2 (1999), 173-188.
3 *Aberdare Leader*, 22 January 1916.
4 *Llais Llafur*, 1 January 1916.
5 Robert Pope, 'Christ and Caesar? Welsh Nonconformists and the State, 1914–1918' in Matthew Cragoe and Chris Williams (eds), *Wales & War: Society, Politics and Religion in the Nineteenth and Twentieth Centuries* (Cardiff: University of Wales Press, 2007), pp. 165-183.
6 Ibid.
7 Ilana R. Bet-El, *Conscripts: Lost legions of the Great War* (Stroud: Sutton publishing, 1999), p. 2.
8 *Forty-fifth Annual Report of the Local Government Board, 1915-1916*, PP 1916, XII, Cd 8331, 22-24.
9 Thomas C. Kennedy, *The Hound of Conscience: A History of the No-Conscription Fellowship, 1914-1919* (Fayetteville: University of Arkansas Press, 1981), p. 82.
10 K.R. Grieves, 'Military tribunal papers: the case of Leek local tribunal in the First World War', *Archives*, 16/70 (October 1983), 145-150.
11 Quoted in Grieves, 'Leek tribunal'.
12 John Graham, *Conscription and Conscience: a History 1916-1919* (London: George Allen & Unwin, 1922), p. 68.
13 Kenneth O. Morgan, *Rebirth of a Nation: Wales 1880-1980* (Oxford: Oxford University Press, 1982), p. 164.
14 John Rae, *Conscience and Politics* (London: Oxford University Press, 1970), p. 55.
15 A.R. Mack, 'Conscription and conscientious objection in Leeds and Yorkshire in the First World War', (unpublished M.Phil. thesis, University of York, 1982).
16 NLW, CTB 2, Cardiganshire Appeal Tribunal papers and documents.
17 *Carmarthen Journal*, 25 February 1916.
18 *Carmarthen Journal*, 10 March 1916.
19 *Llanelly Mercury*, 9 March 1916.
20 *Llanelly Mercury*, 5 October 1916.
21 *Llanelly Mercury*, 12 October 1916.
22 *Carmarthen Journal*, 18 February, 1916.
23 *Llanelly Mercury*, 16 March 1916.
24 Pembrokeshire Record Office, D/LJ/935.
25 *Carmarthen Journal*, 24 March 1916.
26 *Carmarthen Journal*, 21 April 1916; 2 June 1916.
27 *Carmarthen Journal*, 2 June 1916.
28 *Carmarthen Journal*, 29 September 1916.
29 *Carmarthen Journal*, 20 October 1916.
30 *Carmarthen Journal*, 3 November 1916.
31 *Carmarthen Journal*, 10 November 1916.
32 *Statistics of the Military Effort of the British Empire during the Great War* (London: HMSO, 1922), p. 364.
33 *Parliamentary Debates (Commons), 5th series*, vol. 75, col. 2357, 16 March 1916.
34 Rae, *Conscience and Politics*, p. 71.
35 Davies, *A History of Wales*, p. 500.
36 Rae, *Conscience and Politics*, p. 131.
37 Morgan, *Rebirth of a Nation*, p. 164. See also Dewi Eirug Davies, *Byddin y Brenin* (Swansea: Tŷ John Penry, 1988), pp. 159-60, (in Welsh), for how two conscientious objectors were questioned in Cardiganshire.

Chapter 9

'The Most Literary of Wars'

Literature and the war

—⁓—

'GWAE FI FY MYW MEWN OES MOR DDRENG' (Cursed am I to live in this dire age) are words that still reverberate across the years since Ellis Humphrey Evans penned them in northern France in 1917. The First World War is arguably the most literary of all wars. It produced a vast outpouring of writing in all forms of poetry and prose. Newspapers and journals were full of eye-witness accounts and reportage of events great and small. Poets crafted englynion, sonnets, eulogies and odes that reached a high point in the National Eisteddfod in 1917.

The quality of the literature varied enormously, but one cannot deny that fear, grief and death gave rise to some remarkable works. This study will concentrate on literature produced by both combatants and non-combatants who lived through the war years, writing in either Welsh or English.

The best known Welsh war poet remains Hedd Wyn (Ellis Humphrey Evans) born in 1887 in rural Merionethshire of a farming family. Hedd Wyn was an accomplished poet before the outbreak of war, having won the chair at various local

Hedd Wyn

eisteddfodau; in 1916 he was runner-up in the National Eisteddfod in Aberystwyth. One critic remarked that 'Hedd is a poet of promise who composes verses as easily as breathing. If he can escape the German bullets, more will be heard of him'.[1] He was conscripted in 1917, having declined the opportunity to volunteer, and joined the 15th Battalion Royal Welsh Fusiliers. The new recruits to the Battalion were sent to Litherland, a training camp near Liverpool, where it was described as 'a most pathetic sight to see them having to soldier at all, coming as they did from work of national importance on farms, and leaving their loved ones at home, for hardly one of them appeared to have been cut out for soldiers'. This, apparently, was 'particularly true of Hedd Wyn'.[2] After initial training Hedd Wyn answered the call for temporary ploughmen and returned home for two months, where he devoted all his spare time to writing.

Memorial statue to Hedd Wyn in Trawsfynydd.

On 9 June 1917, Hedd Wyn was drafted to France with his battalion. His initial impressions of the Western Front were grim: 'tywydd trymaidd, enaid trymaidd a chalon drymaidd: dyna drindod anghysurus, onid e?' (Heavy weather, heavy soul and heavy heart: that is an uncomfortable trinity, isn't it?) The battalion was involved in the third battle of Ypres and the assault on Pilckem Ridge on 31 July 1917. Three hours into his first engagement in battle Hedd Wyn was mortally wounded, struck in the chest by a fragment of shrapnel; he was one of 31,000 to die in the battle. In his diary, Field Marshal Douglas Haig described 31 July 1917 as 'a fine day's work'.[3] Hedd Wyn was buried in Artillery Wood cemetery near Boesinghe, with his headstone inscribed in the name E.H. Evans. After the war, a petition was presented to the Imperial War Graves Commission which brought the change of inscription to 'Y Prifardd Hedd Wyn' (The Principal Bard Hedd Wyn). In 1923 a bronze statue of Hedd Wyn as a shepherd-boy was unveiled in Trawsfynydd. It bears an englyn written by Hedd Wyn in memory of a slain friend:

> Ei aberth nid â heibio – ei wyneb
> Annwyl nid â'n ango
> Er i'r Almaen ystaenio
> Ei dwrn dur yn ei waed o.
> (His sacrifice was not in vain – his face
> In our minds will remain
> Although he left a bloodstain
> On Germany's iron fist of pain.)

While on home leave prior to going to the Western Front, Hedd Wyn had largely composed 'Yr Arwr' ('The Hero') which he subsequently entered for the National Eisteddfod in Birkenhead in 1917. This poem was posted from the trenches under the pseudonym 'Fleur-de-lys'. Fact has become intertwined with fiction as to whether Hedd Wyn's commanding officer,

when censoring the homeward post, almost stopped his entry reaching the eisteddfod organizers because he did not understand the Welsh language and feared it was subversive propaganda. On 6 September 1917, in the presence of Lloyd George, just over a month after the poet's death, Hedd Wyn's awdl 'Yr Arwr' was awarded the chair at the National Eisteddfod in Birkenhead. Instead of the usual ceremony, the chair was draped in black and bards came forward in a long procession to place their poetic tributes, in the form of englynion, on the shroud. The chair was then transported to Hedd Wyn's family home, Yr Ysgwrn near Trawsfynydd, where it still resides today. A collection of Hedd Wyn's poems edited by J.J. Williams was published in 1918 entitled *Cerddi'r Bugail* (*Poems of the Shepherd*).

Gerwyn Wiliams argues that 'such a dignified symbol of creativity and

The chair won posthumously by Hedd Wyn at the National Eisteddfod in Birkenhead in 1917. It is displayed at Hedd Wyn's family home, Yr Ysgwrn near Trawsfynydd.

(Courtesy of Gwasg Carreg Gwalch)

vulnerability was automatically at odds with all the philistinism and militarism of war'.[4] Prior to his conscription, Hedd Wyn had written of war in an almost romantic light, for example in 'Gwladgarwch' ('Patriotism'), echoing the sentiments of English poets such as Rupert Brooke. Following his enlistment and experiences in Litherland, he adopted a much more critical and realistic tone. The opening line of 'Rhyfel' (War) is 'Gwae fi fy myw mewn oes mor ddreng' (Woe that I live in this dire age), which neatly mirrors Rupert Brooke's opening line of his poem 'Peace', written in 1914 'Now, God be thanked Who has matched us with His hour'. Hedd Wyn has almost come to symbolise Wales and the First World War, perhaps more so since 1992 and the making of the biographical film *Hedd Wyn* by Paul Turner. It was scripted in Welsh by Alan Llwyd and was to be nominated for an oscar as the best foreign film. Alan Llwyd regards Hedd Wyn as the last great romantic poet to compose in Welsh and that 'Yr Arwr' was possibly the most ambitious eisteddfod winner in the twentieth century.

Robert Williams Parry (1884-1956), born in the Nantlle valley in north Wales, first came to prominence as a Welsh-language poet when he won the chair in the National Eisteddfod in 1910 for his poem 'Yr Haf' ('The Summer'). On the outbreak of war he was employed as an English teacher in Barry, south Wales. He volunteered in 1914 but was rejected because of his poor eyesight. In November 1916 he was accepted as medically fit for general service with an A1 rating, which says far more about the army's need for men than any miraculous improvement in Williams Parry's eyesight. In February 1917 he was posted to Hetherfield cadet school in Berkhamsted and in April transferred to the Royal Garrison Artillery camp at Mornhill, Winchester. He concluded this unhappy period of his life at an anti-aircraft gun station in Billericay, Essex, defending London against zeppelins.

Williams Parry's reputation was based on his first collection of poems *Yr Haf a Cherddi Eraill* (*The Summer and Other Poems*) published in 1924. The second half of this volume was written during Williams Parry's war service and is in stark contrast to the pastoral lyricism of the earlier poems. In his war poems Williams Parry 'moved swiftly from the fanciful to the dismal' and they provide a 'sombre counterpoint to the melodious title poem'.[5] Williams Parry wrote both sonnets and *englynion* on the theme of war, including a series of the latter in memory of Hedd Wyn. One of his best known compositions is the *englyn* 'Ar Gofadail' ('On a Monument') which is inscribed on war memorials in Pen-y-groes and Bethesda:

O Gofadail gofidiau tad a mam!
Tydi mwy drwy'r oesau
Ddysgi ffordd i ddwys goffáu
Y rhwyg o golli'r hogiau.

(O Memorial to the anguish of fathers and mothers!
You alone throughout the ages
Will teach us how to solemnly remember
The wrench of losing the lads.)

His greatest poem was generally held to be the sequence of *englynion* (strict metre poems) in memory of Hedd Wyn:

Y bardd trwm dan bridd tramor, – y dwylaw
Na ddidolir rhagor:
Y llygaid dwys dan ddwys ddôr,
Y llygaid na all agor.

(The sad poet lies under alien soil
In silence forever;
His two hands too still to stir,
Eyes that can see no longer.)

In 1952 Williams Parry published his only other collection of poetry entitled *Cerddi'r Gaeaf* (*Poems of Winter*). Although the number of poems he wrote is not great, his output is generally accepted as being some of the finest written in Welsh during the twentieth century.

T.H. Parry-Williams (1887-1975), from Rhyd-ddu in Caernarfonshire, like Williams Parry, had great success at a young age in the National Eisteddfod, winning both the chair and crown in 1912 and again in 1915. He was a conscientious objector and spent the war lecturing in Welsh at the University College of Wales, Aberystwyth. Parry-Williams was to have an outstanding career as a writer, critic, scholar and philologist, yet he never fully confronted the subject of war in his writing. A colleague of Parry-Williams's in the Welsh department at Aberystwyth was another conscientious objector, T. Gwynn Jones (1871-1949). After elementary

T. H. Parry-Williams.

school, Jones worked as a journalist on Welsh-language weekly newspapers such as *Baner ac Amserau Cymru* and *Yr Herald Cymraeg*. After a brief period as a cataloguer at the new National Library of Wales in 1917, Jones was appointed as reader in Welsh literature in Aberystwyth before promotion to a chair in 1919. Like Parry-Williams and Wiliams Parry, Jones came to prominence in the National Eisteddfod, winning the first of his two chairs in 1902 when still a struggling journalist. Jones became a leading poet of his generation with most of his poems drawing on freely adapted Celtic legends. During the war he became increasingly critical of Britain's slide towards militarism.

He composed a number of concise pieces in which he pointedly satirized the direction of Welsh political and social life. As a more long-lasting testament to his undoubted talents, Jones produced a sequence of seven mythological poems, which chart the transition of his early optimism to bitter disillusionment as the First World War progressed. The second of these poems, 'Madog', was published in 1918 and is written in cynghanedd, conforming to the strict metres of bardic tradition. 'Madog' is set in the twelfth century depicting a fraternal rivalry which leads to the death of one brother. Although Jones thought the poem would not probably be understood at the time of its publication, it was clearly intended as an allegory of the war.

A Welsh-language writer who experienced war at first hand was Albert Evans-Jones (1895-1970), usually known by his bardic name 'Cynan'. He served in France and Salonika in the 86th Field Ambulance, Royal Army Medical Corps, first as an ambulance man then pastor. His experiences undoubtedly shaped much of his writing and he attempted to introduce a specifically Welsh point of view to what he produced. His descriptions of the horrors of war and the impact on man's body and spirit are central to his poems in collections such as *Telyn y Nos* (*The Harp of the Night*) published in 1921. In the same year, his winning entry at the National

Eisteddfod, 'Mab y Bwthyn' ('Son of the Cottage') also dealt with war. This long free-metre poem (pryddest) tells the story of a young man from a rural Welsh community who is confronted by worldly temptations whilst serving abroad in the army. Cynan's descriptions of the atrocities of war are no less vivid than those of Wilfred Owen or Siegfried Sassoon:

> O dan y gwifrau – pigog, geirwon,
> A thros bentyrrau hen o'r meirwon …
> O Dduw! A rhaid im gofio sawr
> Y fan lle'r heidiai'r llygod mawr?
> (Under the sharp barbed wire,
> And over old mounds of the dead
> O God! Must I remember the stench
> Of the place where the rats swarmed.)

After the war Cynan became a Calvinistic Methodist minister in Penmaenmawr, followed by an academic career at University College, Bangor. He is probably best remembered as a reforming archdruid of the National Eisteddfod largely shaping the various ceremonies of the chair and crown as they appear today. Academic critics often have been rather dismissive of Cynan's literary legacy regarding his work as too populist and sentimental.

Another preacher-poet who spent time in the front line during the war was J. Dyfnallt Owen (1873-1956). Dyfnallt (usually known by his bardic name alone) had entered the ministry in 1898. In 1916 he went to Béthune, in northern France as chaplain to the YMCA, where he remained for three months. In 1917 he published *Myfyrion a Chaneuon Maes y Tân* (*Meditations and Songs of the Battlefield*), a short book of poems, diary entries and meditations. Perhaps its most noteworthy feature was that it was the first creative record in the Welsh language to stem directly from the war. Dyfnallt's poems alluded to the crisis of conscience felt by the members of Nonconformist chapels during the conflict, although he always retained a basic belief in the justness of fighting the war.

David James (Gwenallt) Jones (1899-1968) was brought up in a devoutly Nonconformist home in Pontardawe in the Swansea valley. He was a pupil-teacher from 1916-17 and he was briefly taught by Kate Roberts. He was conscripted in 1917 but applied for exemption on both political and religious grounds. After refusing non-combatant service, he was imprisoned in June 1917 and spent time in both Wormwood Scrubs and Princetown prison on Dartmoor. Gwenallt's father suffered insults and persecution because of his son's pacifist stance. In his poem 'Fy Nhad' ('My Father') Gwenallt wrote:

> Eu poer, eu parddu a'u picellau mân;
> Ti ddeliaist ati er pob cnoc a chlwy.
> (Their spit, their vilification and their little spears
> You bore despite each knock and wound.)

Gwenallt was not released until May 1919. He later followed a distinguished academic career at the University College of Wales, Aberystwyth. It was not until the publication of *Plasau'r Brenin* (*The King's Mansions*) in 1934 that Gwenallt first reflected in print on the war and his imprisonment. It has been claimed that Gwenallt and T. Hughes Jones both vowed to write a novel based on the First World War because of the shortage of Welsh-language books on the subject. *Plasau'r Brenin* is clearly autobiographical with the character of Myrddin Tomos acting as Gwenallt's mouthpiece. Gwenallt portrays three very different conscientious objectors who have been imprisoned in the king's mansions: a Welsh nationalist who refuses to take part in a war between the major powers; a communist who sees the war as an imperialist conflict; and a born-again Christian who is an uncompromising pacifist. Saunders Lewis regarded the novel as a 'poet's autobiography' and it is generally accepted that Gwenallt's literary strengths were as a poet rather than as a creative prose writer. This was confirmed in Gwenallt's posthumously published *Fwrneisau* (*Furnaces*) in 1982, based on his youth in Pontardawe and Alltwen. T. Hughes Jones (1895-1966) eventually fulfilled his side of the bargain with Gwenallt, with the publication of *Amser i Ryfel* (*A Time of War*) in 1944. While this describes military life with precision, the novel understandably lacks immediacy and has been described as 'bleak and unadventurous'.[6]

One writer who had a major influence on the writings of the young Gwenallt was T.E. Nicholas, 'Niclas y Glais' (1879-1971). Nicholas was brought up in Pembrokeshire and ordained in the Congregational ministry in 1901. Events such as the Tonypandy riots and the Senghenydd mining disaster shaped Nicholas's political thinking: it was the inhuman

King George V conversing with Major-General Charles Guinand Blackader, Commander of the 38th (Welsh) Division, at Wormhoudt, 13th August 1916. Troops of the Division are along the road.

(Imperial War Museum)

capitalist economic system which caused social injustice, oppression and ultimately war. His early collections *Cerddi Rhyddid* (*Freedom Poems*) 1914, *Y Rhyfel Anghyfiawn* (*The Unjust War*) 1914 and *Dros Eich Gwlad* (*For Your Country*) 1920 all contained anti-war poems with 'Gweriniaeth a Rhyfel' ('Republicanism and War') probably being the most enduring. Critics maintain that his shrill tone and the use of the blunderbuss rather than the rapier, detracted from his central message that it was an imperialist war which was against the best interests of the working classes. Nicholas had become the Congregational minister in Llangybi (Cardiganshire) in 1914 where his Marxist principles led him to organise the agricultural workers and lead miners into collectivist action.[7] Because of his denunciation of the war from the pulpit, Nicholas was regarded as a dangerous subversive and his sermons were monitored by Home Office informers for treasonable sentiments. In 1918, after he had delivered a particularly anti-war sermon in his own chapel there was an unsuccessful attempt to prosecute Nicholas under the Defence of the Realm Act. He founded a local branch of the No-Conscription Fellowship which brought further animosity and many chapels closed their doors to him. He abandoned the ministry in disgust and trained as a dentist, practising in Aberystwyth for many years. In the general election of December 1918, Nicholas stood as the Independent Labour Party candidate in Aberdare with the backing of the trades council, the Labour party and the co-operative movement. It is an indication of how far his views were at odds with the locality when he polled only 6,229 votes. His opponent, the ex-miners' leader turned patriot Charles B. Stanton polled 22,834.

When war broke out, Lewis Valentine (1893-1986) was only twenty-one, having entered University College Bangor in 1913 with the intention of joining the ministry on graduation. However, he served in the Welsh Student Company, Royal Army Medical Corps as a non-combatant, witnessing front-line fighting in northern France in 1917. The war had a direct physical effect on Valentine when a shell blast left him deaf, dumb and blind for three months. The war was also crucial to Valentine's political development as he saw religion hi-jacked in the interests of national aggrandizement. He co-founded the Welsh Nationalist Party in 1925 and was imprisoned for nine months in 1937 for his part in the demonstrations against the siting of the bombing range on the Llŷn peninsula. *Dyddiadur Milwr* (*A Soldier's Diary*) is regarded as Valentine's finest prose work, chronicling his experiences during the war. However, this was not published until 1969-72, when it appeared in the Baptist periodical *Seren Gomer*. Meic Stephens regarded the diary as one of the very few works from Wales which approached the 'stellar quality' of Robert Graves's work (the others being Cynan, R. Williams Parry, Hedd Wyn and Kate Roberts).[8] In the middle of the third battle of Ypres, Valentine wrote 'Uffern! Uffern! Uffern! Cnawd drylliedig, esgeiriau yn ysgyrion. Atal Dduw y dwymyn wallgof, atal boer y mallgwn!' ('Hell! Hell! Hell! Torn flesh, shattered bones. Halt, O God, the mad fever, halt the spitting of the demented dogs').

While this survey is in no way exhaustive, the sum total of enduring Welsh-language literature produced by those with direct experience of the conflict, either at home or abroad, is not particularly extensive. As far as Anglo-Welsh writing is concerned, the situation is very much the same. There are a number of eye-witness accounts and autobiographical musings written in most cases long after the war had ended: *Abercynon to Flanders and Back* by W.G. Bowden[9]; *Taffy Went to War* by Emlyn Williams[10]; *From Khaki to Cloth* by Morgan Watcyn-Williams[11]; and, *The Hungry One* by Charles P. Clayton[12] While these accounts have some interesting detail on training, military life, the front line and so on, they have little literary merit compared to *Memoirs of an Infantry Officer* by Siegfried Sassoon,[13] *Undertones of War* by Edmund Blunden[14] or *Goodbye to All That* by Robert Graves.[15] It is worth noting at this point that the claims to include writers such as Siegfried Sassoon, Robert Graves, Wilfred Owen, Ivor Gurney and T.E. Lawrence in collections of 'Welsh' writers are rejected in this study, even though Alan Llwyd does offer a convincing counter-argument for their inclusion.[16] For example, Graves's connections with Wales are tenuous at best. His father was a school inspector, half Irish and half Scots, whilst his mother was German. The family lived in the middle-class London suburb of Wimbledon. Graves was educated in the south of England, firstly at a succession of preparatory schools before entering the public school, Charterhouse. Before he could enter university, war was declared; Graves enlisted immediately, aged nineteen. The Graves family did own a summer house in Harlech, and it was the secretary of the local golf club who pushed Graves to enlist in the Royal Welsh Fusiliers, but this is really the extent of any Welsh connection.

Robert Graves.

Indeed in *Goodbye to All That*, Graves writing of himself and his sister said that 'having no Welsh blood in us, we felt little temptation to learn Welsh, still less to pretend ourselves Welsh'.[17] Furthermore, it is generally accepted that *Goodbye to All That* is not an autobiography which can in any way be relied upon as a true account of actual events. Paul Fussell describes it as 'a satire, built out of anecdotes heavily influenced by the techniques of stage comedy'.[18] Graves admitted that he wrote the book to 'make a lump of money', making sure that he included all the obligatory ingredients of a popular memoir such as 'food and drink, murders, ghosts, kings, one's mother, T.E. Lawrence and the Prince of Wales'.[19] Frank Richards (1883-1961) was born in Machen, near Newport and brought up by his grandparents. He was a regular soldier and joined the Royal Welsh Fusiliers in 1902, serving in India from 1902-7, before joining the reserve in 1909. On the outbreak of war, Richards was recalled to the 2nd Battalion Welsh Regiment and fought in the battles of Loos, the Somme and third Ypres. He was awarded the Distinguished Conduct Medal and the Military Medal but refused promotion because he claimed that he preferred mixing with ordinary soldiers. In the 1920s Richards read various war memoirs, mostly by officers, but he felt that what was described was a very different war to the one he had fought in.[20] Although writing did not come easily to him, in 1930 he began putting down his recollections of the war with his own particular slant on events. He sent the resulting manuscript to Robert Graves who had been an officer in his battalion. Graves 'licked it into shape' and arranged for its publication as *Old Soldiers Never Die*.[21] The writing is neither sophisticated nor analytical, but his blunt and opinionated comments on military stupidity, staff officers, military chaplains and war correspondents engage the reader. The memoir is very much 'emotion recollected in tranquility' and the influence of Graves hovers throughout, but it is one of the few books on the war not written by an officer.

Llewelyn Wyn Griffith (1890-1977) was educated at Dolgellau Grammar School where his father was headmaster, before entering the civil service working in the Inland Revenue. On the outbreak of war he enlisted in the 7th Battalion Royal Welsh Fusiliers as a private soldier, before being commissioned into the 15th Battalion of the same regiment in January 1915. His descriptions of the battle of Mametz, written immediately after the war but not published until 1931, are as haunting, vivid and brutal as any writing on the conflict. Griffith's brother Private Watcyn Griffith, 17th Battalion Royal Welsh Fusiliers, was killed on 10 July 1916 carrying a message sent by Wyn Griffith. He wrote that 'I had sent him to his death, bearing a message from my own hand, in an endeavour to save other men's brothers'.[22] He returned to work in the civil service continuing to write, translate and broadcast, becoming the captain of the Welsh team in 'Round Britain Quiz'.

One of the most interesting characters to put pen to paper after the war was James Ira Thomas Jones (1896-1960), known unimaginatively as 'Taffy'. He was in the territorial force on the outbreak of war but soon transferred to the newly formed Royal Flying Corps, working as a mechanic. In January 1916 Jones began flying combat missions as an observer, before beginning pilot training in August 1917. He joined 74 Squadron in early 1918 recording thirty-seven 'victories' in just three months. He was awarded the Military Medal, Distinguished Service Order, Distinguished Flying Cross and bar and the Military Cross. As befits an ex-London Welsh scrum-half, Jones was a harum-scarum character with a reputation for crashing aircraft on landing; he reportedly survived twenty-eight accidents of varying severity. After the war, he volunteered to fight the Bolsheviks and was posted to the Archangel front but he did not see combat. Remaining as a regular pilot, Jones became the commanding officer of 74

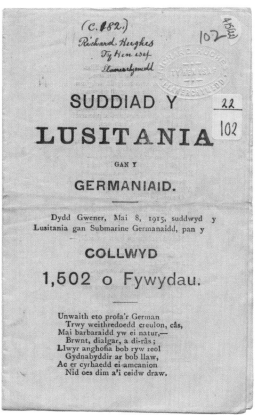

A Welsh ballad, composed to mark the sinking of RMS Lusitania by a German submarine on 7 May 1915.

(Courtesy of Archives and Special Collections, Bangor University)

Squadron retiring in 1936. Despite being forty-three, Jones was recalled to serve in the Second World War, once attacking a German Junkers bomber with a Very pistol as he was flying an unarmed Hawker Henley. In 1954 Jones published *Tiger Squadron*, a history of 74 Squadron. Without any pretensions to literary merit, this entertaining account is best known for Jones's forthright views on war and the enemy.[23] On one occasion Jones was quoted as saying:

> My habit of attacking Huns dangling from their parachutes led to many arguments in the mess. Some officers of the Eton and Sandhurst type, thought I was 'unsportsmanlike' to do it. Never having been to a public school, I was unhampered by such considerations of form. I just pointed out that there was a bloody war on, and that I intended to avenge my pals.[24]

Mention should also be made of E.H. Jones's (1883-1942) *The Road to En-Dor*, although this is a work which is so atypical that it is hard to classify.[25] Elias Henry Jones was a lawyer from Aberystwyth who joined the Indian army on the outbreak of war. He was taken as a prisoner of war by the Turks after the fall of Kut-el-Amara. He survived a march of 700 miles and was imprisoned in Yozgad camp in. With Lieutenant C.W. Hill, an Australian serving in the RFC, Jones managed to convince their captors that they were mediums for a ouija board and descending into insanity, securing their release and repatriation. It is a tale of adventure and cunning, a 'ripping yarn' which was reprinted seventeen times and ran into three editions.

It is generally accepted that one of the most original and innovative works published by a First World War combatant was *In Parenthesis* by David Jones (1895-1974).[26] Jones was born and raised in Brockley, Kent, to a Welsh father and an Anglo-Italian mother. Jones always regarded himself as Welsh and interweaves Welsh legends and language into his work. Indeed, the sub-title of *In Parenthesis* is 'Seinyessit e gledyf ym penn mameu' ('His sword rang on mothers' heads') taken from Aneirin's sixth-century epic poem, *Y Gododdin*. After studying at the Camberwell School of Art, Jones enlisted in the 15th Battalion Royal Welsh Fusiliers, but unlike Graves and Sassoon, as a private soldier. He served in France, notably at the battle of Mametz Wood, before being invalided home with severe trench fever in 1918. He went on to become a noted artist, poet and engraver.

Jones began writing *In Parenthesis* in the late 1920s, but the work was not published until 1937. It covers the period from December 1915, when Jones was posted to France, to July 1916, after the battle of Mametz. Jones thought this period marked a change in the character of the lives of those in the infantry: 'the wholesale slaughter of the later years, the conscripted levies filling the gaps in every file of four, knocked the bottom out of the intimate, continuing, domestic life of small contingents of men'.[27] *In Parenthesis* charts a journey: the old order is destroyed and is replaced by a new disorder represented by shells, 'the stinking physicist's destroying toy'. T.S. Eliot regarded *In Parenthesis* as a 'work of genius' which used language in a new way. Paul Fussell's less charitable view is that it is an 'honourable miscarriage' by a 'turgid illusionist'.[28] It is a difficult work which uses the narrative structure of the novel, with language that takes on the allusiveness and momentum of poetry. Jones referred to *In Parenthesis* as 'writing', refusing to be drawn on whether it was poetry or prose.

Saunders Lewis (1893-1985) was born in Cheshire to Welsh Nonconformist parents, with Welsh always being the first language of the home. After starting in Liverpool University, where Lewis met his future wife Margaret Gilcriest, Lewis volunteered for military service in 1914. He was commissioned as a lieutenant in to the South Wales Borderers, receiving commendations for bravery. He was severely wounded in 1917 necessitating a year's convalescence. After the war, Lewis was to become arguably one of Wales's finest writers. In his obituary, *The Guardian* ranked him alongside W.B. Yeats in Ireland and T.S. Eliot in England. Like Lewis Valentine, Saunders Lewis was a founder member of the Welsh Nationalist Party and he was similarly imprisoned for his opposition to the proposed bombing range on the Llŷn peninsula. Lewis wrote regular letters home (in English) to Margaret Gilcriest which provide a vivid, personal and contemporary account of the war. Lewis showed great early enthusiasm for the war and expressed it in language which is almost reminiscent of Rupert Brooke. He was glad to go to war, 'dreaming of how his personal qualities would be enhanced by the conflict'. Realism soon replaced his early romanticism:

I can't hope to describe to you the mixture of horror and grotesque humour of this line. Nothing at all of what I have seen before of trench warfare was at all like this. In the line we held we were in shell-holes waist-high in slime, without even the semblance of a trench; dead men were as common as the living. They had died in all kinds of positions – numbers had merely drowned, – until your attitude towards them became one of mingled tenderness and sympathy and humorous acceptance. One joked with them and often joined them.[29]

He realises that of his dreams it was 'hollower than most.' He concluded: 'I have gained no more than if I'd spent three years in the rose garden at Wallasey, discussing Rousseau among the mail-carts'.[30]

The most celebrated Anglo-Welsh poet of the First World War, Edward Thomas (1878-1917), was born in London of Welsh parents but never resided in Wales. In *The South Country* he calls himself 'mainly Welsh'. However, he frequently visited relatives and friends in Newport, Swansea and Pontarddulais. Thomas called Wales 'my soul's native land'.[31] At the age of twenty-one he wrote of Wales as a calling: 'it is like a homesickness, but stronger than any homesickness I ever felt – stronger than any passion.'[32] When pressed on the subject he once said that he was '⅝ Welsh'. After graduating from Oxford in 1900, Thomas failed to get a teaching or librarian's post in Wales despite the support of O.M. Edwards; economic necessity forced him to become a prolific book reviewer. He also wrote country books, essays, guidebooks and folk tales and in 1914 his first celebrated poem 'Up in the Wind'. In July 1915, Thomas joined the Artists' Rifles as a private soldier before being commissioned as an officer in to the Royal Garrison Artillery in 1916. He volunteered for overseas service and was posted to northern France in January 1917. He began his service with high ideals, writing home in December 1916, 'I do hope peace won't come just yet. I should not know what to do, especially if it came

Edward Thomas.

before I had really been a soldier'.[33] He was killed during the first hour of the battle of Arras on 9 April 1917. His daughter vividly remembered receiving the news: 'I saw the telegraph boy lean his red bicycle against the fence. Mother stood reading the message with a face of stone. "No answer" came like a croak, and the boy rode away'.[34] In the last two years of his life Thomas had written over 140 poems which were published in *Poems* (originally under his pseudonym Edward Eastaway), *Last Poems* and *Collected Poems*.[35] While Thomas is always known as a 'war poet', all his poetry about the war was written in England before he was exposed to the death and bloodshed of the trenches. His war poems are those of a countryman reacting to the violent destruction of the natural order of things.

Kate Roberts (1891-1985) was born in a slate-quarrying area of Caernarfonshire (Rhosgadfan), the daughter of a quarry-man. Despite never returning to the area after 1915, the locality defined much of her writing. She qualified as a teacher and held posts in Ystalyfera and Aberdare. In 1928 she married Morris Williams; in 1935 they bought Gwasg Gee, a printing and

Kate Roberts.

publishing house in Denbigh, and with it the Welsh weekly newspaper *Banner ac Amserau Cymru*. Roberts wrote regular columns for the paper for over forty years. She thought the years around the First World War were her major creative influence and that it was the death in action of her youngest brother David that prompted her to write. After publishing three volumes of well-received short stories, Roberts produced her first full length novel, *Traed Mewn Cyffion* (*Feet in Chains*) which was awarded joint first prize at the Neath National Eisteddfod in 1934. Set in Moel Arian, a thinly disguised Rhosgadfan, in the period 1880-1918, Roberts depicts how the local community had no understanding of the causes of the war or why it was being fought, beyond a vague understanding that Great Britain 'was going to the help of smaller nations'.[36] Twm, the eldest son of Ffridd Felen, trains to be a teacher and feels that the war would have no effect on him or his brother Owen. Soon Twm felt restless and 'the attraction of joining up was growing all the time'. He saw a 'spirit of adventure abroad', while his world was too languid and walled-in.

By enlisting he would 'be able to see something of the great outside, something other than these eternal mountains, and the sour face of his headmaster'.[37] By 1916 the people of Moel Arian came to realise that the war was only being fought to promote the selfish interests of 'the ruling class' – the same ones 'who oppressed them in the quarry, who sucked their blood and turned it into gold for themselves'.[38] Roberts is equally scathing about the preachers, 'who a short time beforehand felt like little gods to them, were now condemned because they were in favour of the war'.[39]

In 1967 Roberts published *Tegwch y Bore* (*One Bright Morning*), her longest and most discursive novel, drawing heavily on her own experiences of the war from the perspective of the home front. The book tells the story of Ann Owen, a forthright young teacher from Caernarfonshire who, like Roberts, loses her brother Bobi in the war. Ann constantly refers to the futility of the war and how 'nations had lost sight of the war's original purpose, the defence of small nations, and that now it was about other things, about power, and the loss of power.'[40] When Ann visits her brother Roland in hospital in London, she tries to explain her view to the doctor:

> 'Yes, but my brother is not fighting for his own country'. The doctor looked at her for the first time. Till that moment he had been examining his papers. He took his time before speaking.
> 'Who is he fighting for?'
> 'Not for his country. Wales is our country.'
> The doctor stared at her now …
> 'I do not understand you.'
> 'No an Englishman would not understand … The English know what they are fighting for, but the Welsh do not, because we are a separate nation.'

Kate Roberts remains one of the few women from Wales to have written about the First World War. In two recently published anthologies of women's writing and the First World War, there are respectively sixty-nine entries and eighty-seven entries: none is by a Welsh woman.[41] In recent years, English novelists Susan Hill, Deborah Moggach, Jane Thynne and most notably Pat Barker, have all published successful and well-received novels dealing with the war. In Wales, little has been published of note other than Siân James's *A Small Country* and *Return to 'Hendre Ddu'*.

NOTES

1   Bethan Phillips, 'A fine day's work', *Planet*, 72 (1988-9), pp. 59-64.

2   Ibid.

3   Gary Sheffield and John Bourne (eds), *Douglas Haig: War Diaries and Letters* (London: Weidenfeld & Nicolson, 2005), p. 307.

4   Gerwyn Wiliams, 'The Literature of the First World War', in Dafydd Johnston (ed.), *A Guide to Welsh Literature, c1900-1996* (Cardiff: University of Wales Press, 1998), pp. 22-49

5   Ibid., p. 27.

6   Ibid., p.43.

7   See David A. Pretty, *The Rural Revolt that Failed: Farm Workers' Trade Unions in Wales 1889-1950* (Cardiff: University of Wales Press, 1989), pp. 81-2.

8   Book review in *Planet*, 191 (2008), pp. 107-8.

9   W.G. Bowden, *Abercynon to Flanders and Back* (Risca: Starling Press, 1984).

10 Emlyn Williams, *Taffy Went to War* (Knutsford: Knutsford Secretarial Bureau, 1976).

11 Morgan Watcyn-Williams, *From Khaki to Cloth* (Caernarfon: Caernarfon Methodist Book Agency, 1949).

12 Charles P. Clayton, *The Hungry One* (Llandysul: Gomer Press, 1978).

13 Siegfried Sassoon, *The Complete Memoirs of George Sherston* (London: Faber and Faber, 1937).

14 Edmund Blunden, *Undertones of War* (London: Richard Cobden-Sanderson, 1928).

15 Robert Graves, *Goodbye to All That* (Penguin Books: London, 1960).

16 See Alan Llwyd (ed.), *Out of the Fire of Hell: Welsh Experience of the Great War 1914 in Prose and Verse* (Llandysul: Gomer Press, 2008), pp. ix–xxii.

17 Graves, *Goodbye to All That*, p. 34.

18 Paul Fussell, *The Great War and Modern Memory* (Oxford: Oxford University Press, 1975), p. 207.

19 Quoted in Arnold D. Harvey, *A Muse of Fire: Literature, Art and War* (London: Hambledon Press, 1998), p. 139.

20 Frank Richards, *Old Soldiers Never Die* (London: Faber and Faber, 1933), p. 4.

21 Ibid., p.5

22 Ll. Wyn Griffith, *Up to Mametz and Beyond* (Barnsley: Pen & Sword, 2010), p. 114.

23 Ira Jones, *Tiger Squadron* (London: W. H. Allen, 1954).

24 Quoted in Dave English, *The Air Up There: More Great Quotations on Flight* (New York: McGraw-Hill, 2003), p. 203.

25 Elias Jones, *The Road to En-Dor: A True Story of Cunning Wartime Escape* (London: John Lane The Bodley Head, 1933).

26 David Jones, *In Parenthesis* (London: Faber and Faber, 1937).

27 Ibid., p. ix.

28 Fussell, *The Great War*, p. 144.

29 Mair Saunders Jones, Ned Thomas, Harri Pritchard Jones (eds), *Saunders Lewis: Letters to Margaret Gilcriest* (Cardiff: University of Wales Press, 1993), p. 238.

30 Ibid., p. 241.

31 Quoted in Llwyd, *Out of the Fire of Hell*, p. xx.

32 Quoted in Matthew Hollis, *Now All Roads Lead to France: The Last Years of Edward Thomas* (London: Faber and Faber, 2011), p. 161.

33 Myfanwy Thomas, *One of These Fine Days* (Manchester: Carcanet New Press,1982), p. 56.

34 Ibid.

35 Edward Thomas, *Collected Poems* (London: Selwyn and Blount, 1920).

36 Kate Roberts, *Feet in Chains* (London: Corgi, 1977), p. 32.

[37] Ibid., p. 34.

[38] Ibid., p. 144.

[39] Ibid., p. 144.

[40] Kate Roberts, *One Bright Morning* (Llandysul: Gomer Press, 2008) p. 126.

[41] See Angela K. Smith (ed.), *Women's Writing of the First World War: An Anthology* (Manchester: Manchester University Press, 2000); Agnès Cardinal, Dorothy Goldman, Judith Hattaway (eds), *Women's Writing on the First World War* (Oxford: Oxford University Press, 1999).

Chapter 10

The Home Front

—⟋⟍—

AGRICULTURE

IN DECEMBER 1916, the President of the Board of Agriculture, Rowland Prothero, declared: 'it is my sincere conviction that it may be on the corn-fields and potato lands of Great Britain that victory in the Great War may be lost or won'.[1] At the outbreak of war, Britain was certainly not self-sufficient in food; farmers produced only a fifth of the wheat consumed, the remainder being imported. Nearly half of the meat supply and over three-quarters of cheese were also imported. British farmers provided enough food for only 125 days of the year. Wales was traditionally a corn growing nation and evidence of ploughed land has been discovered in uplands at an altitude at which it is scarcely conceivable that any cereals would yield even a scanty return. Throughout the nineteenth and early twentieth centuries there was a significant move away from arable production to grass farming and stock rearing. Between 1890 and 1914, the total acreage of land used for arable production fell by 26 per cent, whilst the acreage of grass for grazing and hay rose by five per cent and rough grazing by 40 per cent. In the same period, the number of cattle increased by seven per cent and the number of sheep by 17 per cent.[2]

In the early years of the war, this changing pattern of land use in Wales was halted, if not reversed, in some counties. The acreage of land used for grass and hay barely altered from 1914-16, while the acreage used for cereal crops rose from 340,000 acres in 1914 to 377,000 acres in 1916 (see Table 1). This occurred largely because of individual decisions by farmers on the expectation of higher prices for wheat, barley and oats

Table 1: Land Use in Wales, 1912–21

	Total grass for grazing & hay, '000s acres	Total corn & pulse crops, '000s acres	Wheat, '000s acres	Barley, '000s acres	Potatoes, '000s acres	Turnips & Swedes, '000s acres	Total cultivated area, '000s acres
1912	2,224	360	47	95	27	61	2,998
1913	2,262	347	43	92	26	60	2,991
1914	2,257	340	43	87	26	59	2,982
1915	2,251	347	56	83	28	54	2,978
1916	2,210	377	56	90	30	56	2,992
1917	2,167	425	71	98	36	54	2.993
1918	1,970	637	113	109	39	56	2,958
1919	1,958	552	85	107	30	62	2,907
1920	1,998	457	61	103	29	60	2,885
1921	2,004	380	47	83	28	54	2,822

Anonymous diary of a soldier in France, 1915.   *(Courtesy of Gwent Record Office)* while imports were disrupted. There was no intervention by either local or national government in agricultural policy in this period, and food supplies from both home and abroad were well maintained. Throughout Wales, agriculture prospered with the prices of all farm products rising, especially those of wool and cereal crops. Between August 1914 and July 1915 the price of corn increased by 42 per cent.[3]

Two factors were to cause this *laissez-faire* policy to be abandoned. Firstly, the winter of 1915 and spring of 1916 were marked by atrocious weather with frosts and heavy rain, which subsequently affected the harvest of 1916. There was also a poor harvest in the Americas, which was the chief source of imported food. Secondly, the German High Command was known to be planning a new, unlimited submarine campaign with the aim of sinking as much shipping as possible thus curtailing imports of food and other war materials and forcing a British surrender. The government's response was to boost home food production by expanding the area devoted to crops at the expense of that previously devoted to grassland. The rationale behind this 'plough policy' was simply that more mouths could be fed from a given area devoted to crops than if the same area were to be devoted to livestock. On 1 January 1917 a new sub-department of the Board of Agriculture, the Food Production Department was created to implement this policy.

At a local level, government policy was to be carried out by the County War Agricultural Committees. In most counties of Wales, these committees were based on the existing Agricultural Committees of the County Council, with additional co-opted members. In the first two years of the war, the work of persuading local farmers to voluntarily plough more land was carried out via campaigns in the local press, and by holding meetings in rural areas. It was feared that many farmers would be reluctant to give up a pattern of land use which had proved profitable in the immediate past, but as has already been shown, Welsh farmers had already begun to plough more and graze less. Government intervention after 1916 simply sped up the process.

In 1917, amid fears that food stocks were reaching dangerously low levels, the government felt compelled to intervene still further in agricultural policy. Under the Corn Production Act farmers were given the incentive of a six-year guarantee of corn prices and rent increases were restricted. New wages boards were initiated to set legally enforceable minimum rates of pay (initially 25s. per week) and hours of work for agricultural workers. The County War Agricultural Committees were to appoint executive committees, with a maximum of seven members, which were given new powers to compel farmers to cultivate arable land where this was deemed necessary. The committees appointed officers to survey all farms in each county, to give each farm a quota of land to be cultivated and finally to ensure the orders served on the farmers were carried out. There were aggregate quotas of newly cultivated land for each county: 18,000 acres in Anglesey, 27,000 acres in Glamorgan and 11,000 acres in Merioneth for example.[4]

Despite many objections by farmers about their quotas of land to be cultivated (in Caernarfonshire, for example, over a thousand appeals against quotas were made), the campaign was successful. In Wales, from 1916-18 the land used for grazing and hay fell by 240,000 acres and that used for corn and root crops rose by 260,000 acres. In the same period the total number of cattle in Wales fell from 868,648 to 830,573 and the number of sheep fell from 4.12 million to 3.70 million. The yield of wheat rose from 1.63 million bushels to 3.36 million bushels, and the yield of potatoes from 142,000 tons to 234,000 tons (see Table 2). As the yield of other crops such as barley, oats and turnips/swedes also rose slightly and the total cultivated area remained virtually constant, Welsh farmers were

Table 2: Estimated yields of principal crops, Wales

	Wheat, '000s bushels	Barley, '000s bushels	Oats, '000s bushels	Potatoes, '000s tons	Turnips/Swedes, '000s tons
1912	1,230	2,839	7,050	131	848
1913	1,171	2,773	6,923	144	907
1914	1,244	2,748	7,453	153	938
1915	1,600	2,471	7,309	163	799
1916	1,630	2,723	8,228	142	891
1917	1,906	2,789	8,681	206	815
1918	3,360	3,408	14,056	234	847
1919	2,408	3,288	11,416	170	815
1920	1,488	2,928	7,608	104	770
1921	1,344	2,000	6,400	154	675

clearly farming more efficiently and thus productively. A major change in land use in Wales had taken place, specifically because of the involvement of government in agricultural practice, prompted by the exigencies of war.

The County War Agricultural Committees were also given responsibility for co-ordinating the supply and distribution of tractors, ploughs, horses, fertilisers and seed wheat and potatoes. For example, in Glamorgan forty-four tractors were made available and sixty-three tractor drivers, ploughmen and mechanics. Ninety-seven horses were supplied by the government and accommodated at a central stable in Bridgend. To assist smallholders lacking equipment, fourteen ploughing gangs made up of ploughmen and teams of horses were formed. The Food Production Department supplied twenty-seven ploughs, ten disc harrows, twenty sets of three-harrows, twenty corn drills, forty-five binders and twenty rollers. The Committee distributed over 3,000 tons of fertilisers and 160,000 bushels of seed corn.[5]

The final area of responsibility for the War Agricultural Committees was to try and ensure that there was an adequate supply of labour for agriculture. The civilian labour market was subject to acute shortages, chiefly due to the demands of the Army for manpower. Some 272,000 men from Wales enlisted in the armed forces out of a pre-war employed male labour force of 808,500. In 1911, there were 95,966 males employed in agriculture and 20,181 females. The Board of Trade estimated that 28-33 per cent of the male agricultural workforce throughout England and Wales was lost by 1916.[6] While this is almost certainly an overestimation as far as Wales is concerned, there is evidence that the War Agricultural Committees in rural counties were concerned at the loss of labour both to the armed forces and to better paid employment in industrialised areas. The Carmarthenshire Committee for example, passed a resolution in November 1916 that there would be 'a disastrous shortage in the home production of wheat and other essential foods if farms were further depleted of skilled and indispensable labour', and that if milk and food supplies fell, 'the War Office and not agriculturalists would be responsible'.

The County War Agricultural Committees, usually in close co-operation with the military authorities, established a range of schemes to ensure sufficient labour was available. Firstly, soldiers were made available to work on farms, especially at harvest time and if they had some experience of agricultural work. Secondly, prisoners of war were directed to work on farms. For example, over 1,000 German prisoners of war from Fron Goch Camp near Bala worked on local farms. In Magor, about sixty prisoners of war arrived in the town in August 1917 and were housed in Pencoed Castle (owned by D.A. Thomas, later Lord Rhondda) and placed at the disposal of the government for the duration of the war. The men were soon put to work and helped with the harvest, but were then moved to the Isle of Man in November 1917. The farmers, who had been initially suspicious of the prisoners of war, found them invaluable as workers and drew up a petition for their return.[7] Thirdly, once conscription had been introduced, the War Agricultural Committees ensured that there was a prominent agriculturalist present at local and county tribunals, to offer evidence in support of farm workers who were appealing against their call-up.[8]

The final strategy for ensuring an adequate labour supply was to encourage local women to take up work on farms, or to return to work on farms from the industrialised areas. Initially, some farmers were sceptical of the value of such labour, holding meetings to express their view of the absurdity of offering them women as labourers. However, women soon proved their worth and farmers who had taken on women for harvest work in 1917, intending to release them after the crops had been brought in, retained them in many cases for winter stock work. It was estimated that 5,782 women worked on the land in Caernarfonshire and 2,699 in Anglesey. A small proportion of these women would have been members of the Women's Land Army, formed in January 1917. The aim had been to supply a full-time, trained and disciplined force of women which would be available throughout the year. Selection standards were very high, and of the first 45,000 applications for membership only 5,000 were selected. In Cardiganshire, 150 women from the Land Army were allocated to the county, recruited mainly from Glamorgan, Durham and Denbighshire. In Gwynedd, only 224 members of the Land Army were employed throughout the war, a tiny proportion of the pre-war workforce of 21,854.[9] The women received a month's training, with a guaranteed minimum wage of 20s per week, plus free uniform and footwear.[10]

Members of the Women's Land Army in Montgomeryshire, c1918.

(Courtesy of Archives and Special Collections, Bangor University)

While no statistics are available specifically for Wales, one estimate is that the 'conventional' labour force on farms in England and Wales fell to approximately 90 per cent of pre-war levels in 1916-18. Replacement labour of women, soldiers, prisoners of war, and the Women's Land Army gradually filled this gap during 1916-17, reaching 97 per cent of pre-war levels by 1918. The County War Agricultural Committees played an important role not only in maintaining the labour supply, but also in encouraging – and then compelling – a change of land use, and organising and distributing scarce resources and machinery. In doing so they helped to ensure that the food supply of Wales, and the United Kingdom, was well maintained throughout the war.

A new development, spurred on by the conditions of war was the spread of the Agricultural Organization Societies, originally founded in Bangor for north Wales in 1911 and in Brecon for south Wales in 1914. The societies encouraged farmers to join together and work on a co-operative basis for both buying and selling. By 1917 there were seventy societies in south Wales with nearly 12,000 members and sixty branches in the north with 6,000 members.

The change in land ownership in Wales, sometimes referred to as the 'green revolution', straddled the First World War. At the end of the nineteenth century land ownership in Wales was concentrated in the hands of a relatively few families. In 1872, the whole of the agricultural land of Wales was owned by 16,000 people, with 55 per cent of the land in Gwynedd in the possession of just thirty-seven families.[11] Only 10 per cent of land was owner-occupied, the remaining 90 per cent was in the possession of landowners who rented their land. This pattern of land ownership had remained virtually unchanged and unchallenged for three hundred years. Half of all estates were between 3,000-5,000 acres, but there were still major landowners with vast estates. Edwinsford (Carmarthenshire) and Stackpole (Pembrokeshire) each occupied 10,000-15,000 acres, whilst the Wynns of Wynnstay owned 142,000 acres. Much of this land was farmed by tenants, with the Morgans of Tredegar, for example, controlling the tenancies of more than one thousand farms. In the nineteenth century, the ownership of land still conferred social prestige and a degree of political power and influence upon its owners. However, by the outbreak of the Second World War, 34 per cent of holdings were owner-occupied and by 1970 this figure had reached 60 per cent. John Davies regards this as 'a change of the greatest significance in Welsh rural society'.[12]

Leading up to the First World War, this change in land ownership from tenanted farms to owner-occupiers had begun, albeit slowly. This changing pattern of ownership reached its peak during the years 1909-22, with the key period being from 1918-22, in the immediate aftermath of the First World War. In 1909, there were 443 agricultural holdings with more than 300 acres of cultivated land; by 1922 this figure had fallen to 320. In 1915, parts of the Kemeys-Tynte estates in Glamorgan and Monmouthshire were put on the market; in 1916 vast swathes of land in Monmouthshire were sold by Lord Tredegar and the Marquess of Abergavenny.[13] It would be wrong to conclude that the war caused such a change in that the economic, political and social factors outlined above had their genesis in the pre-war period. Indirectly, it can be argued, the war accelerated a changing pattern of ownership by undermining the financial viability of owning and renting land. From 1914-20, agricultural prices rose by 300 per cent, and while gross rents rose, net rents fell.

The agricultural labourer, sometimes known as the 'forgotten man of the Welsh agrarian debate' had benefited from a guaranteed minimum wage from 1917 onwards, which meant that the wages of agricultural labourers rose by 75 per cent in the period 1914-18.[14] Given that the cost of living had increased by 115 per cent for foodstuffs and 103 per cent for all items in the same period, it was understandable that labourers felt that they were being denied a share in the huge profits farmers were accruing. David Howell has argued that 'the first serious breakdown in relations [between farmers and labourers] in Welsh counties came during the later years of the First World War and must be attributed to the particular circumstances of wartime'.[15] Howell also cites other bones of contention: farmers' children were often able to stay working on the family farm, so that farmers suffered less personal tragedy from deaths at the front than did other occupational groups. Farmers were accused of electing themselves onto military tribunals to shelter their own families, and also of bringing home their sons from the towns to take the place on the farm of a local boy, who would then be eligible for military service.

These grievances added to poor accommodation and long hours, meant that Welsh farm labourers were in an increasingly confrontational mood. The most obvious manifestation of this was the move towards unionization from 1917 onwards. The major impetus for this was the passing of the Corn Production Act in August 1917, which regulated the wages of farm labourers via wages boards. The wages boards allowed for equal representation of employers and men, which meant that a trade union representing all the men would have much more negotiating muscle. As the *Welsh Gazette* commented, after centuries of 'disinterestedness and natural subservience', the Welsh labourer was undergoing an awakening.[16] The nature of the awakening varied from county to county. The relationship between farmers and labourers in the industrialized counties of Glamorgan and Monmouth was especially rancorous, but in Breconshire and Radnorshire, for example, things were much more amicable. In Cardiganshire and Pembrokeshire farmers threatened to release for military service any worker who dared to join a union. In Anglesey, David Pretty has argued that three years of war had united the ranks of labour, 'moreover a combination of working class consciousness and wartime sacrifices meant they would be unwilling to return to former conditions.'[17] Howell concluded his analysis of agricultural workers and labour organization with the comment that 'the "awakening" of the Welsh farm labourer came during the war years'. This is not to say that there was a causal relationship between the two, but clearly the economic situation in the later war years, coupled with government legislation, created the right conditions for unionization to prosper. For the first time, the agricultural labourer began to understand the value of his own worth.

AFTERMATH

In 1920, confronted by a deepening economic crisis, the government repealed the legislative machinery which had promised a four-year guarantee of prices for selected items of farm output. The so-called 'great betrayal' exposed British farming to world prices and the national market became a dumping ground for world food products. In Wales, the new owner-occupiers who had purchased their farms during the war years when prices of agricultural products had risen by some 300 per cent soon found that their seemingly acceptable mortgage rate of 4-6 per cent was actually a financial millstone. Farmers saw the value of their land decline sharply throughout the 1920s. As Richard Moore-Colyer concluded, 'some abandoned the struggle and sold out to neighbours, but for the majority there was little alternative but to cleave to the wreckage by progressive belt-tightening, exploiting unpaid family labour or even taking in paying guests'[18] Agricultural labourers fared equally badly: their wages had reached a peak in 1921 of 44s. 2d per week, an increase of 145 per cent on the pre-war level. However, by 1924 the average wage had fallen to 28s. 11d. It was not until the later 1930s that matters began to improve for Welsh farmers.

COAL MINING

In 1913, the Welsh coalfield produced 56.8 million tons of coal, which accounted for virtually 20 per cent of all British output, while employing 232,800 men, or 21 per cent of the national workforce.[19] A spectacular boom in the coal mining industry in the late nineteenth and early twentieth centuries had seen production and employment double. Looking back to the outbreak of war Lloyd George commented, 'coal was everything for us'.[20] Initially the war helped to sustain this boom, but in the immediate post-war period the industry was confronted with the problem of excess capacity. Put simply, output proved to be too large for the available markets and decline was inevitable. The First World War was to prove to be a watershed in both the economics of the industry and its internal politics.

In 1913, the south Wales coalfield dominated the British supply of anthracite, dry steam and stoking steam coal. Over 60 per cent of Welsh output was exported, which accounted for 41 per cent of all coal shipped from British ports. However, the high quality of the abundant reserves of steam coal ensured that the demands of the Royal Navy would more than compensate for the loss of export trade when war was declared. Experiments in the 1860s and 1870s had persuaded the naval authorities to rely almost totally on Welsh coal, which generated more steam power than other coals, left little clinker and had the strategic advantage in war of being virtually smokeless. Twenty-eight collieries in south Wales, mainly in the Rhondda and Aberdare valleys, were on the 'Admiralty List' meeting the stringent criteria on the quality of steam coal. In 1913, the Navy had purchased 1.5 million tons of coal; by the spring of 1915, this figure was to reach 15 million tons per annum.

It soon became apparent that the south Wales valleys would be fertile recruiting grounds for Kitchener's army, whether for reasons of patriotism, economic hardship or a desire to escape from the unremitting toil of the workplace. This proved equally true of the mining areas of both England and Scotland, causing concerns that the output of coal, especially for the Royal Navy, might be

Abraham Howells, a miner from Bedwas, who served with both the Royal Welsh Fusiliers and the South Wales Borderers.

threatened. Consequently, in early 1915 a committee was set up to inquire into 'Conditions prevailing in the coal industry due to the war' under the chairmanship of R.A.S. Redmayne and including Vernon Hartshorn as one of the seven members. They sought to determine the extent of the depletion of labour caused by the 'patriotism of the miners' in volunteering, how far replacement labour had made good the loss and therefore how output could be maintained. The outcomes were as expected: there was a shortage of labour with losses to the armed forces and a fall in output.

In July 1914, 999,424 men were employed in the mining industry in the UK; by the end of February 1915, 184,659 (18.5 per cent) had enlisted in the armed forces. In Wales, 31,172 (18.7 per cent) had enlisted, while the workforce had fallen by 19,198, giving a figure of approximately 12,000 who had moved in to employment in the industry. While some would have been experienced floating mining labour, the vast majority were not and thus were unable to replace the coal getters and hauliers. The effect on output was grave: the total number employed in Welsh mines fell by 11.49 per cent between the outbreak of war and February 1915, but output fell by 16.01 per cent. This can be explained by the fact that the persons most physically fit and able to undertake arduous work were the most likely to volunteer: it was estimated that 40 per cent of miners aged nineteen to thirty-eight had enlisted. The fall in output in Wales in the first six months of the year was markedly different to the situation in England, where the fall in the workforce (13.29 per cent) was broadly matched by a fall in output (12.47 per cent). In Scotland, the workforce fell by 16.63 per cent yet output fell by only 2.16 per cent.

The Welsh miner was slightly more willing to enlist (18.7 per cent of the workforce had enlisted by February 1915) than his English counterpart (18.0 per cent), but less likely than his Scottish counterpart (21.3 per cent). Although the numbers of miners employed in counties other than Glamorgan was small by comparison, the more rural counties such as Flintshire (12.1 per cent), Denbighshire (14.4 per cent) and Breconshire (8.0 per cent) lost a smaller percentage of their workforce to enlistment than the average for Wales as a whole. Clearly the rural areas of Wales were not supporting the war to the same extent as the industrialized areas.

The committee of inquiry's report was conciliatory in tone, constantly referring to the patriotic, self-sacrificing and hard-working nature of the miners. Given a predicted loss in output of thirty-six million tons per annum, the report concluded:

> The evidence before us is conclusive that if labour is further withdrawn from the collieries ... the output will be so seriously reduced as to seriously affect the industrial position of the country, and the time appears to the Committee to have arrived when very full consideration should be given to the question as to whether further recruiting among the miners should be encouraged.[21]

The committee had considered and rejected suggestions such as suspending the Eight Hours Act, employing women as surface workers and reducing the age at which boys could work underground from fourteen years of age to thirteen. The one factor which, it was felt, would improve output was a reduction in the rate of absenteeism, which was running at an average of 9.8 per cent across the UK in the first six months of the war and at 10.5 per cent in Wales. It was calculated that if there was no avoidable absenteeism (i.e. other than for sickness) output would be increased by thirteen to fourteen million tons per annum. If this was combined with the loss of exports of twenty-four million tons, the annual loss of output of thirty-six million tons would be restored, providing the workforce was not further depleted by calls from the armed forces. [22]

Crowds on Llandeilo station awaiting a troop train in 1918.   *(NLW, D. C. Harries Collection)*

In the years preceding the war the south Wales coalfield had gained a reputation as being a hotbed of militancy and syndicalism; whether this was justified or not, disputes in 1875, 1898, 1910 and 1912 suggest that there was a tendency to support extremism. In July 1915, to the disbelief and approbation of many both within Wales and outside, the south Wales miners went on strike. At the heart of their grievances was the belief that the colliery owners were using the cover of war to exploit the workforce, while making vast profits for themselves. For this, there is ample evidence. In March, 1915 a headline in the *Western Mail* announced 'Boom in the coal trade', reporting that steam coal had risen in price from 21s. 6d in October 1914 to 30s. by March 1915, a rise of almost 40 per cent. Shares in Powell Dyffryn collieries had risen from 49s. to 56s. 6d in the first three months of 1915.[23] Joseph Shaw, chairman of the company, announced record profits at the annual meeting in March 1915, but then caused deep resentment by suggesting that all public houses should close earlier to reduce absenteeism at the pits. The miners had been confronted by a 24 per cent rise in food costs between July 1914 and March 1915, while working-class living costs had risen by 20 per cent. Consequently, to try and maintain their standard of living the miners sought a substantial wage rise, which they were sure the mine owners were quite capable of paying. In addition, the new wage rates would have no upper limit, they would apply nationally and a daily minimum of 5s. both for underground and surface workers would be introduced.

Wage rates in the south Wales coalfield had last been fixed in 1910 for a period of five years and were due to expire on 1 July 1915, preceded by a three month period of negotiation. As early as February 1915, the South Wales Miners' Federation (SWMF) had set out its stall with a call for a 20 per cent wage increase. The *Western Mail* commented: 'It is difficult to believe that members of the South Wales Miners' Conference want to initiate industrial war whilst the country is engaged in a life and death conflict with a powerful and implacable foe'.[24] The mine owners refused to meet or negotiate, claiming that a new wage agreement was not appropriate in war-time; they offered a simple 10 per cent bonus to alleviate the effects of inflation.

As the deadline of 1 July approached, there was a flurry of meetings involving, at various times, the miners' leaders, the President of the Board of Trade (Walter Runciman), the Chief Industrial Commissioner (George Askwith) and the Minister of Munitions (David Lloyd George). The latter was clear on his standpoint: 'I am not going to have any conflict with miners'.[25] He was to be true to his word. In the first two weeks of July, the situation became increasingly fraught with the colliery owners and miners' leaders displaying self-righteous intransigence. On 13 July, the Munitions of War Act was applied by proclamation to the South Wales coalfield, making it illegal to take part in a strike or lock-out unless certain stringent conditions had been met. This was like a red rag to a bull. The miners felt that they were being singled out by a coercive and unsympathetic government, which only served to stiffen their resolve. In direct contravention of the Act, on 15 July a strike began and by 17 July, 200,000 miners and 700 collieries had stopped working. This had a knock-on effect on the railways and docks, putting a further 250,000 men out of work. For the *Western Mail*, 'a strike would be disastrous to the nation and to the Welsh coalfield, and would be a perpetual reproach against the south Wales miners.'[26] The *South Wales Daily News* was equally critical: 'nothing can defend [the] decision. It is against every interest and conception of patriotism … it is a negation of patriotism and common-sense'.[27] A J.M. Staniforth cartoon in the *Western Mail* showed a collier wallowing in a sewer of 'Disloyalty, Greed and Treachery'. Dame Wales says 'Shame on you! I am disgusted at your conduct, look you! Indeed now, you can be no son of mine to act in such a shocking manner.'[28]

When the strike began, there were 100,000 tons of Welsh coal above ground and another 700,000 tons held in ships, bunkers or ashore. The navy was burning 412,000 tons a month, so the Admiralty calculated that if the strike lasted any longer than seventy-one days, the vast majority of the navy's ships would be immobilised or forced to burn inferior fuel.[29] When the Cabinet met on 19 July, it seemed at first that they would confront the miners, but then softened their line and decided to send Lloyd George to south Wales to make a final appeal on 'patriotic grounds'. The Minister of Munitions, accompanied by two senior Labour Party members, arrived in Cardiff by special train. On 20 July a settlement was reached which effectively conceded all the miners' demands, including new minimum wages (ranging from 33s. per week for a labourer, to 42s. for a ripper), the application of the agreement to SWMF members only, and that the agreement should last beyond the end of the war. Lloyd George, ever the pragmatist, realized that it would be impossible to imprison 200,000 miners for contravening the Munitions of War Act, and therefore a settlement – at whatever cost – had to be reached. On 22 July Lloyd George addressed an open meeting of the miners, showering them with praise for their hard work.

Barry Supple, the foremost historian of the modern coal mining industry, maintains that the 'unyielding and stiff-necked employers' bore a large part of the responsibility for their own humiliation. Their obduracy in the negotiations had 'inflamed the miners, and lost the owners any public sympathy they might have enjoyed'.[30] However, contemporary reactions to the strike were much more hostile. It was claimed that the strike had been fostered by German secret agents and that £60,000 in gold sovereigns had been used to bribe the miners. Bonar

A detachment of the Royal Army Medical Corps marching through Cardiff.

Law, the leader of the Conservative Party and a member of Asquith's coalition government, thought that it would be better to shoot one hundred men in suppressing a strike than to lose thousands in the field as a consequence of it.

Anthony Mòr-O'Brien persuasively argues that the strike of 1915, far from showing the miners to be unpatriotic, was actually due to 'an excess of patriotism which, in the emotion-charged atmosphere of wartime, needed official acknowledgement and reward'.[31] The miners went on strike, he maintains, 'to achieve the higher wages that would be a badge of patriotism, and which would advertise to the world at large the vital contribution which miners were making to the national cause'. Hywel Francis and David Smith, in their history of the SWMF, argue that the strike was a clear expression of 'a growing anti-war feeling', although there is little evidence to support this view.[32]

In 1917, the government set up a 'Committee of Inquiry into Industrial Unrest' which examined the cause of the strike in 1915. The Committee concluded:

> The men were driven to strike by the belief on their part that the owners were 'exploiting' the patriotism of the miners, believing it would inevitably prevent them from pressing home their claim by actually striking. It was this suspected exploitation of their patriotism for the gain of others, and not any lack of patriotism or of a failure to appreciate the national difficulties, that caused them to strike … it is our opinion that, strong as is the men's attachment to certain views as to the future of their industry, their patriotism is stronger.[33]

While one can argue that the south Wales miners were probably more radical than those in other parts of Britain and there was a small but vociferous syndicalist element, the relations between miners and owners were riddled with distrust, suspicion and resentment. The overriding factor which precipitated the strike was an economic one: wartime inflation had pushed prices ahead of wages for the majority of miners. While they might have accepted this in the national interest they were not prepared to do so against a backdrop of increased profits for the mine owners. The miners were not alone in finding difficulties in making ends meet. In the spring of 1915, railwaymen, dockers, council employees, policemen and postal workers in south Wales, had all submitted claims for higher wages – but none was to take strike action.

The most significant outcome of the events of July 1915 was that it led the way towards eventual government control of the mining industry. Following Lloyd George's brokered settlement, disputes between the miners and owners rumbled on. In June 1916, a further 15 per cent wage rise was negotiated, but this was immediately followed by a provocative increase in the price of coal. In turn, this stimulated a new claim by the SWMF for a further 15 per cent increase, submitted on 31 October 1916. They also demanded the right to examine colliery accounts to determine the true level of company profits. The owners then countered with a claim for a 10 per cent reduction in wages because of rising production costs. While *The Times* referred to the 'Curse of South Wales' and the feud which was imperilling the nation's safety, the blame was laid squarely at the door of the owners: 'in no other coalfield is there such strife and distrust of the owners ... They have taken upon themselves to conduct the industry and they have drawn immense wealth from it ... If they cannot conduct it, the sooner it is transferred to someone who can the better'. [34]

The long-running and rancorous dispute had convinced the government that action had to be taken to protect essential supplies of coal for the navy and munitions industry. On 1 December 1916, under the Defence of the Realm Act, the government assumed control over the south Wales collieries. The remainder of the British coal-mining industry followed in March 1917 and formal control was to last until March 1921. The purpose of government control in south Wales was twofold: firstly, to oversee production and distribution, ensuring decisions were always in the national interest; and secondly, to remove the chief cause of industrial unrest by making the miners feel that they were contributing positively to the war effort, rather than lining the pockets of mine owners and shareholders.

The need to balance the mines' requirement for men with the nation's requirement for soldiers remained a constant problem until the end of the war. By January 1917, 26 per cent of the industry's workforce had joined the armed forces, being replaced by entrants from other industries, school leavers or the unemployed. Despite this, the coal mines remained one of the last pools of young, physically fit men on which the government could draw. In January 1917, the War Cabinet decided to call up 20,000 miners throughout Britain, starting with the unskilled and those who had joined the industry since the outbreak of war. The SWMF recommended acceptance of the 'comb-out' scheme, but it was overwhelmingly rejected by a coalfield conference on 2 August 1917, by 236 votes to 25. It was also resolved to hold a coalfield ballot to establish whether or not membership would be in favour of strike action should the government attempt to implement the scheme. The War Cabinet, fearful of strike action and coal supplies being interrupted, thus decided to launch a patriotic campaign in south Wales, to counteract the pacifist and syndicalist attitudes they perceived as being predominant amongst the workforce. General Smuts was dispatched to Wales to organise a series of 'War Aims' meetings in late October and early November 1917 prior to the ballot. He was assisted by a number of MPs from south Wales, including two prominent Labour members, William Brace (immediate past-president of the SWMF) and John Williams (previously miners' agent for the western district of the SWMF). The government campaign was aided by the support of the *South Wales Daily Press* and indeed by a majority of the SWMF executive. The result showed 98,948 votes against and 28,903 votes for strike action should the comb-out scheme be introduced. The historian David Egan concluded that this pro-strike vote of nearly 25 per cent 'represented a firm launching-pad for the anti-war movement in the SWMF to continue the struggle for the rest of the war'.[35]

The miners continued to flex their industrial muscle. In September 1917, they demanded an increase of 1s. 10d per shift to counteract the rising costs of food, which it was estimated had doubled since the outbreak of war. To avoid a protracted dispute they accepted 1s. 6d per shift. In 1918 the coal industry faced its most threatening wartime crisis with a predicted 10 per cent shortfall in output. The government's only real option was to reduce the supply of coal to industry, which it was estimated would cause unemployment of 500,000. In June 1918 the miners demanded a further wage increase of 1s. 6d per shift knowing full well that any threat to production would not be countenanced by the government. By mid-August 1918, the stark reality was that the only way to maintain coal supplies was for men to be released from the armed forces. Throughout Britain, by the time of the armistice, 38,000 former miners were back in the pits from fighting in the war. The political and economic balancing act meant that the war ended with coal supplies being maintained to both the armed forces and essential industries.

AFTERMATH

Barry Supple argues that the greatest effects of the war were felt in wages, profits and industrial relations: 'in these respects the consequences of the War and the way coal was controlled were to be irresistibly long-lasting'. Following the strike in July 1915, the power and influence of the south Wales miners in matters relating to wages, hours, conditions of work and the control of labour supply were all considerably enhanced; this was to remain the case for the duration of the war. For example, the SWMF successfully reduced the hours of surface workers from eleven (including ninety minutes for meals) to eight hours thirty minutes (plus twenty minutes for meals), while successfully resisting any changes in the regulations concerning the employment of women and boys.

At the Miners' Federation of Great Britain annual conference in August 1918, the delegates unanimously accepted a south Wales motion in favour of the state ownership of coal mines with joint control by the workforce and the state. The war had not only boosted the confidence and expectations of the miners, but had also enhanced their economic power. The mine owners had continued to make handsome profits throughout the war. This, coupled with an assumption that future demand was assured, led to complacency and chronic under-investment. From 1918-20, the market for Welsh coal remained buoyant and employment was above pre-war levels. In 1921 the market for coal collapsed, when foreign competition from France, Germany and Poland increased and

Royal Welsh Fusiliers recruiting poster.

government control was withdrawn. After defeat in a bitter and protracted national strike from April-July 1921, wages were significantly reduced. The advances of the war years disappeared.

SLATE QUARRYING

The north Wales slate industry, despite a rapid expansion in the nineteenth century, had faced a depression (despite temporary improvements in 1902 and 1909) in the years leading up to the outbreak of war. This was caused by a decline in demand consequent upon a distressed building trade and also from the competition for a shrinking market from foreign-produced slates and tiles. Unemployment and emigration to such places as Liverpool, south Wales and the United States defined the period. Between 1906 and 1913, the number of employees in the quarries in the Ffestiniog district fell by 28 per cent; in Dyffryn Nantlle the number fell by 38 per cent.[36] The labour force in the Gwynedd slate quarries fell from 17,053 to 11,970 between 1900 and 1914, while the number of operating quarries declined from 84 to 53. This depression marked the first stage in the slate industry's long-term decline and its effects also 'ensured that the pressures of war critically accelerated that decline'.[37]

The effects of the war were immediate and severe. A significant decline in the number of new houses built in the period 1914-16 resulted in the demand for slates falling by 60 per cent. Thereafter, house-building all but ceased until 1919. In addition, the export trade had virtually collapsed (Germany had been a good market) and restrictions on shipping and rail transport hindered sales further. By the end of August 1914, many of the larger quarries operated on a part-time basis, while smaller quarries simply closed down.

In an area with few prospects of alternative employment, the immediate effect was a sharp increase in unemployment. By the end of August 1914, 800 men were out of work in Nantlle, by September 1,100 were unemployed in Caernarfonshire and by October, 400 were unemployed in the Ffestiniog area. This had two effects: firstly, by mid-1915, the North Wales Quarrymen's Union reported that 1,200 of its 8,475 members had moved to seek work in other parts of Britain; secondly, unemployment gave a spur to recruitment for the armed forces. Economic necessity temporarily outweighed any antipathy to the war. In January

1915, the quarrymen's union estimated that 23 per cent of its members of military age had enrolled voluntarily in the armed forces. The manager of the Rhosydd quarry in Ffestiniog formed a small unit of quarrymen to serve in the army, and C.H. Derbyshire, the owner of the Penmaenmawr Quarry formed a 'quarry battalion' of stone-workers from Penmaenmawr, Llanfairfechan and Trefor.[38]

In 1916, the slate industry took an unexpected upward turn with an increased demand for roofing slates, largely for government munitions factories. In 1917 demand increased further as merchants began to build up stocks in anticipation of a post-war boom in house-building. The main problem in satisfying demand was a depleted skilled labour force as a result of enlistment and migration. This situation was further exacerbated in March 1917 when the Director of National Service listed slate-quarrying as a non-essential industry, resulting in quarrymen being sent to carry out essential war work in other areas of Britain. Quarries such as Rhosydd, Craig Ddu, Rhiwbach and Diphwys closed immediately for the remainder of the war.[39] By 1918 the slate industry 'had rarely been in such a parlous state'. The First World War came close to destroying the slate industry; by the end of the war scarcely one-third of the original workforce remained in the quarries.[40] From 1914-18 the number of operating quarries in north Wales fell from 53 to 24 and annual production fell from 256,417 tons to 101,315.[41]

AFTERMATH

The end of the war brought an unexpected and dramatic boom to the slate industry. By July 1920 the price of slates was treble that of wartime; output rose from 164,098 tons in 1919 to 237,350 tons in 1921, while the number of men employed rose from 6,604 to 9,520 in the same period.[42] The minimum rate of pay for a quarryman was 8s. 3d per day in 1919 rising to 12s. 6d by 1920. This boom was largely caused by domestic demand for slates for new houses; export markets had been almost totally lost. The industry flourished until the winter of 1920-1 and then entered a long period of stagnation and crisis. Minimum pay fell to 9s. 4d per day by 1922. The war had not only highlighted the shortage of skilled labour available to the industry, but also had a 'more critical impact as a catalyst affecting the rate of the industry's long term decline.[43] The war hastened the industry's decline and shaped the course of development of slate quarrying in north Wales during the inter-war period.

Politics

When war broke out a political truce between the main political parties was immediately called which lasted until the armistice was signed in 1918. Political and religious differences were subsumed to the greater needs of winning the war. On the national stage, the war totally transformed the career of Wales's foremost politician, David Lloyd George. In 1914 he was still best known as a headstrong radical, on the left of British politics, the arch enemy of privilege and landed wealth. By the time of the armistice he was portrayed as the saviour of the nation, 'the man who won the war'. In O.M. Edwards's journal, *Cymru*, he was depicted as a valorous leader in the Arthurian mould, defending the realm against the barbarian Huns.[44] As both Minister of Munitions from May 1915 and Prime Minister from December 1916, Lloyd George had shown a deftness of political touch which helped to bring victory. His brilliant war-time speeches apparently astonished even Hitler and certainly caught the mood of the nation in need of inspiration. Some would argue that Lloyd George never played down his Welshness and consequently the Welsh nation took great pride that the 'Welsh Wizard' was in Downing Street. Others maintain that 'the Goat' cynically manipulated the account of his background and upbringing to his own political advantage.

The political map of Wales was totally transformed in the years spanning the First World War, with the dominance of the Liberal Party at both local and national level being replaced by that of the Labour Party. The question still being debated by historians is the extent to which the war actually caused changes in Welsh (and British) politics and which therefore explain Labour's triumph over the Liberals. Put another way, if the First World War had not taken place would the Labour Party still have replaced the Liberal party as the dominant force in Welsh politics? Supporters of the 'political change' argument point to the essentially illiberal measures, such as conscription, which had to be introduced by the Liberal Party to win the war. The consequent division between the supporters of Lloyd

Coastal C6, the larger of two types of airship used in the First World War. It was based at Pembroke Royal Naval Air Station, now RAF Carew Cheriton.   *(Courtesy of Adrian James)*

George and Asquith caused a split in the Liberal Party from which it never recovered. The counter-argument stresses structural factors, pointing to the emergence of class politics in late-Victorian and Edwardian Britain as the key factors in the rise of the Labour Party. Following the growth of class tension and conflict and the greater politicization of industrial relations, the decision of trades unions to affiliate to the Labour Party is seen by some historians as a crucial turning point.[45] Chris Williams is even more exact and dates 'the political collapse of the Liberal edifice in the Rhondda valleys' as coming with the Tonypandy riots and the Cambrian Combine strike of 1910.[46] D. Gareth Evans argues that on 'the threshold of the First World War the foundations for Labour's post-war advances had been laid: the Labour movement was organizationally prepared and its infrastructure secure.'[47] The credibility of the Labour Party was also aided by the success of various collectivist measures adopted during the war. The collieries, shipping and the railways all came under government control, exports were restricted, rationing adopted, prices and wages controlled, the opening hours of public houses reduced – even the clocks were put forward an hour in summer. The power of the state was being positively used to defeat an external enemy, giving weight to the Labour Party's assertions that the same power could be used to fight poverty and social injustice.

The war experience, others argue, was not one which automatically benefited the Labour Party. The historian Eddie May maintains that the outbreak of war 'exposed profound differences within the leadership of the party.'[48] There is no evidence that opposition to the war was prevalent amongst the Welsh working class. Army recruitment was higher from within the ranks of the south Wales miners than all other occupational groups. This was at odds with the pacifist views of many members of the hierarchy of the Independent Labour Party. This split was clearly shown in the by-election held in November 1915 on the death of Keir Hardie in the dual-member Merthyr Boroughs constituency.[49] James Winstone, a loyal member of the Independent Labour Party was nominated by the SWMF and Labour Party. His opponent was the former firebrand and extremist Charles Stanton, who in 1893 had been indicted at the Glamorgan assizes for allegedly firing a revolver at the police during a demonstration of striking miners. On the outbreak of war, Stanton became the arch jingoist and patriot. He resigned his position as a miners' agent and stood against Winstone as an independent but with the support of the British Socialist Party.

The campaign was fought primarily on the extent of each candidate's support for the war and who could tap the jingoistic barometer the hardest. Winstone's patriotism was questioned and his followers were accused of being pro-German pacifists. Unbeknown to his supporters and opponents, Stanton received covert financial support from a group of prominent members of the Conservative Party such as H.A. Gwynne (editor of the *Morning Post*), Arthur Steel-Maitland (chairman of the Unionist Party) and Lord Milner (chairman of the National Service League).[50] Stanton comfortably defeated Winstone, securing 10,286 votes to his opponent's 6,080. Stanton commented: 'I interpret my election, which has been contributed to so largely by the south Wales miners, to signify that there is an end for one and for all of lukewarmness or contempt for the great unifying idea of country and Empire'.[51] When Stanton made his maiden speech in the House of Commons on 21 December, he said he was in Westminster to back up the war party, to do all he could as a humble individual to bring the war to a successful conclusion and 'to bring as much trouble, disaster and tribulation as possible to the German "Huns"'.[52] Mòr–O'Brien concluded that 'even in such a constituency, which was reputed to be hostile to the war, the great majority of the voters wanted the war effort to be pursued with unabated vigour'.[53]

While the debate over the explanation for the rise of the Labour Party continues, there is little doubt of the political outcome in parliamentary terms. Put simply, the war was a disaster for the Liberal Party in Wales. In the election of December 1910 the Liberal Party won 26 seats out of 34, with the Conservative Party winning 3 (with majorities of 9, 54 and 299) and the Labour Party 5 seats. In the 'coupon' election of December 1918, called hours after the signing of the armistice, Wales now had 36 constituencies. The country's mandate for a continuation of coalition government was reflected in the Welsh results: the coalitionists won 20

Tea break at a training camp in Pembrokeshire c. 1919.   *(Courtesy of the Roger J. C. Thomas Collection)*

seats (19 Liberal and 1 Conservative), the Labour Party won 10 seats, the Liberal Party 3, the Conservative Party 2 and the National Democratic Party 1. The preponderance of Liberal coalitionists in Wales differed from the national picture, illustrating the residual but waning strength and depth of loyalty to the pre-war Liberal Party. By 1922, the Labour Party had increased its grip winning 18 seats compared to the National Liberals' 9, Conservatives' 6, Liberals' 2 and Independent Labour's 1. Electors who had shown a reluctance to abandon the Liberal Party in 1918 had no such qualms in 1922. The Labour Party dominance of the Welsh political landscape had begun.

NOTES

[1] Quoted in Colin Dakers, *The Countryside at War, 1914-18* (London: Constable, 1987), p. 130.

[2] J. Williams (ed.), *Digest of Welsh Historical Statistics* (Cardiff: Welsh Office, 1985).

[3] Cyril Parry, 'Gwynedd and the Great War, 1914-18', *The Welsh History Review*, 14/1 (1988), 78-117.

[4] Ivor Nicholson and Lloyd Williams, *Wales: Its Part in the War* (London: Hodder and Stoughton, 1922), pp. 210-218.

[5] Ibid., pp. 209-10.

[6] Peter Dewey, 'Agricultural Labour Supply in England and Wales During the First World War', *Economic History Review*, 28/1 (1975), 100-112.

[7] Peter Strong, 'Magor and Undy in the Great War', *Gwent Local History*, 86 (1999), 36-46.

[8] Parry, 'Gwynedd and the Great War'; Nicholson and Williams, *Wales*, pp. 210-11.

[9] Parry, 'Gwynedd and the Great War'.

[10] Nicholson and Williams, *Wales*, pp. 222-6.

[11] John Davies, 'The End of the Great Estates and the Rise of Freehold Farming in Wales', *The Welsh History Review*, 8/2 (1974-5), 186-211.

[12] Ibid.

[13] Ibid.

[14] A.W. Ashby and I.L. Evans, *The Agriculture of Wales and Monmouthshire* (Cardiff: Gwasg Prifysgol Cymru, 1944), p. 87.

[15] David Howell, 'Labour Organization Among Agricultural Workers in Wales, 1872-1921', *The Welsh History Review*, 16/1 (1992), 63-92.

[16] Ibid.

[17] David A. Pretty, 'Undeb Gweithwyr Môn: Anglesey Workers' Union', *Transactions of the Anglesey Antiquarian Society and Field Club*, 1988, 115-148.

[18] Richard Moore-Colyer, 'The End of the Gentry Estates', *Planet*, 172 (2005), 73-82.

[19] Barry Supple, *The History of the British Coal Industry, Vol. 4, 1914-1946: The Political Economy of Decline* (Oxford: Oxford University Press, 1987), p. 11.

[20] Quoted in Supple, *Coal Industry*, p. 43.

[21] *Report of the Departmental Committee Appointed to Enquire into the Conditions Prevailing in the Coal Mining Industry due to the War, 1915*, PP 1914-16, XXVIII, Cd 7939.

22 Ibid.
23 *Western Mail*, 6 March 1915.
24 *Western Mail*, 8 February 1915.
25 Quoted in Supple, *Coal Industry*, p. 66.
26 *Western Mail*, 14 July 1915.
27 *South Wales Daily News*, 16 July 1916.
28 *Western Mail*, 17 July 1915.
29 J.D. Davies, *Britannia's Dragon: A Naval History of Wales* (Stroud: The History Press, 2013), p. 196.
30 Supple, *Coal Industry*, p. 65.
31 Anthony Mòr-O'Brien, 'Patriotism on Trial: The Strike of the South Wales Miners, July 1915', *The Welsh History Review*, 12 (1984), 76-104.
32 Hywel Francis and David Smith, *The Fed: A History of the South Wales Miners in the Twentieth Century* (London: Lawrence & Wishart, 1980), p. 22.
33 *Commission of Enquiry into Industrial Unrest, 1917*, PP 1917-18, XV, Cd 8668.
34 *The Times*, 22 November 1916, 27 November 1916.
35 David Egan, 'The Swansea Conference of the British Council of Soldiers' and Workers' Delegates, July 1917: Reactions to the Russian Revolution of February, 1917, and the Anti-war Movement in South Wales', *Llafur*, 1/4 (1975), 12-37.
36 R. Merfyn Jones, *The North Wales Quarrymen, 1874-1922* (Cardiff: University of Wales Press, 1982), p. 295.
37 Parry, 'Gwynedd and the Great War'.
38 Ibid.
39 Ibid.
40 Jones, *North Wales Quarrymen*, p. 259.
41 Parry, 'Gwynedd and the Great War'.
42 Ibid.
43 Ibid.
44 Quoted in Geraint H. Jenkins, *A Concise History of Wales* (Cambridge: Cambridge University Press, 2007), p. 252.
45 Eddie May, 'Charles Stanton and the Limits to "Patriotic" Labour', *The Welsh History Review*, 18/3 (1997), 483-508.
46 Chris Williams, *Democratic Rhondda: Politics and Society 1885-1951* (Cardiff: University of Wales Press, 1996), p. 83.
47 D. Gareth Evans, *A History of Wales 1906-2000* (Cardiff: University of Wales Press, 2000), p. 84.
48 Eddie May, 'The Mosaic of Labour Politics', 1900-1918', in Duncan Tanner, Chris Williams and Deian Hopkin (eds), *The Labour Party in Wales, 1900-2000* (Cardiff: University of Wales Press, 2000), 61-85.
49 Anthony Mòr-O'Brien, 'The Merthyr Boroughs Election, November 1915', *The Welsh History Review*, 12 (1984-5), 538-566.
50 Barry M. Doyle, 'Who Paid the Price of Patriotism? The Funding of Charles Stanton during the Merthyr Boroughs By-Election of 1915', *English Historical Review*, Nov 1994, 1215-1222.
51 *Western Mail*, 29 November, 1915.
52 *Western Mail*, 22 December 1915.
53 Mòr-O'Brien, 'Merthyr Boroughs Election'.

Chapter 11

VADs, FANYs and Munitionettes

Women and the challenges of war

—⟋⟋⟋—

WOMEN PLAYED A VITAL ROLE in the First World War whether in the manufacture of shells, as a munitionette, as a nurse or Voluntary Aid Detachment behind the front line, as a tram conductor supporting the transport system, or as a wife or mother keeping the home fires burning. Without their contribution the war could not have been won. However, historians are still debating about the effects that the war had on women's social and economic status and how far any positive changes carried through to the post-war world. Some argue that the war eventually brought about a transformation in the lives of women, while others, often labelled the 'new feminist pessimists' thought that the war changed absolutely nothing.

In 1911 there were 215,681 females in Wales (23.6 per cent) classified as 'occupied' (i.e. in employment) and 696,687 (76.4 per cent) as 'unoccupied'. This economic activity rate was considerably lower than that of England which was above 32 per cent. This can be explained by the limited job opportunities available to women in Wales, especially in manufacturing and the fact that in many parts of the country, women gave up paid employment on marriage. There were regional variations within Wales also: in 1911, one in three Cardiganshire women was in paid employment but in Glamorgan it was only one in five. In a study of Pontypridd in war-time, Lisa Snook found only 18 per cent of women were classified as occupied. The locality was dominated by heavy industry considerably reducing job opportunities. Additionally, the prevailing attitude was against women – and especially married women – working outside the home.[1] Of those in employment in Wales, 42 per cent worked in domestic service, with 15.5 per cent working as dressmakers, 13.1 per cent in food, drink and tobacco, 9.4 per cent in agriculture and 8.5 per cent in professional occupations. About 90 per cent of women employed before the war were single and they were overwhelmingly working class. It should also be noted that 17 per cent of women in Wales in this period did not marry and a high proportion of them would have had to earn a living.

The immediate effect of the outbreak of war was to cause an increase in women's unemployment in Wales. In September 1914, it was reported that women and girls were losing their jobs in Cardiff as those from the upper socio-economic classes cut back on their expenditure; domestic servants, dressmakers, milliners, shop assistants and hotel workers all suffered. Fourteen prominent firms had put women workers on half-time.[2] In Swansea, women's unemployment doubled between December 1913 and December 1914. Although it was unforeseen in the period before October 1914, there were soon indications that the war-time economy would need to tap into the female labour pool to make up for the shortfall in the workforce caused by enlisting men. Furthermore, the war brought with it a stimulus to the economy which also benefited female employment. For example, the Ben Evans store in Swansea won a contract to supply 15,000 blankets and thousands of shirts, pants, vests and service-caps. In October 1914, the West Wales Flannel Manufacturing Company was contracted to supply 150,000 shirts.[3] These were, of course, related to the traditional fields of peace-time employment for women, but in 1915 women began to be employed in non-industrial jobs that were new to them, such as in transport or office work.

Substitution, the extensive use of women in place of men in the workplace, really took hold from the summer of 1915 onwards. From August, for example, the Cardiff telephone exchange was entirely staffed by women and in September, Barry saw female 'postmen'. Women were employed on the trams in Cardiff, Swansea and the Rhondda. Cardiff Corporation Tramways employed some sixty women conductors by

November 1915 and also some female tram drivers, despite the initial refusal of men to work with them.[4] The Cardiff Tramways Association had been particularly vociferous in protesting against the employment of married women whose husbands were in regular work. Women took up driving delivery vehicles for the Co-operative Society and in Cardiff, the first woman taxi driver took to the road in November 1915.[5] Employed women also moved from traditional areas of employment such as domestic service and textiles and clothing to the more lucrative munitions and engineering work. Also, new women workers were brought into the workplace, predominantly young, working class and single. Another group which came into its own in war-time was married women who had

Group of female workers employed at a brickworks in south Wales, c1917.   *(Imperial War Museum)*

previously been told that their place was in the home; some firms had a definite policy of employing soldiers' wives.[6] It is hard to find specific evidence for Wales, but in Britain as a whole, it was estimated that the average pre-war pay for women was 13s. 6d per week which rose to 30-35s. by the end of the war.[7] Even allowing for wartime inflation and wage rates being lower in Wales than England, it is clear that women were being better paid than they had been previously. It was not only the economic benefits which were attractive to Welsh women; they also enjoyed the social benefits of working as part of a team, making new friends and a new-found independence.

Female munitions workers, Queensferry, 1917.

(Courtesy of Flintshire Record Office)

The greatest demand for women workers, and the area where most opportunities for employment existed, was in munitions factories. As Gail Braybon has identified, 'the process of dilution (the breaking down of a task previously done by a skilled men into a number of smaller operations), agreements admitting women to work "customarily done by men" and large scale recruitment by the Ministry of Munitions led to the major influx of thousands of women into the munitions factories from 1915 onwards'.[8] Government run National Shell Factories were set up in Cardiff, Llanelli, Newport, Uskside, Swansea, Porthmadog and Wrexham. There was an explosives works in Queensferry and Alfred Nobel's works in Pembrey, both of which were taken over by the government. It was estimated by the Board of Trade that at least 5,000 women were employed in munitions' production in south Wales, but these numbers were dwarfed by those who worked in the explosives factories: 2,500 were employed in Queensferry and 8,000 or so in Pembrey.[9] The working conditions in munitions factories were variable, with the best National Factories providing canteens, proper changing and wash rooms and welfare and recreational facilities. However, the Factory Acts were effectively put aside for the duration of the war, meaning that many women worked in dangerous and insanitary conditions reminiscent of the worst Victorian factories. The most dangerous workplaces were the factories producing high explosives in Queensferry and Pembrey. In 1916 *The Lancet* itemized the dangers of manufacturing TNT: 'nasal discomfort, nose bleeds, smarting eyes, headaches, sore throat, tight chest, coughs, pains in the stomach, nausea, constipation alternating with diarrhoea and skin rashes'. These were followed by 'anorexia, giddiness, the swelling of hands and feet, drowsiness and finally death'. In 1917 and 1918 at Queensferry, 3,813 acid burns, 2,128 eye injuries, 763 cases of industrial dermatitis were treated and 12,778 accidents occurred. Fatal accidents were not uncommon.

The working conditions in Pembrey were described by Miss G.M. West, a member of the Women's Police Service, with a supervisory role over the women in the factory: 'the TNT stinks, no other word describes it, an evil sickly chokey smell that makes you feel sick'. However, this was nothing compared to the area where nitric acid was turned into oleum:

The air is filled with white fumes and yellow fumes & brown fumes. The particles of acid land on your face & make you nearly go mad with a feeling like pins & needles, only more so, & they land on your clothes & make brown spots all over them and they rot your hankies so that they come back from the laundry in rags & they get up your nose & down your throat & into your eyes, so that you are blind and speechless by the time you escape ... Each time you emerge ... you feel like Dante returning from hell.[10]

West described Pembrey as 'the back of beyond ... the most desolate spot in the world'. The factory was built in the sandy hills known as The Burrows, a few miles outside the town. The workforce came from all over south Wales; some were from 'the lonely little sheep farms in the mountains' and spoke only Welsh, 'or a very little broken English & are very good sorts though rough'. Others were 'the wives and relations of the miners from the Rhonda Valley'. They were 'full of socialistic theories and perpetually getting up strikes in true Tonypandy style'. However, they 'were very easily influenced by a little oratory & as soon as they ... made up their minds to "go back" they became as meek as little lambs'. There were also some women from the Swansea docks area, 'bad characters ... a mixed lot & are to some extent a different type from the other Welsh girls with a good deal of German blood with a large admixture of other races, including blacks'. Overall, West thought the workers were 'very rough' and their language was 'sometimes too terrible'. They were 'very impressionable, quite friendly one moment & shrieking with rage, & almost ready to tear one in pieces the next'.[11]

Despite the appalling working conditions and risks to health, for many women work in the munitions and explosives factories offered an escape and a degree of social and economic independence previously denied to them. Certainly compared to domestic service (the most common pre-war employment for women in Wales) munitions work offered an escape from badly paid drudgery and servility to far better paid employment, a reliable income and an improved standard of living. The woman's role in making weapons of war also placed them directly at the forefront of the war effort; they were doing their bit in what was previously a totally male environment. Angela Woollacott argues that munitions workers became 'a powerful symbol of modernity'.[12]

The significant expansion of women's uniformed services offered a plethora of new employment and volunteering opportunities. On the outbreak of war, there were two organizations for military nurses: the Queen Alexandra's Imperial Military Nursing Service and the Territorial Force Nursing Service, which jointly employed 3,000 women across Britain. In addition, there were opportunities for volunteers to serve in the First Aid Nursing Yeomanry (FANYs) established in 1907 and the Voluntary Aid Detachments (VADs) formed in 1910 under the auspices of the Red Cross and St John's Ambulance Brigade. One Voluntary Aid Detachment consisted of 23 women, but 'VAD' soon came to mean an individual nurse. In Glamorgan, 112 detachments were formed to staff 48 hospitals which opened in the county during the war, treating 30,000 men. Some 74,000 women from Britain were to become VADs and the number of military nurses rose from 2,600 in 1914 to 18,000 by 1918.

Margaret and Gwendoline Davies, grand-daughters of David Davies, Llandinam, nineteenth-century industrial magnate and politician, managed to achieve something which few other women did – they got out

Gwendoline and Margaret Davies (Llandinam) with French soldiers outside a cantine in northern France in 1916. The sisters are the two women centre right. Dora Herbert Jones, who became their Secretary at Gregynog, is the woman on the extreme right.

to France. The sisters volunteered through the London committee of the French Red Cross, wearing the Red Cross uniform of a blue or white dress, a white apron with a large red cross and a headdress of a gauze veil and a dark blue nurse's cap. They were not in any way qualified as nurses and were mainly concerned with the welfare of the ordinary soldier, or *poilu*, in the French army. Groups of women operated canteens at railway stations, convalescent hospitals and transit camps, supplying the troops with coffee, snacks and cigarettes. The volunteers had to meet the costs of the huts from which they operated and fund their own accommodation and living expenses. This inevitably meant that only women from the upper classes could afford to do such work. In July 1916, Gwendoline Davies set up a canteen on the outskirts of Troyes, a transit camp for soldiers on their way up the line to Verdun, which became known as the 'Cantine des Dames Anglaises'. It offered a reading room and a refreshment room complete with gramophone. Les Dames Anglaises had to buy food for the canteen and keep it clean, but their main task was to serve endless cups of coffee and to distribute cigarettes. They also 'provided writing paper and magazines, decorated the canteen with flowers and pictures, kept the gramophone going with a mix of patriotic songs and popular music, washed the dishes, talked to the soldiers, and coped where necessary with the amorous or drunk *poilu*'.[13] Margaret Davies kept a journal throughout this period, vividly describing not only the mundane work in the canteen but also her visits to the battlefields of the Somme and Ypres and the destroyed city of Verdun. The sisters also faced physical danger when working at a canteen in Châlons-sur-Marne, a few miles from the front line and within the sounds of gunfire. In her journal Margaret Davies reflects that she found her time in Troyes a liberating experience, as she was respected by the soldiers and her fellow workers for herself and not for her wealth or social position.[14]

While wearing a nurse's uniform was deemed perfectly acceptable and womanly, the appearance of women in more masculine and militaristic uniforms offended many and even led to accusations of lesbianism. However, the exigencies of war-time necessitated more police, especially in supervisory roles such as that of Miss G.M. West at Pembrey. Many regular police constables had volunteered for service in the army leading to a shortage of police officers throughout Wales. For example, in July

1917 there were 26 vacancies in the Carmarthenshire county police force, rising to 44 by October 1918.[15] In Wales, two organizations recruited women: the Women's Patrols of the National Union of Women Workers (NUWW), which was a middle class, voluntary organization, had a primarily moral function rescuing homeless girls from railway stations, flushing out courting couples from the shadows of doorways and parks and trying to stop prostitutes plying their trade; and, the Women's Police Service (WPS), an altogether different type of organization, being paid, with a uniform and official authority.

For those women preferring a more rural environment, the shortage of agricultural labour became critical from 1916 onwards. There was both a need to replace those men who had joined up in the armed forces, and also to fill the places of women who had left the land to seek higher wages – and perhaps greater freedom – working in munitions factories or other work in the war-time economy. In March 1917 a new Women's Land Army (WLA) was established, open to women of all classes with the aim of providing a permanent skilled and mobile female labour force. Significantly, WLA members were to be paid less than unskilled male agricultural labourers. The WLA's own handbook reminded its members that they were 'doing a man's work' and would be dressed 'rather like a man', but were warned 'that just because you wear a smock and breeches you should take care to behave like a British girl who expects chivalry and respect from everyone she meets'.[16]

A milestone was reached in 1917 with the introduction of National Service for Women (NSW), which Deirdre Beddoe has called 'the most startling innovation of the First World War'.[17] It was the first time that the state had made an official demand on women, saying in effect 'Your Country Needs You'. Through the National Service Scheme women were recruited not only for the Women's Land Army, but also the new Women's Army Auxiliary Corps (WAAC), the Women's Royal Naval service (WRNS) and the Women's Royal Auxiliary Air Force (WRAAF). The arrival of the Wrens in the naval base in Holyhead caused a stir, when a senior naval officer discovered that his coding office was 'full of them'. He opined that if he had his way he 'wouldn't have a woman within a hundred miles of any naval base'. He promptly issued strict orders about what the Wrens could and couldn't do, where they could and couldn't go and so forth. Apparently within a few months the same senior naval officer married one of the Wrens.[18]

Margaret Haig Mackworth, daughter of D.A. Thomas (later Lord Rhondda), was appointed as commissioner of the NSW organization in Wales. She had been a militant suffragette prior to the war, attacking Prime Minister Asquith's car in the general election of 1910 and being imprisoned in 1913 for committing arson by setting light to a pillar box. In May 1915, returning from America, she was aboard the *Lusitania* when it was torpedoed off the Irish coast. She was rescued after hours in the freezing water and having survived the ordeal, she was determined to play her own part in the war. She organized meetings and rallies throughout Wales to try and encourage women to join the NSW. Despite her efforts she was disappointed with the small number of Welsh women who volunteered. The first contingent of some fifty women left Cardiff for France in June 1917 to work as clerks. Lord Penrhyn's daughter, Violet Douglas-Pennant, was appointed as the second commandant of the new Women's Royal Air Force (WRAF) in June 1918. This organization had superseded the WRAAF in April 1918 and was beset with difficulties from the outset. Her predecessor as commandant had lasted just one month in post. Douglas-Pennant found 14,000 WRAF supervised by only seventy-five officers, scattered over 500 camps. Many girls were without their promised uniforms, living in poor conditions and were undisciplined and prone to strike. Despite throwing herself into her work Douglas-Pennant was dismissed two months after her appointment; this owed more to her refusal to kow-tow to senior Air Force officers than to any deficiencies on her part.

The vast majority of women in Wales during the war were not employed or in uniform, but either chose or had no alternative but to 'keep the home fires burning'. The most immediate effect on the families of those who had enlisted in 1914 was to cause hardship. Although some employers such as the Ocean Coal Company in the Rhondda paid a reduced wage to those who enlisted, most families had to rely on the newly introduced separation allowances. The administrative structure for payments creaked and groaned under the weight of applications, in much the same way as the machinery for enlistment had done. Women had to prove their marital status by sending in their marriage licence and this frequently led to a delay in payment. It was indicative of the status of women at the time that payments were only to be made on their good behaviour. Police forces across Wales were instructed to monitor the behaviour of women as it was feared that this new financial independence might lead to drunkenness and debauchery. W. Picton Philipps, Chief Constable of Carmarthenshire, issued a general order entitled 'Cessation of Army Separation Allowances to the Unworthy':

> The allowances granted to the wives and dependants of soldiers are now on a more liberal scale than hitherto, and the result has been to put into the hands of many of them larger sums than they have ever previously enjoyed; this has happened at a time when these women are deprived of the company and guidance of their husbands and are subject sometimes to extreme anxiety, at other times to natural feelings of pride and exultation. In these circumstances, many who ordinarily are quiet and well conducted are exposed to special temptations, and may be led momentarily to careless spending of money and excessive drinking not in accordance with their ordinary habits.[19]

The police officers were instructed not to arrest women immediately, but to give a clear warning in the first instance and only proceed to lay charges if it was clear that a warning would have little effect. The chairman of the bench in Tredegar wrote to the *Caerphilly Journal* saying that he thought it was 'full time to make an example of some of the women whose husbands were at the front' and that 'it was a scandalous thing how some of these women misconducted themselves both as regards drink and misbehaviour'.[20]

Rapidly rising food prices were a challenge to the women who had to feed a family. By the spring of 1915 most basic foodstuffs had risen in price by 60-75 per cent. By November 1918, retail food prices were 133 per cent higher than in July 1914 and the working-class cost of living was calculated to have risen by 120-125 per cent in the same period. While wages also rose, often they did not keep pace with prices: between July 1914 and November 1918, the average wage per shift in the south Wales and Monmouthshire coalfield, for an adult working underground, rose from 7s. 8d to 15s7d, a rise of 103 per cent.[21] Shortages of basic foodstuffs such as bread, potatoes, butter, milk, meat and eggs, especially in the towns, became a progressively greater headache as the war continued. The severe

NATIONAL SERVICE
WOMEN'S
LAND ARMY

GOD SPEED THE PLOUGH
AND THE WOMAN WHO DRIVES IT

APPLY FOR ENROLMENT FORMS AT YOUR NEAREST POST OFFICE OR
EMPLOYMENT EXCHANGE

A recruiting poster for the Women's Land Army, part of the National Service for Women introduced in 1917.

winter of 1916-17 devastated the potato crop, a staple of the Welsh working-class diet. In March 1917, a shopkeeper in Caernarfon had his scales smashed by angry women and the next week faced a militant crowd who fought over his two sacks of potatoes. A riot broke out in Wrexham when women fought over a cartload of potatoes in the town square; some women fainted and the police had to be called to disperse the mob.[22]

The psychological pressures of war, caused by the pain, anxiety and uncertainties of loved ones fighting abroad, are impossible to measure. For nearly all women, this was a completely new set of circumstances, with no established pattern of response or support network to fall back on. Elizabeth Mundy from Llanelli became severely depressed because of her husband's absence in the army. She walked into the sea, drowned her two-year-old son and unsuccessfully tried to commit suicide. She was rescued and subsequently charged with murder and remanded in custody. Her husband, Sergeant Frank Mundy, 13th Battalion Welsh Regiment, returned from France and pleaded his wife's case at a second hearing; she was acquitted.[23] The Scott family of Aberavon was hit by tragedy unimagined in 1914; Private John Scott, 1/4th Battalion Welsh regiment, apparently committed suicide by drowning in Port Talbot docks on 3 September 1915. He was aged fifty-one and working as a cook at Vivian Camp in Port Talbot. In the previous month both of his sons had been killed: Sergeant John Scott, of the same Battalion as his father, was killed in action at Gallipoli on 14 August 1915, while his brother had died of wounds at sea three days earlier. Private John Scott was buried with full military honours and at the inquest into his death the coroner sympathetically recorded an open verdict. This would have given his wife some small degree of solace, having lost a husband and two sons within the space of three weeks.[24]

Pamela Michael described the case of Janet W., a mother of thirty-five with three young children. She had received a telegram informing her that her husband was 'missing in action', followed by a second telegram reporting that he had been killed in action. The shock of the news left her in such a distraught state that she was committed to Denbigh Asylum. She claimed that someone had tried to poison her and that the room was full of poisonous gas. Her husband had in fact survived the war, returning home to find his wife in the asylum and his children taken to Liverpool. Janet W. remained in the asylum until her death in 1957 and apparently her children visited her once a year.[25] The uncertainty and unreliability of news from the front line, even in official communications, caused untold stress to women and families at home. The mother of Private David Jones from Carmarthen was told in September 1914 that her son was missing in action. It was not until two years later she was officially informed that her son had been killed in action on 26 September 1916. Mr and Mrs William Parry received a telegram from the War Office on 11 May 1917 which stated 'deeply regret to inform you that 2nd Lieut H. Parry, King's Royal Rifle Corps, was killed in action on 6 May 1917'. The parents had actually received a letter from their son also dated 6 May, saying that he was in hospital where he had been for some weeks, but that he was making a good recovery. They received a further letter from him on 8 May confirming this and Lieutenant Parry survived the war. Myfanwy Thomas, daughter of the poet Edward Thomas, remembered the reaction of her mother to the devastating news of the death of her father: 'Mother fetched our coats and we went shivering out into the sunny April afternoon. I clutched her hand, half-running to keep up with her quick firm step, glancing continually up at the graven face that did not turn to meet my look ... I waited with dry mouth and chilled heart, outside the post office, while wires were sent off to Mother's sisters.[26]

Apart from paid employment, Welsh women threw themselves into the war in all sorts of ways, whether it was knitting socks for soldiers at the front, arranging accommodation for Belgian refugees or raising funds for local and national war charities. The Davies sisters of Llandinam, before their work in the *cantines* of northern France, had focused their efforts on the plight of Belgian refugees. Their plan was to bring Belgian artists to Wales where they could work in safety and also inspire the country's art students. Two representatives travelled to Belgium in September 1914 and assembled a group of ninety-one refugees including the sculptor George Minne and the painters Valerius de Saedeleer and Gustave van de Woestijne. All three families were to spend the rest of the war as refugees, largely dependent on the Davies family for support. Isolated from the Belgian community and with no contact with other artists, the war years proved to be not only lonely but also artistically unproductive. However, the later work of all three artists was to be profoundly influenced by their Welsh exile.[27]

The women's suffrage movement in Wales, and the rest of Britain, responded to the outbreak of war by officially suspending its campaign of action and militancy. This brought a reciprocal response from the Home Secretary, Reginald McKenna, on 10 August 1914 to unconditionally release all suffragette prisoners. The Women's Social and Political Union (WSPU) then began a fervent anti-German campaign and subordinated women's interests to war propaganda; the National Union of Women's Suffrage Societies (NUWSS) adopted a similar patriotic stand. Emmeline Pankhurst spoke in Aberdare in October 1915, calling for the people of Wales 'to rally round the old flag as one man [sic] with only one aim – that of annihilating German militarism and its concomitant oppression and savagery'.[28] Sylvia Pankhurst was critical of the WSPU, as it was 'entirely departed from the suffrage movement' concentrating its energies 'wholly to the prosecution of the war ... its Chauvinism unexampled amongst all other women's societies.'[29] When Christabel Pankhurst spoke in Llandrindod Wells on 4 August 1917, she denounced any open 'talk of peace and compromise urging renewed and substantial determination to secure complete victory'.[30] It was indicative of the change of direction of the WSPU that in October 1915 its journal changed title from *The Suffragette* to *Britannia*. In November 1917 the WSPU became the Women's Party.

The question of how far women's contribution to the war effort related to their achievement of the franchise is open to debate. Few politicians supported women's suffrage on the grounds of the work they had performed during the war; essentially, the argument for female enfranchisement had been won before 1914 and all that was required was

Soldiers and staff at Plas Trescawen, Anglesey, a military convalescent hospital.

(Courtesy of the Anglesey Archives, WSH/15/2)

specific terms acceptable to Parliament. However, Ryland Wallace argues that 'women's vital contribution to the war effort as munitions workers and in other roles won universal recognition, accelerated social change, made female involvement in the public sphere less threatening and shifted opinion in favour of enfranchisement'.[31] Deirdre Beddoe argues that women did not achieve the vote as a reward for their wartime services: 'winning the franchise was the result of sixty years of campaigning. What their contribution to the war effort did was to make it impossible to deny them their rights any longer'.[32]

The support that WSPU gave to the prosecution of the war certainly did not harm the cause of reform to the franchise either. Also, the part played by Lloyd George should not be underestimated in that he had consistently supported the principle of female enfranchisement. In March 1918 when a deputation of women's organizations met with him, Mrs Edward, speaking on behalf of the women of Wales, went as far as to say that if women gained the vote 'the Wales of the future will be cheerier and brighter than the Wales of the past, and that a crown of blessing would be placed on the Prime Minister's head'.[33] As Prime Minister, Lloyd George had feared that electoral reform might cause a split in the coalition, with the Conservatives arguing that domestic party controversies were not the business of the coalition. He stuck to his guns, but with characteristic wiliness ensured that the he distanced himself from the actual legislation.

The Representation of the People Act (1918) will always be synonymous with votes for women, yet the act primarily dealt with male suffrage, seeking to put right an unexpected consequence of the war: that men who had lost their residential qualifications for twelve months' continuous occupation through service overseas, would be potentially disenfranchised. The Act extended the franchise to women aged over thirty who were themselves ratepayers or were married to a ratepayer. The intention was to only give the vote to stable, mature women rather than the single, young, impressionable munitionettes. The Act was passed with barely a ripple, the pre-war activists being unable to claim a resounding victory for their pre-war campaign. The Welsh electorate expanded from about 430,000 to over 1,172,000, although women remained significantly in the minority.

AFTERMATH

There is no doubt that the expansion of the war economy allowed women to make a positive and valued contribution to the war effort. As a consequence, the whole emphasis of a woman's role in society changed; she was granted an enhanced status for the period of the war. The central question is whether the war years laid the foundation for a new pathway to the future for women, or whether the period was an inconsequential and temporary detour, almost taking women back to the point where they had started. In terms of employment for women, there was depressingly little change. As already stated, in Wales in 1911, 215,181 women (23.64 per cent) were classified as occupied; by 1921 this figure had fallen to 213,149 (21.18 per cent). Wales still fell some way behind England where the female participation rate was over 32 per cent in 1921. As in pre-war days, there were significant regional variations due to both economic and social factors: 24 per cent of women were in paid work in Cardiganshire, whereas in the Rhondda the figure was only 12.5 per cent. This pattern of falling female participation rates in Wales continued in the decade 1921-31. Where some small change did take place was in the type of work in which women were employed. In 1921, domestic service still remained the single largest occupation, employing 78,471 women, showing a fall of 12,025 since 1911. Domestic servants made up 36.8 per cent of the occupied female workforce, a fall of 5.2 per cent since 1911. Those working in textiles and fabrics fell by 2 per cent and those involved in dressmaking fell by 7 per cent in the same period. Areas of growth were in professional occupations which employed 8.5 per cent of the female workforce in 1911 rising to 11.2 per cent in 1921. The number of female employees involved in transport rose from 683 (0.3 per cent) in 1911 to 4,214 (2.0 per cent) in 1921. Although this sector only employed a small number of women, it

Female munitions workers walk beside the horse-drawn hearse of one of their colleagues, killed at work in Pembrey. They are wearing their factory uniforms as a sign of respect during the funeral procession through Swansea. *(Imperial War Museum)*

was symbolically important that this rise had occurred, given what had happened during the war. Agricultural employment fell from 9.4 per cent of the workforce in 1911 to 5.3 per cent in 1921, a reduction of 8,826 employees. It should be remembered that many women, both married and single, would have been working full-time on family farms, but would not have been classified as 'occupied'.

These figures show a depressing lack of progress in terms of both the number of women employed in Wales and also the type of work they were doing. While working women had been rightly lauded during the war for their contribution to the war economy, no sooner had the armistice been signed than the expected role of women in society altered dramatically. Working women were criticized for being 'pin-money girls' and for stealing men's jobs. Across Wales, women were dismissed as they were expected to make way for men and to revert to their primary role as wives, mothers and daughters. Beddoe concluded that the 'old patriarchal attitudes had merely been put on ice for the duration of the war ... women were seen as having got above themselves and had to be knocked back into shape and into a position of dependency on men'.[34] Men's conception of the role of women in society remained largely what it was before the war. The foundations of the male-dominated society had experienced a brief tremble; it would be many decades before the edifice tumbled.

NOTES

1 Lisa Snook, '"Out of the Cage": Women and the First World War in Pontypridd', *Llafur*, 8/2 (2001), 75-88.
2 *Western Mail*, 26 September 1914.
3 Deirdre Beddoe, *Out of the Shadows: A History of Women in Twentieth Century Wales* (Cardiff: University of Wales Press, 2000), p. 57.
4 Ibid., p. 58.
5 Deirdre Beddoe, 'Munitionettes, Maids and Mams: Women in Wales 1914-1939', in Angela V. John (ed.), *Our Mothers' Land: Chapters in Welsh Women's History 1830-1939* (Cardiff: University of Wales Press, 1991), 189-209.
6 Gail Braybon, *Women Workers in the First World War* (London: Routledge, 1989), p. 49.
7 Ibid., p. 116.
8 Ibid., p. 116.
9 Beddoe, *Out of the Shadows*, p. 61.
10 IWM, The Diary of Miss G.M. West, 77/156/1.
11 Ibid.
12 Angela Woollacott, *On Her Their Lives Depend* (London: University of California Press, 1994), p. 3.
13 Oliver Fairclough, '"Knocked to Pieces": The Impact of the Great War', in Oliver Fairclough (ed.), '"Things of Beauty": What two Sisters did for Wales' (Cardiff:: National Museum of Wales Books, 2007), 61-80.
14 Ibid.
15 Carmarthenshire Archives Service (CAS), Carmarthenshire County Council (CCC) Minutes, Standing Joint Committee, 10 July 1917, 8 October 1918.
16 www.womenslandarmy.co.uk
17 Beddoe, *Out of the Shadows*, p. 68.
18 J.D. Davies, *Britannia's Dragon: A Naval History of Wales* (Stroud: The History Press, 2013), p. 202.
19 CAS, CCC, Minutes of the Joint Standing Committee, 30 November 1914.
20 *Caerphilly Journal*, 4 January 1915.
21 A.L. Bowley, *Prices and Wages in the United Kingdom 1914-19* (Oxford: Clarendon Press, 1921), p. 157.
22 Beddoe, *Out of the Shadows*, p. 50.
23 *Llanelly Mercury*, 16 August 1917, 6 September 1917, 13 September 1917.
24 *Carmarthen Journal*, 9 September 1915.
25 Pamela Michael, *Care and Treatment of the Mentally Ill in North Wales, 1800-2000* (Cardiff: University of Wales Press, 2003), p. 117.
26 Myfanwy Thomas, *One of These Fine Days* (Manchester: Carcanet New Press, 1982), p. 62.
27 Fairclough, "Knocked to Pieces", p. 65.
28 Ryland Wallace, *The Women's Suffrage Movement in Wales, 1866-1928* (Cardiff: University of Wales Press, 2009), p. 221.
29 Ibid., p. 220.
30 *Radnorshire Standard*, 11 August 1917.
31 Wallace, *The Women's Suffrage Movement*, p. 248.
32 Beddoe, *Out of the Shadows*, p. 72.
33 Wallace, *The Women's Suffrage Movement*, p. 245.
34 Beddoe, *Out of the Shadows*, p. 74.

Chapter 12

'A Righteous War ... a Holy Crusade'

Organised religion and the war

—⟋𝒲⟍—

THROUGHOUT THE NINETEENTH CENTURY, Welsh Nonconformity had been a by-word for international peace and co-operation. In most parts of Wales, and especially in rural areas, the chapels still exercised great moral and social authority. In 1914, approximately 20 per cent of the total population of Wales was a Nonconformist communicant and there was a chapel for every 400 persons living in Wales. There were 124,800 members of the Baptist Church, 184,800 Calvinistic Methodists, 42,000 Baptists and 159,750 Congregationalists. In addition, there were 155,500 Easter Day communicants of the Anglican Church.[1] The actual numbers do not give a complete picture: the tentacles of the chapels reached far wider than their membership; virtually every facet of Welsh life was subject to their influence. Chapels and churches remained the centre of social life for many communities.

When the First World War broke out the response of the churches and chapels in Wales was one of near unanimous support, most surprisingly including the Nonconformist denominations. While there were a number of individual ministers in Wales who voiced serious doubts about Britain's entry to the war, such as Thomas Rees, John Puleston Jones, Herbert Morgan and T.E. Nicholas, they were the exception. One, now notorious, photograph taken in the garden of 11 Downing Street, of Chancellor of the Exchequer David Lloyd George with Sir Henry Jones (philosopher

Battle of the St Quentin Canal (Saint-Quentin). Prisoners in a Clearing Depot, Abbeville, 2nd October 1918.

(Imperial War Museum)

and former Calvinistic Methodist minister) and Revd John Williams, in full Welsh Army Corps uniform and clerical collar, encapsulates how Welsh Nonconformity had come to be associated with the political establishment of the day. The influence and rhetorical skills of the honey-tongued Lloyd George have often been cited as a major reason why so many Nonconformists pushed aside their long-held pacifist views and discarded all that was distinctive in the Christian faith and ethic. Lloyd George was able to put forward convincing arguments that Britain was fighting a just war against bourgeois militarism which was almost an incarnation of evil. Furthermore, in entering the war to support Belgium, Lloyd George argued that the motive was one of 'purest chivalry to defend the weak ... [the] poor little neighbour whose home was broken into by a hulking bully'.[2] In August 1914 the local and national press reported that references to the war were made from most pulpits in the Principality, with the government being commended for 'enforcing the moral and religious obligations of citizenship in the present national crisis'.[3] Lloyd George succeeded in 'making a bloody war into a holy crusade'.[4] However, it should be remembered that Lloyd George did not speak out openly in favour of the war until 19 September 1914, whereas many ministers and denominational periodicals up and down the country had defended Britain's honourable action in taking up arms against Germany's aggression long before this date. It is still open to considerable debate why all the major denominations endorsed the war. The outcome, D. Densil Morgan argues, was clear: 'rather than providing a moral code, a set of values and a knowledge of God which could transcend temporal and merely national considerations, institutional Christianity appeared to have become a function of the imperial cause.'[5]

Public proclamations of support for the war were widespread. John Gwili Jenkins claimed in the Baptist denominational journal *Seren Cymru*, that the government 'could be trusted when it claimed war had been inevitable'.[6] Revd J. Edwards, a Congregationalist minister in Porthmadog, preached his first sermon after the outbreak of war with a message that was repeated in chapels throughout Wales:

> There is one bright spot in international affairs in Europe today and that is that England [sic] has seen its way clear to interfere in a war

that has been thrust upon peaceful people by the spirit of tyranny. It is a war that is nothing less than a great struggle between the Prince of Peace and the God of War. England today is fighting for international justice and ultimate peace.[7]

H.M. Hughes, the Congregationalist minister of Capel Ebeneser in Cardiff asserted that the war had been inevitable given the rise in German militarism and that the British conscience would be clear for pursuing it. *Y Goleuad*, the journal of the Calvinistic Methodists, maintained that militarism had to be opposed at all costs and the rape of the nations which had started with Belgium had to be countered.[8] In Denbighshire, Nonconformist ministers 'did not waver from their conviction of the justice of Britain's cause'.[9] The *Wrexham Advertiser* reported one Congregational minister who was firmly in favour of peace and neutrality, but he argued that Britain could not stay on the sidelines 'without losing honour and self-respect and our obligation to a weaker nation'.[10] A Methodist minister in Gwynedd called it a 'righteous war', adding that if any young man felt it his duty to take up arms, 'the blessing of heaven be upon you, and on the gun you are carrying'.[11]

The Anglican Church, as one would have expected with the close relationship between church and state, fully supported the decision to go to war; Germany had flouted international law and left Britain with no alternative but to honour her treaty obligations to Belgium. Bishop Joshua Hughes of Llandaff wrote:

> We cannot as a nation break our plighted word. We cannot stand by in our sea girt isle and see the weak trampled upon, robbed and outraged by a cruel and relentless horde as long as we have power to hold out our helping hand to support and protect those who call to us for help.[12]

Canon Brown, preaching in St Peter's Church, Carmarthen on 9 August argued that 'no nation ever entered upon a war with a clearer conscience than we do now, can we not send our forces to the front in confidence and hope that God, who is a God of righteousness, will be their aid'.[13] The vicar of Bwlchgwyn in Denbighshire described the conflict as 'a Holy War', while his colleague in neighbouring Minera declared it to be a just war because 'this country had no alternative but to declare war on Germany'.[14]

Revd John Williams, Brynsiencyn, Anglesey, Calvinistic Methodist Minister and 'recruiting sergeant'.

Some Nonconformist ministers were prepared to take things one stage further than verbal support from the pulpit and became active recruiting officers for the armed forces. None were more well-known than two Calvinistic Methodist ministers from north Wales, both personal friends of Lloyd George, Thomas Charles Williams, Menai Bridge, and John Williams, Brynsiencyn. T.C. Williams was 'debonair and intellectual, whose fashionable pulpit delivery was as revered in the bourgeois world of London Nonconformity as it was among the chapelgoers of north Wales'.[15] He was known for his lively imagination, a rich resonant voice and great fluency of speech. He utilized these qualities to great effect at recruiting meetings throughout north Wales. John Williams began his ministry in Horeb chapel, Brynsiencyn, Anglesey in 1878 before moving to Liverpool in 1895 to become pastor of Prince's Road chapel. He retired in 1906 moving back to Brynsiencyn but he was still extremely active within the Calvinistic Methodist church. John Williams was recognized as the great master of pulpit oratory. He had a powerful voice, was articulate, eloquent and possessed a rich vocabulary, preaching in both Welsh and English. Williams was a curious mix of the progressive and the reactionary: he lived in considerable luxury and in his lifestyle he almost took on the role of the local squire; however, in his retiring address as moderator of the Calvinistic Methodist assembly in May 1914, he confronted social and economic issues such as a living wage for all workers and the need for decent housing.[16]

When the Welsh Army Corps (WAC) was established in September 1914, Lloyd George made sure that John Williams was appointed as chaplain-general with the honorary rank of colonel. The sight of Williams in full military uniform and clerical collar became well-known not only in the pulpit, but also in recruiting meetings throughout north Wales. Griffith Jones, from Y Ffôr near Pwllheli, was a member of Ebeneser chapel where Williams came to preach early in the war. From the pulpit, Williams urged all the young men from the congregation to join up and even placed an enlistment form on the communion table. Griffith Jones was swept along by the preacher's rhetoric and moved forward to volunteer his services. His mother tried to pull him back but she was rebuked by Revd Williams.[17] Jones joined the 13th Battalion Royal Welsh Fusiliers and was killed on 10 July 1916 in the battle of Mametz Wood. He is commemorated on the Thiepval memorial. The minister of Penbryn Congregational chapel in Wrexham refused to follow Williams's lead stating that 'while I believe

Frank Richards.

wholeheartedly in our cause, as a Christian minister I do not feel impelled by the dictates of my conscience, much less by those of the Town Council, to act as a recruiting sergeant'.[18]

The presence of Anglican and Nonconformist chaplains at the front may have caused some to query the relationship between Christianity and militarism and the seeming hypocrisy of the situation. Frank Richards had little good to say about the clergymen he met, describing them as drunkards, cowards or philanderers. He thought that church parade was detested by 95 per cent of his battalion.[19] Robert Graves, writing about the Royal Welsh Fusiliers, thought that 'hardly one soldier in a hundred was inspired by religious feeling of even the crudest kind. It would have been difficult to remain religious in the trenches even if one survived the irreligion of the training battalion'. Graves thought that there was little respect for Anglican regimental chaplains and 'if they had shown one-tenth the courage, endurance, and other human qualities that the regimental doctors showed ... the British Expeditionary Force might well have started a religious revival'. Graves thought the chaplains were generally happy to hide behind the order that they should not go on the front line, but 'occasionally, on a quiet day in a quiet sector, the chaplain would make a daring afternoon visit to the support line and distribute a few cigarettes before hurrying back'. While praising the Roman Catholic chaplains for being involved 'wherever the fighting was', Graves concluded that 'Anglican chaplains were remarkably out of touch

D. Cynddelw Williams

with their troops'.[20] Perhaps such views offer a distorted picture, owing more to the hyperbolic style of the writers than actuality.

Lloyd George had fought a hard battle with Lord Kitchener to ensure that Nonconformist chaplains could minister to the moral and spiritual needs of those who had joined the WAC. While this was largely intended to help stimulate recruitment because of the influence of the chapels, it also brought forth many brave, dedicated and committed men who were to serve with distinction. Perhaps the most celebrated Welsh minister was D. Cynddelw Williams, a Calvinistic Methodist from Capel Saron in Penygroes, near Caernarfon.[21] He volunteered for service in the autumn of 1914 when he was already in his late forties. Williams worked first with the 10th Battalion Royal Welsh Fusiliers, 10th Battalion Welsh Regiment and 6th Battalion South Wales Borderers in a training camp in Bournemouth. He organized services in a local cinema and regularly attracted congregations of over one hundred. He also formed a Welsh choir which sang in the town's churches in the winter of 1914-15. Williams saw his mission as trying to turn men away from drink, women and swearing and to turn to God. He felt that he was more successful in this with the south Walians than the north Walians. When Williams was posted to France in September 1915 he instigated a swear-box in the officers' mess, the proceeds of which purchased a primus stove. His steadfast but sometimes naïve character endeared him to the front line soldiers, especially as he was willing to share with them the dangers of the trenches. Williams tried to organize simple services of hymn singing and bible readings wherever he was. Morgan Watcyn-Williams was present at many of his hastily arranged services:

> I heard the padre constantly for twelve months, now in a ruined house, now in an orchard behind Arras with the apple tree in bloom, and again inside the walls of a little French school, and he had ever the same straightforward message – a Power greater than war, love stronger than death, and sacrifice the very gate of heaven'[22]

Williams's bravery was well-illustrated by his insistence on giving a proper burial to Lieutenant William Hughes, 10th Battalion Royal Welsh Fusiliers, who had died on 2 March 1916. His body had been roughly located in no-man's-land on 14 March. In his diary, Williams describes going through the barbed wire and into mud so thick and cloying that it was sucking his boots off, with enemy star shells constantly bursting around him. The body of Lieutenant Hughes was found, properly buried and a short service held at the graveside. Williams was awarded the Military Cross in 1916 for his bravery on the Somme. Morgan Watcyn-Wiliams was also witness to Revd Williams's bravery: 'all around Delville and Longueval and Guillemont the wounded came pouring in, but the padre never hesitated, and out among the falling shells and flying splinters carried on with the work of rescue.'[23] The official citation stated that his award was for 'conspicuous gallantry and devotion to duty' when 'he accompanied the battalion [10th Battalion Royal Welsh Fusiliers] to the front line, and performed most valuable service in the rescue and tending of the wounded under an intense fire. He has on many previous occasions done fine work'. At the end of the war Williams surprisingly chose not to return to the ministry in Wales but stayed as a chaplain in various army camps in the south of England. He was devastated to find that hardly anyone attended his services. In September 1919 Williams answered the call to Capel Caersalem in Penmaenmawr, where he remained until his retirement.

The Calvinistic Methodist David Morris Jones was another Welsh minister to be awarded the Military Cross.[24] Like Cynddelw Williams, he was highly respected for his willingness to share the dangers of the front line with the soldiers. He had joined the Welsh Student Company of the Royal Army Medical Corps (RAMC) in 1916, which was a unit enabling those holding pacifist convictions to serve their country in a non-combatant role. He then felt the call to offer himself as a commissioned chaplain, but before a position became vacant, he was posted to the Balkan front with the RAMC. Following this, he was appointed as chaplain to the Royal Welsh Fusiliers. Jones was posted to northern France in the spring of 1917 where he spent time with the 13th, 14th and 16th Battalions. Jones threw himself into his work arranging a regular Sunday evening *Cymanfa Ganu* (hymn singing festival) which frequently attracted over 300 participants. How many attended because of the religious dimension of the hymn singing and how many were attracted by the ritual familiarity of something from home, it is impossible to gauge. While at the front, Jones would also have been taking services and parades, preaching, organizing educational classes, writing to the families of the deceased and visiting men in the trenches to support them in any way possible. For his actions during the attack on Gouzeaucourt on 18 September 1918, Jones was awarded the Military Cross. In the official citation Jones was described as displaying 'the greatest gallantry and absolute disregard for personal danger'. On three occasions he went out into no-man's-land to attend to wounded men and his 'cheerfulness and determination under heavy fire inspired the whole battalion'. Following the war, Jones ministered in Skewen, Blaneau Ffestiniog and Swansea before being appointed Professor of Philosophy at the Theological College, Aberystwyth.

Peter John Roberts, a Wesleyan minister from Bangor also made a strong impression on those with whom he came into contact. Ll. Wyn Griffith (referring to him as 'old Evans the padre') described how Roberts

2nd Battalion Monmouthshire Regiment, in the trenches at Le Bizet, April 1915. The Regiment was originally part of the Territorial Force.

lost one of his sons at the battle of Mametz and was unable to find his grave: 'he walked about for hours, but couldn't find any one who knew where it was, nor could he find the padre who buried him. He was going to bury other people's boys ... since he couldn't find his own boy's grave to pray over'. The brigade signalling officer says to Griffith:

> But there's a man for you, Gruff ... off to bury other men's boys at five in the morning, and maybe his own son not buried yet, a couple of miles away. There was some shrapnel overhead, but I saw him going up the slope as if he were alone in the world. If I come through this bloody business, I'd like to go to that man's church.[25]

Others who made a lasting impression on front line troops for their bravery and sincerity were A. Rhys Morgan, the Baptist minister who was also awarded the Military Cross, Congregationalists Evan Mathias and Peris Williams who were both mentioned in dispatches and churchmen William T. Havard and Timothy Rees, who were both awarded the Military Cross and subsequently became the bishops of St Asaph and Llandaff respectively. In total 14 Welsh Anglican clergymen, 8 Calvinistic Methodists, 10 Baptists and 14 Congregationalist ministers served in a full-time capacity with the various Welsh regiments. In addition there was a considerably higher number who volunteered for occasional service with the YMCA. It would seem that Wales was well served by its military chaplains and the caricatures portrayed by Robert Graves and Frank Richards were little more than that.

While the war would undoubtedly have seriously tested the faith and religious beliefs of many combatants, D. Densil Morgan has assembled an impressive body of evidence to show that 'faith under fire' was vitally important to many soldiers. Private Thomas Jones, 16th Battalion Royal Welsh Fusiliers, from Pennal, Merioneth regularly wrote home describing the help he received from prayer and worship and assuring his family of his faith in God's protection. In early 1916 he was struck by the sight of a crucifix standing unscathed outside a wrecked church, which he perceived as a sign of God's providence. Private W.G. Jones, a medical orderly in the Royal Welsh Fusiliers, found that although there were no religious services, he experienced the presence of God more strongly than he had ever before, allowing him to move amongst death without any fear whatsoever. He accounts for this 'only by reference to this power and consolation of my religion'.[26] When Revd Cynddelw Williams met a young volunteer, Private Lewis from south Wales, the clergyman asked him whether soldiers in the trenches were praying. Lewis replied 'you can be sure that they are, what else would you do with men dying all around you'?[27] For many in the front line, taking Holy Communion became a vitally important and moving experience. Private B.J. Evans took communion in Salonika and found it had a 'peculiar effect' on him and his spirit was 'well blessed in that service'. He wrote home that:

> ... it is a glorious fact for me that although I am far from home, far from friends and relatives, yet heaven is as near to me here as it was in Wales, and God is as eager to hear and answer our prayers out in this wild country as he was in the quiet, comfortable home amongst the hills of Wales.[28]

Corporal Frank Reed, 6th Battalion Welsh Regiment, wrote home that 'every Sunday morning at 7.30 we have Holy Communion which is a great help to men leaving for the trenches in the night'.[29] As Densil Morgan concluded, such experiences 'bear poignant witness to the effectiveness of the churches in inculcating true experiential Christianity. Whereas nominal Christianity was shown to be worthless in the trenches, true faith, often when reinforced by the objective potency of sacramental symbolism, was revered by many.'[30]

AFTERMATH

It is a commonly held assumption that returning soldiers, having witnessed the brutality and horrors of war, turned against organized religion in vast numbers. David Russell Barnes, for example, remembers that his grandfather 'never set foot in the chapel again after returning home from the battle of the Somme'.[31] When Will Arthur returned to Glynneath after the war, he found that he could not reconcile the teachings he had received in chapel with his experiences in the war:

> There was [sic] our doubts, that our teaching had reached a kind of chasm ... We couldn't cross it, on that side we could see what we had been taught and on this side our experience in the army, and of course there was a big gap between the two you see.[32]

The war not only caused difficulties concerning religious teaching, but it also widened the experiences of many men who had never previously left the confines of their community; they had a new perspective on life. In the cold light of the post-war world, the churches found it hard to defend the extent to which they had compromised their principles in readily supporting the war. Charges of hypocrisy flew at them from all directions. There is no doubt that the Nonconformist denominations faced enormous challenges in 1918, but then they had also done so in the immediate pre-war period. The question to answer is how far the war magnified these challenges and hastened change?

Despite many claims to the contrary, one thing the war did not do was cause a significant decline in membership of the church and chapels; bereaved families and disillusioned soldiers did not turn their backs on the chapels in response to the horrors of war. In Wales, the Calvinistic Methodists registered 184,843 communicants in 1914, rising to a peak of 189,727 in 1926 before beginning a slow, gradual decline. The Congregationalists recorded 159,753 members in 1914, climbing to a peak of 174,908 in 1933 before also beginning a gradual decline. The Baptist membership was 124,795 in 1914, rising to 130,098 in 1926 before falling at approximately 2,000 per year throughout the 1930s. The Anglican Church recorded 155,532 Easter Day communicants in 1914, rising to 159,316 in 1919 followed by a steady rise to 193,668 at the outbreak of the Second World War. Nonconformist statistics are notoriously difficult to interpret because membership does not necessarily mean attendance at chapel, nor even residence in the locality. Similarly, those attending services were not always members and membership and attendance tells us nothing about faith. However, despite these shortcomings, the statistics suggest a clear pattern in the first half of the twentieth century. Following the religious revival of 1904-5, there was an increase in chapel membership to 1907, followed by a slight decline. During the First World War and up to 1926, there was a steady increase in membership followed by a gradual decline. There was no significantly sharp movement, either up or down, at any time.

To explain these patterns of movement is more problematic. Robert Pope argues that in the uncertainty of war, some people may have turned to religion 'as the tried and tested stronghold against the onslaught of

Men of the 15th Battalion Royal Welsh Fusiliers (London Welsh) queuing for a meal in the trenches at Fleurbaix, 28 December 1917. *(Imperial War Museum)*

diabolical powers'. Later in the war some may have turned to religion in search of divine intervention, but this does not explain the continued growth in membership from 1918-26. Similarly, Pope argues, if religion had been seen as a comfort against the hardships of war, then 1926 should have brought an increase in membership also. His 'tentative conclusion' was this: 'Nonconformity still exercised a significant influence over many Welshmen during this period'.[33] Densil Morgan maintains that the religious legacy of the First World War was 'ambiguous'. Whereas the death and destruction had turned many against God, it was through the war that others found their faith. Morgan Watcyn-Williams provides a good example: his fervent Christian convictions were strengthened greatly by his experiences on the Somme. Many others returned with a new resolve to serve God and their fellow man and to do all they could to prevent the tragedy of war from ever happening again. Returning soldiers were led to believe that they stood on the threshold of a new age with a fairer, more equal society to look forward to. This, Densil Morgan argued, was 'the most significant aspect of the change to have affected Welsh religion by 1918: Christianity would be forced to respond to the social challenge'.[34] An even greater challenge lay ahead in the 1920s and 1930s.

NOTES

[1] Geraint H. Jenkins, *A Concise History of Wales* (Cambridge: Cambridge University Press, 2007), p. 272.

[2] Robert Pope, 'Welsh Nonconformists and the State 1914-1918', in Matthew Cragoe and Chris Williams (eds) *Wales and War: Society, Politics and Religion in the Nineteenth and Twentieth Centuries* (Cardiff: University of Wales Press, 2007), 165-183.

[3] For example, *Carmarthen Journal*, 14 August 1914.

[4] Dewi Eirug Davies, *Byddin y Brenin: Cymru a'i Chrefydd yn y Rhyfel Mawr* (Swansea: Tŷ John Penry, 1988), p. 35.

[5] D. Densil Morgan, *The Span of the Cross: Christian Religion and Society in Wales, 1914-2000* (Cardiff: University of Wales Press, 1999), p. 46.

[6] *Seren Cymru*, 7 August 1914.

[7] *Cambrian News and Merionethshire Standard*, 14 August 1914.

[8] Pope, 'Welsh Nonconformists', p. 172.

[9] Eric Griffiths, 'Denbighshire Coalminers and their Agent during the Great War', *Denbighshire Historical Society Transactions*, 50 (2001), 116-161.

[10] *Wrexham Advertiser*, 29 August 1914.

[11] Griffiths, 'Denbighshire Coalminers'.

[12] Morgan, *Span of the Cross*, pp. 42-3.

[13] *Carmarthen Journal*, 14 August 1914.

[14] Griffiths, 'Denbighshire Coalminers'.

[15] Morgan, *Span of the Cross*, p. 43.

[16] Robert Pope, *Building Jerusalem: Nonconformity, Labour and the Social Question in Wales, 1906–1939* (Cardiff: University of Wales Press, 1998), p. 57.

[17] *www.peoplescollection.co.uk*

[18] Griffiths, 'Denbighshire Coalminers'.

[19] Frank Richards, *Old Soldiers Never Die* (London: Faber and Faber, 1933), pp. 83-6.

[20] Robert Graves, *Goodbye to All That* (Penguin Books: London, 1960), pp. 197-8.

[21] D. Densil Morgan, '"Ffydd yn y ffosydd": Bywyd a Gwaith y Caplan D. Cynddelw Williams', *The National Library of Wales Journal*, 29/1 (1995), 77-99.

[22] Morgan Watcyn-Williams, *From Khaki to Cloth: the Autobiography of the Revd. Morgan Watcyn-Williams MC* (Caernarfon: Calvinistic Methodist Book Agency, 1949), p.54.

[23] Ibid., p. 95.

[24] See J.E. Wynne Davies, 'Professor David Morris Jones, MC, MA, BD, (1887-1957): War Diaries', *Cylchgrawn Hanes, Cymdeithas Hanes y Methodistiaidd Calfinaidd*, 22 (1998), 35-54.

[25] Llewelyn Wyn Griffith, *Up to Mametz and Beyond* (Barnsley: Pen & Sword, 2010), pp. 98-9.

[26] Morgan, *Span of the Cross*, p. 49.

[27] Ibid., p. 65.

[28] Quoted in Morgan, *Span of the Cross*, p. 51.

[29] Ibid., p. 49

[30] Ibid., p. 49.

[31] See *Planet*, 118 (1996), p. 102.

[32] Pope, *Building Jerusalem*, p. 94.

[33] Ibid.

[34] D. Densil Morgan, '"Christ and the War": Some aspects of the Welsh Experience, 1914-18', *The Journal of Welsh Religious History*, 5 (1997), 73-91.

Conclusion

—◊◊◊—

O N 3 AUGUST 1915, the National Eisteddfod for the first time in its history dispensed with the great ritual of the partial unsheathing of its ceremonial sword and the audience response of 'Heddwch' ('Peace'). Instead, the festival of literature and music became a paean to militarism. W. Llewelyn Williams, MP for Carmarthen Borough, delivered an 'exhilarating oration' on the prowess of the Welsh soldier over the previous six hundred years.[1] Brigadier-General Owen Thomas (the only Welsh-speaking General in the British army), in full uniform, presided in the pavilion, accompanied by Colonel Fox Pitt, 15th Battalion Royal Welsh Fusiliers and Revd Colonel John Williams, Brynsiencyn. Thomas 'roused his fellow countrymen to a pitch of patriotic fervour that should have borne fruit outside the pavilion, where recruiting officers were busy'. He called for new eisteddfod competitions in military skills such as rifle shooting, while Revd Ceitho Davies, also clad in khaki, offered the Gorsedd prayer. Lloyd George was received with 'an overpowering outburst of enthusiasm' and to the disgust of T.H. Parry-Williams, winner of the crown (one of the two major poetry competitions), the Minister of Munitions proceeded to laud Wales's contribution to the war.

The events of August 1915 encapsulate how in one year Wales had changed from being a society dominated largely by the Nonconformist traditions of peace, to one of overt support for jingoistic militarism. By 1918, it became clear that the war marked a watershed in Wales not only in social, political and economic terms, but also for every individual within that society. In simple terms, for the 272,000 Welshmen who fought in the war, life would never be the same again. Some were physically scarred by the events of war, others were mentally scarred; the days of diagnosing and treating post-traumatic stress disorder were far in the future. For the families of the 31,000 Welshmen who died, coming to terms with the

David Lloyd George inspecting volunteers at the National Eisteddfod in Bangor, August 1915.

loss of a husband, father, brother, grandson or fiancé was heartbreaking; the war's tentacles reached into virtually every village and town in the Principality. The vast majority who died were buried on a foreign field which meant further grief for the families at home, denied the finality of a funeral or a grave to visit.

The break with the past was nowhere more obvious than in the countryside, with the accelerated break-up of the old landed estates and the demise of the power of the gentry. Agricultural labourers had for the first time received a guaranteed minimum wage and their general standard of living had risen. Equally importantly, their economic value had been recognised. In the coalfield, the miners' unions became increasingly assertive and class-conscious and the last rites of the Lib-Lab class collaboration had been read; furthermore, the gradual shift in power from the chapels to the unions was given greater impetus. The war provided women with the opportunity to enter the workplace in occupations previously denied to them. Some would argue that this liberated women and set them on the path to social equality and emancipation; others would point to the patterns of employment in post-war years being much the same as pre-war. Apart from a narrow group of women receiving the vote in 1918, little else had changed.

Just as the National Eisteddfod in 1915 symbolised the change in Wales from peacetime to wartime, so did the election to Parliament of George Maitland Lloyd Davies in 1923 embody the post-war mood. Davies, a member of the Fellowship of Reconciliation, had suffered imprisonment, prejudice and revulsion during the war because of his pacifist views. In the 1923 general election, Davies stood as a Christian Pacifist candidate in the constituency of the University of Wales (a seat previously held by the Liberal party). Although he was elected with a majority of only ten votes, his success caused a sensation. It was a public proclamation that the ideals of war and militarism were of the past and that the days of Lloyd George's Liberalism were numbered. The war was now viewed with disgust and shame. Post-war Wales was a new country.

NOTE
[1] See *Western Mail*, 4-6 August 1915.

Chronology of the War

—⁓ഡ⁓—

1914

June 28: Archduke Franz Ferdinand, heir to the throne of the Austro-Hungarian Empire, and his wife are assassinated in Sarajevo, Bosnia by Gavrilo Princip.

July 28: Austria-Hungary declares war on Serbia.

August 1: Germany declares war on Russia. Italy and Belgium announce neutrality.

August 3: Germany declares war on France and invades Belgium and France. Great Britain gives order for troops to mobilise.

August 4: Great Britain declares war on Germany. United States declares neutrality.

August 6: Royal Navy cruiser HMS *Amphion* is sunk by German mines in the North Sea, causing the death of 150 men who are the first British casualties of war.

August 7: First members of the British Expeditionary Force (BEF) land in France. Lord Kitchener calls for the first 100,000 men to enlist.

August 10: France declares war on Austria-Hungary.

August 13: The first squadrons of the Royal Flying Corps arrive in France.

August 24: British and Belgian troops retreat from Mons.

September 6: The Battle of the Marne checks the German advance at the cost of 13,000 British, 250,000 French and 250,000 German casualties. Trench warfare begins.

September 10: Germans retreat, stabilising their line along the River Aisne.

September 15: The Battle of the Aisne begins.

September 19: Lloyd George makes his 'Queen's Hall' speech which leads to the formation of the Welsh Army Corps.

October 10: The Welsh Army Corps is officially established.

October 12: First Battle of Ypres begins.

October 29: Turkey enters the war on the side of the Central Powers.

November 22: Trenches are established along the entire Western Front.

December 16: The German First High Sea fleet shells Hartlepool, Whitby and Scarborough, killing 137.

December 25: Unofficial truce declared by soldiers along the Western Front.

1915

January 19: In the first airborne attack on British soil, Zeppelins bomb Great Yarmouth and King's Lynn, killing five civilians.

January 24: The Battle of Dogger Bank; the British Navy sinks the German cruiser *Blücher*.

February 4: German U-boats begin attacks on allied and neutral shipping; Germany declares a blockade around Britain and Ireland.

February 19: Allied naval bombardment of the Dardanelles and Gallipoli begins.

March 10: The British Offensive at Neuve Chapelle begins with heavy allied losses. Some of the blame falls on the poor quality and lack of British shells, initiating the 'Shell Crisis'.

April 22: Second Battle of Ypres begins. First use of poison gas by Germany.

April 25: Allied landings on the Gallipoli Peninsula; 70,000 British, Commonwealth and French troops are under heavy fire.

May 2: Austro-German offensive on Galicia begins.

May 7: German U-boat torpedoes British liner *Lusitania* with the loss of 128 American lives, creating a US-German diplomatic crisis.

May 9: Battle of Aubers Ridge on the Western Front; British attack is unsuccessful.

May 23: Italy declares war on Austria-Hungary.

May 26: The 'Shell Crisis' exposes the failings of the British Government in supporting front line troops. Discontent over rising casualty figures grows and a coalition government is formed as Prime Minister Asquith struggles to maintain control of the House of Commons. Lloyd George becomes Minister of Munitions.

May 31: The first Zeppelin raid on London kills seven and injures thirty-five.

June 4: The Third and final Battle of Krithia begins at Gallipoli as Allies attempt to push inland from their beach-heads. British losses amount to 6,000 men.

June 21: British troops reach the Euphrates in Mesopotamia, and re-occupy Aden.

August 6: Allies land two divisions at Suvla Bay, Gallipoli. They opt not to take the strategic heights overlooking the beaches and are eventually pinned to the coast by Turkish troops.

August 16: A U-boat bombards Whitehaven, showing that Britain's maritime defences can be breached by German submarines.

August 21: The Battle of Scimitar Hill, Gallipoli, is the final British offensive in the Dardanelles. They are repelled and lose 5,000 men.

September 25: The Allied offensive focuses on Loos and Champagne. At the Battle of Loos the British use gas for the first time.

September 27: British and Canadian regiments take Hill 70 at Loos and break the German line, but lack of reserves to exploit the breach results in limited success.

September 28: British forces advancing along the River Tigris in Mesopotamia capture Kut-al-Imara.

October 6: Lord Derby becomes Director of Recruiting.

October 12: British nurse Edith Cavell is executed by German firing squad for helping POWs escape from Belgium to Holland.

October 15: Britain declares war on Bulgaria.

October 31: Steel helmets introduced on the British Front.

November 22: Battle of Ctesiphon, 25 miles south of Baghdad. Allies inflict heavy casualties on the Turks, but are forced to retire to Kut-al-Imara due to lack of supplies. The Turkish soldiers give chase and besiege the town.

December 19: Sir Douglas Haig replaces Sir John French as Commander-in-Chief of the British Expeditionary Force.

December 20: Allies complete the evacuation of 83,000 troops from Suvla Bay and ANZAC Cove in Gallipoli. Not a single loss of life in the withdrawal, with the Turks unaware of the evacuation.

1916

January 8: Allied evacuation of Helles marks the end of the Gallipoli campaign.

January 24: The Military Service Act is passed, introducing conscription for unmarried men.

February 21: The Battle of Verdun starts with a German offensive against the Mort-Homme Ridge. The battle lasts ten months and over a million men become casualties.

April 5: The Battle of Kut-al-Imara. The third and final Allied attempt to relieve the town flounders in the mud along the Tigris, with 23,000 Allied casualties.

April 29: Besieged garrison at Kut-al-Imara in Mesopotamia surrenders after 143 days and 3,000 British and 6,000 Indian troops go into captivity. The majority of these die of disease and starvation in prison camps.

May 31-June 1: The Battle of Jutland. The German High Seas Fleet is forced to retire despite inflicting heavier losses on the Royal Navy (14 ships and 6,100 men), but the German fleet remains irreparably damaged for the rest of the war.

June 4: The Russian Brusilov Offensive begins on the Eastern Front. It nearly cripples Austria-Hungary out of the war.

June 5: Lord Kitchener sails for Russia on board HMS *Hampshire*. The ship is mined off Orkney and Kitchener is lost along with 643 other crewmen and general staff.

June 8: Second Military Service Act is passed extending conscription to married men.

July 1: The Battle of the Somme begins involving 750,000 allied soldiers. There are 60,000 British casualties on the first day, with 20,000 dead.

July 4: Lloyd George becomes Secretary of State for War.

July 7: Battle of Mametz Wood begins.

July 14: The Battle of Bazentin Ridge marks the end of the first Somme Offensive. The British break the German line but fail to deploy the cavalry fast enough to take full advantage.

July 23: The Battle of Pozières Ridge marks the second Somme offensive. The action to take the village costs 17,000 Allied casualties, the majority of whom are Australian.

August 27: Italy declares war on Germany.

September 2: The first Zeppelin is shot down over Britain. The Royal Flying Corps uses a new combination of explosive and incendiary bullets to great effect.

September 9: The Battle of Ginchy. The British capture Ginchy – a post of vital strategic importance, as it commands a view of the whole Somme battlefield.

September 15: The Battle of Flers-Courcelette signifies the start of the third stage of the Somme offensive. Tanks are used for the first time. Despite initial gains the Allies fail to break through German lines.

September 26: The Battle of Thiepval. Tanks play a crucial role in the capture of this strategic village.

November 13: The Battle of Ancre. The fourth phase of the Somme offensive is marked by the British capturing Beaumont Hamel taking nearly 4,000 prisoners.

December 7: David Lloyd George becomes Prime Minister forming a coalition government.

December 18: The Battle of Verdun ends. It is the longest and costliest battle on the Western Front.

1917

February 3: The United States severs diplomatic relations with Germany as U-Boats threaten US shipping.

February 21: The great German withdrawal begins, falling back twenty-five miles to establish stronger positions along the Hindenburg Line.

February 24: Turkish retreat to Baghdad, abandoning Kut-al-Imara in Mesopotamia.

March 11: Baghdad is taken by the British after three days fighting.

March 15: Tsar Nicholas II abdicates as Moscow falls to Russian Revolutionaries. The demise of the Russian Army frees German troops for the Western Front.

March 26: The First Battle of Gaza, Palestine, as the British attempt to cut off the Turkish forces in Mesopotamia from their homeland. They fail to take the town and are forced to withdraw.

April 6: US declares war on Germany. Troops begin to mobilise immediately.

April 9: The Battle of Arras.

April 16: The Second Battle of Aisne begins as part of the 'Nivelle Offensive'. Heavy losses spark mutinies within the French Army.

April 19: The Second Battle of Gaza begins in Palestine but it is eventually called off due to mounting casualties.

June 7: The Battle of Messines Ridge. There are few allied casualties, as the attack is preceded by the detonation of nineteen mines under the German front lines. The explosions are reportedly heard in England.

June 13: Germans launch the first major heavy bomber raid over London, killing 135 people.

June 25: First US troops arrive in France.

July 16: T.E. Lawrence and the Arabs liberate Aqaba in Jordan after crossing the Nefu desert. This opens the route north for the Arab Army and isolates the Turkish Army in Mesopotamia.

July 31: The Third Battle of Ypres (Battle of Passchendaele) begins along a fifteen-mile front in Flanders. Initial attacks are successful as the German forward trenches are lightly manned. Hedd Wyn is killed on Pilckem Ridge.

August 20: The Third Battle of Verdun begins.

October 9: The third phase of the Ypres offensive begins with British and French troops taking Poelcapelle. Heavy rain falls in the next forty-eight hours on already saturated ground. The previous bombardments smashed the drainage systems and the battlefield turns into a quagmire.

October 12: The British launch their latest assaults at Ypres against the Passchendaele Ridge. New Zealand and Australian divisions suffer heavy casualties, then are bogged down in the mud and are forced back to their start lines.

October 26: The Second Battle of Passchendaele begins with 20,000 men of the Third and Fourth Canadian Divisions advancing up the hills of the salient. It cost the Allies 12,000 casualties to gain a few hundred yards.

October 30: Reinforced with the addition of two British divisions, a second offensive is launched in torrential rains to capture Passchendaele. The Allies hold the town for the next five days in the face of repeated German shelling and counterattacks.

October 31: Battle of Beersheba, Palestine. British forces take the town capturing 1,800 Turkish troops. This leaves the way open for the advance on Jerusalem.

November 7: British capture Gaza.

November 10: Battle of Passchendaele ends. After months of fighting, the Allies have advanced only five miles, but have taken the high ground that dominates the salient. There are half a million casualties, of which around 140,000 have been killed.

November 20: The Battle of Cambrai begins. During the attack, Royal Flying Corps aircraft drop bombs on German anti-tank guns and strongpoints to clear a path for the Allied tanks and ground troops.

December 9: Britain liberates Jerusalem, ending 673 years of Turkish rule.

1918

March 3: Soviet Russia concludes separate peace at Brest-Litovsk with Germany and her allies.

March 21: Germany launches a major spring offensive.

March 28: The German offensive along the River Scarpe is halted at great loss. The American Expeditionary Force plays a vital role.

April 1: Royal Air Force established.

April 5: The German spring offensive halts outside Amiens as British and Australian forces hold the line.

April 22: Allies carry out raids against the harbours of Ostend and Zeebrugge. Obsolete vessels are driven ashore and blown up in order to blockade the entrances. Zeebrugge is partially successful; the Ostend raid fails.

May 10: The British launch a second raid on Ostend. HMS *Vindictive* is this time successfully scuttled in the harbour entrance. German cruisers are no longer able to use the port.

May 27: Operation Blücher, the third German spring offensive, attacks the French army along the Aisne River. The French are forced back to the Marne but hold the river after being reinforced by American troops.

June 9: The fourth German Offensive on the Western Front, codenamed 'Gneisenau', between Noyan and Montdidier. It fails to break the French line and ends four days later.

June 10: Representation of the People Act enfranchises women over thirty.

June 15: The second Battle of the Piave River, Italy, opens with a massive offensive by the Austro-Hungarian Army. Italian and British troops first hold and then push back the attackers. Despite heavy losses the Allies destroy the Austro-Hungarian Army, precipitating the collapse of the Empire.

July 15: The second Battle of the Marne marks the final phase of the German spring offensive. Allied counter attacks inflict irreplaceable German casualties.

August 8: The second Battle of Amiens begins. German resistance is sporadic and thousands surrender.

September 4: On the Western front, Germany retreats to the Siegfried Line.

September 19: The Battle of Samaria marks the end of the British offensive of Palestine.

September 27: Allied offensive on the Cambrai Front leads to the storming of the Hindenburg Line. The Battle of St Quentin results in the Hindenburg Line being breached along the Canal Du Nord and St Quentin Canal.

September 30: British and Arab troops take Damascus, capturing 7,000 prisoners and securing stability in the Middle East. Bulgaria signs an armistice with the allies.

October 4: The German and Austrian peace proposal is sent to the American President, Woodrow Wilson, requesting an armistice.

October 8: The Allies advance along a twenty-mile front from St Quentin to Cambrai and drive the Germans back three miles, taking Cambrai and le Cateau. Over 10,000 Germans are captured.

October 17: British and American troops launch attacks at the Battle of the Selle. The British liberate Lille and Douai. Belgians retake Ostend and reach Zeebrugge the following day. The whole of the Channel coast in the west of Flanders is liberated.

October 23: The British launch a night attack with all three of their armies, the First, the Second and the Fourth. This time the British advance six miles in two days. The British are now 20 miles behind the rear of the Hindenburg Line.

October 30: The Turkish army surrenders to the British in Mesopotamia. Turkey signs an armistice with the Allies.

November 3: Austria-Hungary signs an armistice with the Allies.

November 9: Kaiser Wilhelm II abdicates and flees to Holland.

November 11: The Armistice is signed at 5.00 a.m. and comes into effect at 11.00 a.m.

Index

—꧁—